THE NEW GOLD STANDARD

THE NEW GOLD STANDARD

··········

CHARLIE WEIS AND NOTRE DAME'S RISE TO GLORY

BY
TIM PRISTER

INTRODUCTION BY
LOU HOLTZ

ESPN
BOOKS
a division of
ESPN publishing

ESPN BOOKS

ISBN13: 978-1-933060-20-0
ISBN: 1-933060-20-4

ESPN Books titles are available for special promotions and premiums. For details contact Michael Rentas, Assistant Director, Inventory Operations, Hyperion, 77 West 66th Street, 11th floor, New York, New York 10023, or call 212-456-0133.

FIRST EDITION

10 9 8 7 6 5 4 3 2 1

......

DEDICATION

TO MY MOTHER,

THE ROCK OF MY FAMILY

AND THE INSPIRATION

TO MAKE

MY DREAMS COME TRUE.

TABLE OF CONTENTS

······

INTRODUCTION

BY

LOU HOLTZ

IN 2005, WHEN NOTRE Dame was going through the interview process to hire its next coach, various members of the Board of Trustees called me for my take on Charlie Weis. I made it clear that I didn't know a lot about Charlie, but that a few things about him stood out.

First of all, he is a Notre Dame graduate. That means he knows what the school is all about and what the campus atmosphere is like. And it means he knows and respects the long history and great tradition of Notre Dame.

That's a big plus.

His career in the NFL was also very impressive, considering all the success he achieved with Bill Parcells and Bill Belichick.

Those were the things I stressed.

After doing more study on the team and Charlie, I said on ESPN that Notre Dame would surprise some people and go 9–2, which is how it ended up. Before the season, I predicted that USC's toughest regular-season game would be against Notre Dame. And it was.

Making predictions is fun, and I'm glad I did well with those two, but my faith in the job Charlie would do at Notre Dame was really based on a long conversation I had with him in New York before the season began. We were on a TV show together, and he asked to have breakfast with me. After we spoke for about two hours, I became sold on Charlie Weis.

We talked about his philosophy and approach to football. He knew a lot about Notre Dame football, but he wanted to know more. He asked me what we did when I was there—plus how we did it and why.

He already had a good fix on what he wanted to do. I could see that. He wasn't seeking guidance as much as information and insights that might help him make better decisions.

That impressed me.

The first game, against Pittsburgh, showed me a lot. Charlie had quarterback Brady Quinn throwing short passes, quick screens, and the like. He never put Brady in a position he wasn't ready to handle. As the year went on, and Brady learned the system and started making better decisions, Charlie opened up the offense, and they threw downfield more.

Quite simply, I thought that was the mark of a great coach. He coached his team based on where it was for each game, resisting the temptation to overload his players and try to break fast out of the gate to make a splash.

And he ended up making a splash anyway.

I don't know of anyone other than Ara Parseghian who has made a greater impact on Notre Dame football in his first year than Charlie Weis. They both turned it around immediately. They both understood the pressure and expectations of Notre Dame football. They also both understood how important it is for Notre Dame to be on top.

You see, I believe it's good for college football for Notre Dame to field a good team. When Notre Dame has a good team, millions of people will follow the sport who normally might not.

Among the many smart things Charlie did on the way in was to tell the team that they didn't choose him, he chose them. And he made it clear that if they had played a little better for Tyrone Willingham, he'd still be there.

That's a very smart thing to say to a football team that is dealing with a coaching change. Charlie knows he's a tough, demanding disciplinarian and that the team wouldn't love everything he did or made them do. But he reminded them that it was their failure that brought him in.

His message: "You want the other coach? Well, you should have blocked harder and tackled better. I didn't get the guy fired, you did. But I came here anyway because I believe in Notre Dame and I believe in you."

End of that discussion.

Looking ahead, I expect Notre Dame to be one of the top three teams in the country in 2006. The key will be Brady Quinn, who is a smart and talented player. He's also a very aware and astute young man who is not awed by being the quarterback at Notre Dame. He's not undone by the pressure of that job. In fact, I think he thrives on it. You mix that kind of player with a coach like Charlie, who is constantly challenging players to take it to the next level, and something special could happen.

Usually, a football player's best year is his junior year. Freshmen just want to play and earn a letter. Sophomores want to start. Juniors want to win. And seniors are wondering where they'll go in the NFL draft.

One of the major challenges faced by every college coach is to get his seniors to play the best football of their careers. If Charlie can do that, he'll have a pretty good team. So let me just say it: I think Brady Quinn will have his best season as a senior.

Tradition is always under construction. When I got the job to coach football at Notre Dame, I wasn't looking to become a legend. I just wanted to build the program the way Notre Dame wanted it to be. I'm sure Charlie feels the same way.

At Notre Dame, you're not really just the coach anyway. You're the protector, the caretaker if you will. And right now, I'd say the tradition and history of Notre Dame football are being cared for very, very well.

Chapter 1

A LITTLE BIT
O' NASTY

THE WHEELS OF THE Gulfstream III bit hard into the runway, gained their footing, and then carried the private twin-jet toward the three waiting cars on the tarmac of the South Bend Regional Airport. Local weather forecasters had said the temperature wouldn't dip below 40 degrees, tame for a cloudy December 12, 2004, evening in northern Indiana, but it seemed colder, especially to the Notre Dame greeting party, which included athletic director Kevin White, senior associate athletic director Missy Conboy, associate athletic director John Heisler, senior associate athletic director Bernard Muir, and security personnel.

Farther away, partly shielded by a fence, were the television camera crews and photographers, there to record the arrival of what would be, shockingly and embarrassingly enough, Notre Dame's fourth head football coach in little more than three years.

The pilot steered the plane to a stop, parking it with the cabin door facing away from the cameras. As a brisk wind blew, Notre Dame's newest employee, Charles Joseph Weis, stepped down the plane's stairs and was greeted by the welcoming contingent. Weis' wife, Maura, and son, Charlie, climbed into Conboy's car for the drive to White's house, while Weis rode up front in White's car, with Muir and Heisler in the backseat.

Only a few hours earlier, Weis had been on the New England Patriots sideline at Gillette Stadium, where the defending Super Bowl champions had beaten the Cincinnati Bengals, improved their record to 12–1, and clinched the AFC East title. But at game's end, the Patriots offensive coordinator was quietly whisked away to the Providence airport for the not-so-secret flight to South Bend. Afterward, when asked by reporters for a comment, Patriots owner Robert Kraft said he would respond "tomorrow, when they announce it."

Too late.

Word had already leaked that Weis was the latest coaching centerpiece of a Notre Dame football program not generally comfortable with job turnover. America's most visible college team would now be run by a 48-year-old coach with a New Jersey accent, a buzz cut, three Super Bowl rings (and counting), a Notre Dame diploma, and, most of all, an unspoken mandate from his new bosses not only to rebuild and to win but also to reunite the school's fabled football constituency.

Four seasons earlier, Bob Davie had been Notre Dame's coach. He was fired in favor of George O'Leary, who lasted less than a week after it was discovered (not by Notre Dame, by the way) that he had falsified parts of his résumé. Then came Tyrone Willingham, who provided dignity and stability but not enough victories. Now it was Weis' turn.

Four years, four coaches.

Not since Ara Parseghian was hired, following the 1963 season, had a man with so little national renown been tapped as head coach of the Fighting Irish. Parseghian had established himself at the Big Ten conference's perennial underdog, Northwestern, where he auditioned for the Notre Dame job by beating the Irish four years in a row. But that was pre-cable, pre-ESPN, pre-*USA Today*, and, of course, pre-Internet. Most

Irish fans knew little about Parseghian other than the final scores of those Notre Dame-Northwestern games. It was the nature of the times.

Weis had remained virtually anonymous because, despite solid football credentials, he had never been the head man. He had served as offensive coordinator to Bill Parcells and Bill Belichick, two of the most successful head football coaches and larger-than-life personalities in pro football history. He had been a fixture in the NFL for 15 years, but the public knew little about the man himself, partly because Parcells and Belichick rarely allowed their assistant coaches to speak to the media.

Weis was in the process of adding a fourth Super Bowl ring to his collection, which would make it three in four years with Belichick's New England Patriots. Yet up until a few weeks earlier, most Notre Dame fans had no idea what his qualifications were to be head coach at Notre Dame. Most of those same fans had been infatuated with Urban Meyer, the former Irish assistant who, as head coach, revitalized the dormant Bowling Green program and then led the University of Utah, of the Mountain West conference, to an undefeated season and an appearance in the big-money Fiesta Bowl. It was a given, so said the media, that Meyer would return to South Bend.

Instead, Meyer stunned the college football world when he accepted an offer to become the head coach at the University of Florida. It seemed incomprehensible to Fighting Irish followers that Meyer, a Midwesterner (born in Ohio), a Catholic (he was named after a pope), and someone so familiar with the Notre Dame football culture and tradition, would choose to go elsewhere. By doing so, Meyer made it clear that he thought Florida, not Notre Dame, gave him the best chance to win a national championship.

His decision only added to the insecurities of many of the Fighting Irish faithful, who began to wonder if Meyer might be right. Maybe, just maybe, the program's time had passed. Maybe recruits, mere infants when the Irish had last won a national title (1988), really did consider Notre Dame an also-ran. It didn't help that the school was still smarting over the internal and external criticism aimed at it for the unexpected firing of the classy Tyrone Willingham.

So it was no surprise that a whole nation of inquisitors asked essentially the same question when Notre Dame formally introduced its 28th head football coach in school history: Who is Charlie Weis?

Seeing Weis in a dark suit, white shirt, and blue tie, not the rumpled Patriots sweatshirt or coat that he always wore on the New England sidelines, it was a toss-up as to who was more uncomfortable, him or the Rev. Edward A. Malloy, the outgoing Notre Dame president who just days earlier had wiped his hands clean of the Willingham firing by declaring his "embarrassment" over the university's decision. Yet Malloy handled what could have been an awkward situation with brevity, clarity, and aplomb.

"I am pleased to be able to welcome our new football coach," Malloy said. "He has great pedigree, not only as a Notre Dame graduate, but in terms of his achievements in the professional ranks. I want to say to Coach Weis, you have my wholehearted support. We are really pleased to welcome you and your family back to our community, and I encourage every member of the broader Notre Dame community to give you the support that you deserve."

Next came the Rev. John I. Jenkins, Malloy's successor-elect, who had given his blessing to the controversial change in the football department. Scheduled to take over in the summer of 2005, Jenkins was making his first public appearance representing Notre Dame athletics.

"At the University of Notre Dame, the success in our football program consists of three things: acting with integrity, giving our students a superb education, and excelling on the field," Jenkins said. "Meeting all of these goals is a tremendous challenge. But I believe we have found a person in Charlie Weis who can lead us to such multifaceted success."

The 10-day search that ultimately led to Weis was aided by ex-Notre Dame athletic director and former Atlantic Coast Conference commissioner Gene Corrigan. At least four candidates were interviewed: Meyer, Weis, Buffalo Bills offensive coordinator (and former Notre Dame quarterback and assistant coach) Tom Clements, and Washington Redskins defensive coordinator (and former Irish assistant coach) Greg Blache. But only Weis spoke by phone with what White called, "the student-athlete transition team"—a committee of football players—before the university made its final decision. Weis also met with Notre Dame's executive vice president, John Affleck-Graves, and its NCAA faculty representative, Fernand N. "Tex" Dutile, a 1965 graduate of the Notre Dame Law School and a member of the faculty since 1971. Weis was then offered the position and couldn't say yes fast enough, becoming the first Notre Dame graduate since 1963 to be named head football coach at his alma mater.

After thanking his wife and son, university officials, and his agent, Bob LaMonte, Weis spoke about the long, unexpected journey back to his alma mater. He grew up in New Jersey an avid sports fan and wanted to be a sports announcer during his undergraduate days at Notre Dame, where he earned his degree in speech and drama in 1978 and gained certification as a teacher, just in case he didn't become the next Dick Enberg.

"Here I was, this know-it-all 22-year-old kid, and I had all the answers," said Weis, a smile on his face. "I was one of those guys who could watch the game and tell you all of the dumb things those coaches were doing."

After a five-year stint as an assistant football coach at Morristown (New Jersey) High School under his original mentor, John Chironna, Weis was hired by University of South Carolina head coach Joe Morrison, for whom he served four years as a graduate assistant and a volunteer coach before Morrison's death, at age 51, of a heart attack.

In 1989, Weis landed a head-coaching job at Franklin Township High School in New Jersey, where he led his team to a 10–1 record and a state championship. That's when Al Groh, an assistant under Morrison at South Carolina, recommended Weis to the NFL's New York Giants.

One day the phone rang at Weis' office. His secretary answered the call, jotted down a name, and then told Weis, "Hey, there's a guy by the name of Bill Parcells on the phone."

Sure there was. As if the head coach of the New York Giants would call a high school coach in Jersey. Weis figured it was one of his old college buddies trying to pull another lame practical joke. They had done it before, identifying themselves as Ara Parseghian or Dan Devine. But this was a new low, even for them.

"Oh, sure, put him on the line," an amused Weis told his secretary. He picked up the phone expecting to hear one of his friends laughing on the other end.

"Hey, Bill, how's it going?" said Weis, figuring he'd play along.

"What are you doing?" said the Big Tuna. Himself. Bill Parcells.

Instantly, Weis recognized the gruff voice.

Next thing Charlie Weis knew, he was being interviewed for an assistant coaching job with, yes, the New York Giants.

"It was just like interviewing for a job as head coach at Notre Dame," Weis told friends. "Wouldn't it be something if I ended up getting hired?"

He did. And it was something. Something big.

Weis became a defensive assistant and assistant special teams coach for the Giants. And now—flash-forward 15 years—with a well-established reputation as an offensive mastermind, the kid from Trenton who once pictured himself *announcing* Notre Dame games found himself *coaching* the Fighting Irish.

Weis began his remarks on that December day in 2004 by praising Parcells for the breaks he'd gotten in his career with the Giants. "Bill Parcells gave me an opportunity when I was an absolute nobody, and he groomed me," Weis said. "He started me on special teams, and then he moved me to offense. I coached running backs, tight ends, wide receivers, and quarterbacks. It always seemed like wherever I was with Bill, he always put me at positions that had good players. He kind of set me up for success."

The more Weis talked to the jam-packed audience in the 72–seat Joyce Center football auditorium, the more he sounded like a head football coach. He had paid his dues. He had learned from the best. He knew he was intelligent, and he had a feel for the game. And it was no coincidence that he wore one of his Super Bowl rings that day.

"You all are here today looking at Charlie Weis, and you don't know me," Weis said. "You don't know who I am because of the systems I've been groomed in. I've been groomed under the best, and that puts you in the position to be successful when you're given your opportunity. Well, guess what, folks? I hit pay dirt. The opportunity just struck, so here I am."

Weis outlined his plans for his new job in broad, general terms. As he spoke, his confidence was apparent. Diplomacy also appeared to be one of his assets. There would be no references to the previous regime, other than praise for the job done and the decision by the assistants to coach the Irish in the upcoming Insight Bowl against Oregon State.

"I'm not here to talk to you about anything in the past, but I will say this first: I have the utmost respect and appreciation for Tyrone Willingham and his staff," Weis said. "He is one of the finest men I've come across in this business, and I wish him nothing but the best."

Weis was being diplomatic, but he was also being smart. By acknowledging Willingham and the contributions he made during his three years at Notre Dame, Weis helped start the healing process within the university community.

It was no surprise that Weis made clear he agreed with the Notre Dame academic mantra: "Graduating kids is first and foremost when you bring in a student-athlete to Notre Dame. Bringing in character kids who will make the university proud is important. And yet, it's all about winning games. That's why there was a coaching change."

When Weis met the remaining players from the 2004 football team who had struggled to a 6–5 record during the regular season, he wasn't as diplomatic: "Bill Parcells said it to me years ago: 'You are what you are, folks.' And right now, you're a 6–5 football team. And guess what? That's just not good enough. That's not good enough for you, and it's certainly not going to be good enough for me. So if you think they hired me here to go .500, you've got the wrong guy."

This was a coach who had learned from the best, won against the best, and now insisted on the best from his new team.

This coach's style was markedly different from his predecessor's. Willingham had been calm, composed, almost serene. Weis had some of those same traits, but his voice had a bit of a Parcells edge too—confident, almost dictatorial in tone. There would be one way: Weis' way.

Then, in words that ultimately would serve as the battle cry for Fighting Irish fans from that day forward, Weis said, "How fast or how long it takes to get to the top, I'm not going to predict. But I can tell you this: You're going to have a hard-working, intelligent, nasty football team because the attitude of the head coach will be permeated through the players. I include the 'nasty' because that's part of being a winning football team."

Nasty.

A *nasty* football team.

Notre Dame fans liked the sound of that.

Weis said he would take care of the current players before he would worry about the incoming recruits. His reasoning: "The first thing I've got to do is sell them on the program. Then I've got to clear the slate, be open-minded, and give everyone a fair opportunity to show his wares. Once that happens, and you seed the bottom of your roster with fresh people coming out of high school that raise the talent level from underneath, you've got a chance to establish a system."

Every coach has a system. But Weis had an overarching philosophy to go along with his system. And that philosophy was this: In Weis We Trust.

If you don't trust Weis, go shopping for a different uniform.

"My job then becomes a simple one," he said. "It comes down to X's and O's, and to be honest with you, I think that's when we'll have the greatest advantage. When it comes down to to X's and O's, I have to believe we're going to win most of the time."

Was Weis saying he could outcoach almost any opponent? Uh, yes. You're not supposed to say that at an introductory news conference, are you? Maybe not, but he did say it—and he meant it.

Weis, who had admitted his disappointment when the Giants and Bills top jobs went to other coaches, was adamant about his commitment to his alma mater. He wouldn't use Notre Dame as an audition tape for an NFL head coaching gig. "This is *not* a stepping-stone," he said in a voice charged with you-better-believe-I-mean-it. "This is an end-all for our family. I come to Notre Dame with the intent of retiring here. We didn't come here to bounce somewhere else. If that's what

I was going to do, I wouldn't be taking this job. I'd be waiting until the season ended in the NFL and trying to get one of those jobs. I'm here because I want to be here. I'm proud to be here. I'm thankful to be here."

Weis said he owed both Notre Dame and the Patriots his best effort, and over the course of the next seven to eight weeks, he promised, he would fulfill both obligations: "Once New England's season is over, my NFL career is over, and I'm the head coach of the University of Notre Dame full-time until the day I retire. That is my intent."

Weis already had most of his coaching staff picked out. They would take care of the day-to-day work of recruiting while he shuttled between South Bend and Foxboro. He would make recruiting stops along the way when his Patriots schedule allowed. Most of his Notre Dame work would come late in the evening, when his Patriots work was done for the day.

Weis spoke about his plans for his offense, calling it "a very broad, expansive offensive package." He would fit the offense to the skills of the players he had. If the tight ends were a strength, he would use formations with multiple tight ends. With five offensive linemen and a quarterback, that left him with five other players to use to his advantage.

"How you use formations and personnel groups is what really gives you the advantage, because those defensive guys don't know what you're doing," Weis explained. "That's how we play the game. One week, against a team with poor defensive backs, we might throw more than we run. If we're playing against a team that's not good at stopping the run, we might run a lot more than we throw it. It's really not rocket science when you think about it now. You exploit weaknesses."

Weis admitted that recruiting would be tough for a program that had averaged six losses in its last two seasons. But besides having his greatest asset—Notre Dame—to sell, he would have his NFL success on his résumé. "When players go to front-line programs, they want to play on Saturdays so that they can end up playing on Sundays," Weis said. "I'm coming from teaching guys who play on Sundays, and I think that gives me an advantage because I've been there."

Weis also said he believed he had a recruiting advantage because of his Notre Dame background. No, he hadn't played football as a student, but he knew the game. He'd attended all the home games as an undergraduate. He'd even made a few road trips, like the one to Dallas for the 1978 Cotton Bowl against the No. 1–ranked Texas Longhorns. (When he found out Notre Dame had accepted the bowl bid, he rented a block of rooms at the local Howard Johnson and then sold them to fellow Notre Dame students making the trip.) He understood the academic and social issues at Notre Dame. Plus, he was a living example of just how big someone could dream. "Here's a guy who went to college at the University of Notre Dame and is now the head football coach at the University of Notre Dame," Weis said. "Think about that for a second. That means the sky's the limit, right?"

Weis said he wouldn't make excuses about the school's notoriously tough schedules and tough academics should there be failures on the field. He, the coaching staff, and the players would control their own fate. "They schedule 'em and we play 'em," Weis said. "That's the way it is. I don't make the schedule; I just play it. If I answered that any other way, I would be giving the players an excuse for failure."

And don't forget the "nasty" part.

"It goes back to having that toughness, playing smart, playing disciplined, being nasty, and going out there with an arrogant attitude," he said. "That's the way I have to get the kids thinking, because once they think like that, it doesn't make any difference where you play them. You can call any play in the world. If the kids *know* the play is going to work, they're going to *make* it work."

And what about schoolwork? Weis insisted that his players would be true student-athletes. "As for academics," Weis said, "no one willing to come to Notre Dame expects this to be an easy ride. But what a lot of people don't realize is how great the support system is here at Notre Dame. Once people get in school here, they have a chance to thrive. The most important thing is to find those guys who, academically and character-wise, combined with football ability, give you an opportunity to be proud of them when they end up graduating from Notre Dame."

In other words, Weis got it.

He *got* Notre Dame because he *was* Notre Dame. He had lived it as a student. Now he was about to live it as the head coach.

"There are a lot of hats you have to wear as head coach," he said. "You have to deal with the administration, you have to deal with admissions, and you have to deal with personal problems, family problems, and the press. When you're hired to run an organization like the football program at Notre Dame, you have to view it as a CEO, not just as a football coach. You have to find the right people to delegate responsibilities to. At the same time, you have to understand that you're the one who's ultimately responsible."

When a reporter raised the topic of dealing with the stress of coaching football, Weis talked about his past health issues—specifically, gastric bypass surgery in 2002 to help him control his weight—and how he now dealt with stressful situations much differently than he had earlier in his career. But when someone suggested that Weis had the elective surgery in order to present a better physical image, and thus help him land a head coaching job, he flashed a glimpse of his temper.

"Time out!" Weis snapped. "I didn't say how 'professionally important' the operation was. Let's get this clear right now. Don't put words in my mouth. I said that after the operation my perspective changed and that I learned how to handle things on a much more controlled, much more even keel. That's what I said."

The reporter tried to explain himself: "I read that you talked about becoming a head coach and that it was important to lose weight and that your appearance ... "

"I never said that!" Weis cut in. "A newspaper writer said that was the reason I did it. You want to know why you do gastric bypass? Because for 10 years you're over 300 pounds and your father died at 56 of a second heart attack. You're afraid if you stay at the same level, you're going to drop dead. That's why you do it! It has nothing to do with getting jobs. That's what someone else says because he wants to put words in your mouth. The bottom line is, when you're unhealthy, you do something about it."

Dead silence.

The subject quickly changed to Weis' decision to coach at his alma mater. Why go to downtrodden Notre Dame when his goal of becoming a head coach in the NFL was growing tantalizingly closer each year? His answer instantly endeared him to Fighting Irish fans: "You just said it—it's Notre Dame."

And then he elaborated, although it wasn't really necessary: "When coaching jobs open, you say maybe you can get this job, maybe you can get that job. But this is Notre Dame. If you're going somewhere, you should go where you feel you and your family can be part of something special. I can't think of a better place to be part of something special than to be part of this place."

The nation had now had its first long look at the man charged with bringing Notre Dame back to football prominence.

Was he the right man for the job? He certainly talked a good game.

A bit rough around the edges?

Sure, Charlie Weis still had plenty of blue-collar New Jersey in him. But Notre Dame was in a phase when it needed a little roughness around the edges.

Matter of fact, after hearing Charlie Weis raise the point, everybody agreed that what Notre Dame really, desperately needed was a little bit o' nasty.

Chapter 2

WHY WEIS?

WHEN IT CAME TO choosing a head football coach, no Division I-A program had a smaller margin for error than Notre Dame. It couldn't afford the divisiveness of the Bob Davie years, the public relations mushroom cloud created by the five-day reign of George O'Leary, or the stagnation of Tyrone Willingham's tenure.

The Irish needed a touchdown. They couldn't afford to punt.

Urban Meyer was a touchdown. That's what everyone said. He was young (40), handsome, personable, driven, Catholic, and had the necessary Notre Dame ties, thanks to the five years he'd spent on the Irish staff. It only made sense that he should return to South Bend, this time to end the inertia created during the Willingham regime. How, asked Meyer supporters, could you argue with the symmetry of it all?

Notre Dame was indeed interested in a reunion, but Meyer wasn't the only short list candidate with blue and gold on his résumé. While it's fair to assume that Meyer was Notre Dame's first choice for the job, Weis' qualifications also were formidable, beginning with his three Super Bowl rings (one with the New York Giants, two with the New England Patriots, and another, as it turned out, on the way). Weis had earned a degree from Notre Dame in 1978 and had gone on to become part of the famed Notre Dame alumni network. Weis understood the relationship between Notre Dame and its football program. He understood it because he had lived it. Notre Dame sports was in his blood.

In a 2003 interview conducted by fellow 1978 graduate Mike "Monte" Towle for *Notre Dame Magazine*, former classmate Jim Benenati, a radiologist in Florida who remains one of Weis' friends, remembered his magnetism. "Anyone who knew Charlie at Notre Dame—and he knew a lot of people around campus—had him pegged as a PR guy," Benenati said. "He's a great schmoozer who can talk sports with anyone. He would be a terrific college coach, able to talk the pants off of recruits' parents."

Towle, now the assistant sports editor of *The Tennessean,* in Nashville, knew Weis well during their undergraduate days. Towle was part of a three-man team that interviewed Weis his senior year when he tried out for a position on the student radio station, WSND. Towle said Weis couldn't be stumped when it came to sports trivia, and when he was asked to read a wire story as an audition, he delivered it in a soft, melodious voice.

Born in Vermont and a lifelong Boston Red Sox fan, Towle recalled a conversation he had with Weis, a diehard New York Yankee fan, over the phone. "We got into a big argument," Towle said. "Of course, the Yankees were dominant then, and I didn't have much to back up my argument. But I was yanking his chain. I got him so ticked off, he said, 'Monte, I'm coming over there right now!' He really believed he was right every time he opened his mouth.

"The interesting thing is that when I hear him talk today, he really doesn't look or carry himself much differently than he did back then,"

Towle continued. "He's kind of like a Woody Hayes with a bit of Anthony Robbins polish to him now."

The Notre Dame search committee was high on both coaching candidates, but Meyer was a natural first option, considering his success as a college head coach as well as his familiarity with Notre Dame. Yet Florida's lure proved too great, particularly for a man with three young children and a wife who, when consulted, indicated a preference for the warm climes of Gainesville over the uncertain and inconsistent weather patterns in South Bend. Just as Irish fans had built their hopes to a crescendo for the hottest college coaching name in the business, Meyer and Florida announced their engagement and subsequent marriage to one another.

"This was a family decision that was made prior to the Notre Dame situation," Meyer said. "I heard people say Notre Dame was 'your dream job.' It still is. It just so happens I have three young children and a situation that was well into effect before that one was even on the radar."

Meyer had been counseled by his father, Bud, who told the *Orlando Sentinel* that both Florida and Notre Dame had offered his son a $14 million, seven-year deal. Once the elder Meyer heard the terms, he provided strong, definitive advice for his son.

"If you want a good coaching job, you should go to Florida," Bud Meyer said. "But if you want to be someone immortal with a bronze statue, I don't think that comes with Florida." His son replied: "I just want to coach. I don't want to write books. I don't want to give speeches for $30,000 a pop. I just want to coach."

With Meyer off to Florida, two legitimate candidates remained: Weis and former Irish great Tom Clements. Clements had coveted the job for years, only to lose out to Davie in 1997 and O'Leary and Willingham in 2002.

A 1975 graduate in economics and a 1986 Notre Dame Law School product, Clements had been lauded by fellow Notre Dame alums, most notably Joe Montana and legendary Irish head coach Ara Parseghian. Cerebral, soft-spoken, and low-key, Clements wasn't going to impress the Notre Dame search committee with flamboyance. He had been known for his quiet, steely-eyed confidence as a player. His coaching style was cut from the same cloth. Two days after his December 9 interview, Clements was informed that he had been passed over for the head coaching position for the third time in eight years.

In short order, Notre Dame had zeroed in on Weis. Three days later, in a conference call, Weis spoke with a committee of Irish football players, among them quarterback Brady Quinn, linebacker Brandon Hoyte, defensive end Justin Tuck, tight end Anthony Fasano, offensive tackle Ryan Harris, and defensive end Victor Abiamiri. It was, in a way, like a group of employees interviewing a potential new boss. Questions were asked, issues were discussed. Weis ducked nothing.

About an hour after talking with the players, Weis spoke with the chair of Notre Dame's faculty board on athletics, Tex Dutile. He also talked to provost Nathan Hatch and executive vice president John Affleck-Graves. At about 6 p.m., Jenkins and White formally extended Weis the opportunity to become the 28th football coach in Notre Dame history. Weis accepted. Notre Dame had a new coach.

Weis had been scrutinized like no other coach in the history of Notre Dame football. While White said the research on Weis was no more all-encompassing than what the university had done with O'Leary, whose false claims about his athletic career at New Hampshire and about a master's degree from NYU instantly ended his Notre Dame career, a source told *Blue & Gold Illustrated*, a newspaper devoted principally to Notre Dame football, that the university made more than 200 phone calls while checking Weis' background.

"The reason that it's been tough is because Notre Dame has such a high profile," said Jenkins, who, along with White, had been followed by a television crew from the Salt Lake City airport to their meeting with Meyer at a local hotel. "When we go to visit coaches, the press follows us around. That's not true at every school. We welcome scrutiny. We have it because we have high ideals for our program. We're going to keep those high ideals."

Translation: Notre Dame wasn't going to settle for football mediocrity. Willingham had those same high ideals, but not enough victories.

Now that Jenkins was giving Weis the keys to the Irish football program, there was no confusion about what was expected.

"It's hard for people who are outside Notre Dame to understand the academic challenges of the school, the passion people have about Notre Dame and what it represents, not only on the football field but beyond it," said Jenkins. "Charlie Weis understands all of those things. He can represent them and tell the world about them."

Still, there is little doubt that the national embarrassment created by the O'Leary hiring-firing fiasco pushed Notre Dame to do more than its due diligence regarding Weis. It simply couldn't afford another mistake, another late-breaking revelation.

Oddly enough, a handful of Notre Dame players got a sneak preview of Weis the preceding winter when Willingham invited the then-Patriots offensive coordinator to visit the team. Who knew he was actually inviting his successor?

Willingham had brought Weis to Notre Dame to discuss offensive schemes and philosophy with the coaching staff. But before he left, Weis chatted with some of the players while they were conducting one of their off-season conditioning workouts.

Weis left an impression. One player called him "boastful, abrasive, and self-important," which isn't an altogether unreasonable reaction. At times Weis *is* abrasive, and his personality *is* in marked contrast to Willingham's more understated style.

Other players were amused by Weis' candor. "I can honestly say he was the first guest speaker who wasn't hip-hip-hooray for Notre Dame," said Tuck, who eventually would choose to bypass his final year of eligibility and enter the NFL draft. "He was more of a critical guest speaker. I was kind of surprised."

Weis read the players the riot act that day for their recently completed 5–7 season. He gave them a full serving of the NFL mentality: produce or perish. He could afford to be blunt because he was a Notre Dame alum and because he had been successful at the highest level of professional football. "He was really outgoing and spoke his mind," said Fasano. "A lot of guys were fired up and were like, Wow, it would be neat to play for that guy!"

Little did they know.

A New Jersey native, like Weis, Fasano wasn't put off by Weis' out-spokenness. But a few of his teammates were. "We're a little different on the East Coast," Fasano said. "A lot of guys were kind of shocked by the conversation we had. They came away wondering what it would be like to play for that kind of guy and wondering what his players at New England thought of him. He said he might not be liked, and that's good for a football coach sometimes."

Tuck, shy and reticent by nature, had a different perspective. "At the beginning, I thought he was kind of arrogant, kind of cocky, and kind of confident, flashing his Super Bowl rings around," said the Kellyton, Alabama native. "But if you listened to what he had to say, he was hitting all the right points. He questioned our leadership, and a lot of people didn't take that the right way at first. But after you sat down and thought about it, he was definitely saying the right things. A lot of people forget how physical this game is, and you've got to have a nasty streak in you to play it. If he's going to be a nasty coach, this is going to be a nasty team, and that only benefits us."

No player was affected more significantly by the hiring of Weis than Brady Quinn. Just entering his junior season, Quinn recognized a good recruiter when he heard one. "Once he gets the opportunity to walk into the house of a recruit," Quinn said, "it will be a done deal. He's straightforward. He told us exactly what we needed to do and what he saw out there that we were doing wrong and what we needed to work on as a team."

When word began to spread that Weis had landed the Notre Dame job, several ex-Notre Dame players who had worked for him in the NFL offered their perspective. Former Irish wideout David Givens, who played for Weis in New England, saw him as a perfect fit. "He's been a teacher and coach of high school kids, and he's got so much experience coaching NFL players like myself," said Givens. "There's no doubt in my mind he would be an outstanding recruiter because he relates so well to young people. I can say this because I've played for Charlie and I played at Notre Dame. I understand the pressures of playing and the pressures the coaches had coaching us at Notre Dame. They're all things Charlie would do very well with."

Former Irish tight end Mark Bavaro, who played under Weis with the New York Giants, offered a glowing endorsement, going so far as to compare the new coach to Parcells and Belichick. "I don't think Notre Dame could have made a better decision," said Bavaro. "He's a very straightforward, no-nonsense type of guy. He's not in it for glory or self-promotion. He's in it to win. He's definitely proven he can handle pressure. The Notre Dame job comes with its own type of pressure, but from what I've seen him go through in the past, I think he'll come through just fine."

Former Irish fullback Marc Edwards, who played under Weis in New England, vouched for his offensive creativity: "Charlie doesn't impose his offense on his players. A lot of coaches have a certain ego that their system will outsmart anybody. That's not necessarily the case. You have to use the talent you have. Charlie is so innovative. He was always throwing something at us that was different, some new way of attacking. One of his strengths was how he always used his personnel in the most efficient manner."

Former Irish quarterback, NFL star, and current ESPN analyst Joe Theismann had crossed paths with Weis. As an observer of the game, he felt Weis was on the cutting edge of offensive football, not to mention a good fit for Theismann's alma mater. "He understands throwing the football," said Theismann. "That's what this era of college football is today, the ability to put it in the air. He's been a student at Notre Dame, so he knows the culture of the university. He's worked on a big stage, having been part of world championships with the Patriots. He's a man who will bring a quiet discipline to the program. I think it's a great hire."

No one's endorsement carried more weight than that of the exacting Bill Belichick, who had entrusted his offense to Weis beginning with the 2000 season. In three of the next four years, the Patriots won the Super Bowl. "Charlie is a very smart person," said Belichick. "He really understands what defenses are doing and how to attack them.

He's an outstanding play-caller and has a great sense of timing for when to call certain plays. He's very good at making adjustments during a game. He's not afraid to make tough decisions or to make calls in critical situations. He knows what he wants to do, and he does it with a lot of confidence, and I think that gets conveyed to the people who are executing it."

Indeed, Weis' confidence was out there front and center: "Even though I didn't play football in college or the pros," he said, "I *do* have a clue."

Notre Dame was about to discover that the schmoozer, the guy who thought he was right every time he opened his mouth had more than a clue.

He had a plan.

......

Chapter 3

THE TYRONE WILLINGHAM YEARS—ALL THREE OF THEM

T HE FOUR HORSEMEN. WIN one for the Gipper. Helmets with actual gold dust from the O'Brien Paint Company. Rudy. Pep rallies. The Victory March. Notre Dame's football program has enough history to fill a floor of the Hesburgh Library. That history, that overwhelming sense of tradition, is what separates it from every other Division I-A school.

Or at least, it did, until November 30, 2004, the day Tyrone Willingham, Notre Dame's first-ever African-American head coach, was fired.

Of all of Notre Dame's football traditions, the one that had withstood the test of time is nowhere to be found on any list of official school lore. The school's annual football guide, all 200–plus pages of it, includes no mention of it. And yet, it was as much a part of the

Fighting Irish program as the 11 national championships, the seven Heisman Trophy winners, and even the famed "Play Like a Champion Today" sign the players pat on their way to the field at Notre Dame Stadium.

It was an unspoken yet unbreakable rule: barring scandal, death, or wartime, it was understood that no Notre Dame head football coach would be dismissed until he'd had a minimum of five years to establish his program. It was a noble attempt to create stability, to separate Notre Dame from so-called football factories.

That all changed when athletics director Kevin White announced that Willingham had been fired a few weeks shy of his third anniversary. The decision unleashed a firestorm of criticism from the national media and created a backlash that threatened to incite civil war within the university's extended family.

A day later, Willingham sat at a table inside the Joyce Center Football Auditorium, meeting the assembled media with the same composed demeanor that had become his hallmark in both good times and bad: self-assured, prepared, in charge. Only now, Willingham was not in charge.

A rally that had been scheduled earlier in the week to demand Willingham's resignation had been replaced by a smaller crowd decrying the surprise decision to fire him. A group of 30 to 40 protesters carried signs that read "$ Cost ND Its Integrity," "Never Before, Never Again," and "We Want Ty Back."

Once the news broke that Willingham would not be back, Chandra Johnson, an assistant to Notre Dame president Rev. Edward A. Malloy, shaved her head to protest the firing. Johnson, an African-American, said she would remain bald until Notre Dame won a national title in football "because when we do, that will be justification for some people for why we fired Tyrone Willingham. Not to me, but for some people."

Johnson called the process of firing Willingham "flawed" and claimed that too few people were involved in the decision. "There was little to no consideration of the ramifications," she added. Her stinging remarks—and her unusual gesture of support for Willingham—were soon national news.

You didn't need CSI: South Bend to figure out to whom Johnson was referring to. A pair of powerbrokers—Notre Dame board of trustees chairman Patrick McCartan and trustee Philip Purcell—were considered the ones most responsible for at least initiating the change. They certainly did so without the approval of Malloy and without making their intentions fully known to Notre Dame's faculty board.

In essence, it was a stealth firing.

There were also other movers and shakers involved, to varying degrees. The fingerprints, however faint, of Andrew McKenna, a former chairman of the board of trustees who moves easily within the inner circles of the Chicago business world, could be lifted from the scene. And it is unlikely that trustee Joseph O'Neill III wasn't somewhere in the decision making loop. After all, both men served on the search committee that targeted Weis and Meyer.

The national media ripped Notre Dame to shreds, accusing the school of the worst kind of hypocrisy. Worse yet, members of Notre Dame's own football family made little or no effort to hide their displeasure with the chain of events that had led to Willingham's dismissal.

Former Irish All-American and Lombardi Award winner Chris Zorich, a treasured alumnus and an ambassador of the program, could hardly contain his disgust. During an interview with ESPN, Zorich said, "The firing really tarnishes what Notre Dame is all about." His quote in a *USA Today* column by Jon Saraceno was even more incendiary: "I hate saying this, but I am not familiar with this Notre Dame."

Quarterback Brady Quinn, who had a close relationship with Willingham, had this to say to reporters: "Think about it: It's not even allowing one of his recruiting classes to get all the way through."

Faculty board representative Steve Fallon, in an interview with the *South Bend Tribune*, said there was a concern "about what this teaches student-athletes and students in general about ethical dealings." He also raised the issue of diversity at the school, saying that many of his colleagues were "worried about negative results on recruitment and retention and the quality of life of African-American students and faculty. There's concern about the faculty being overlooked in an important decision. And there's concern about the long-term implications."

Even those who understood the football reasons for the dismissal were upset with the secrecy of the decision. Those critics included Dave Duerson, a member of the board of trustees and a former Irish captain whose son played for Willingham at Notre Dame. "Was I completely surprised Ty was released?" Duerson said in an interview published in the *Detroit News*. "No, not given the win-loss record. But it was the way it was handled. As we all see, it has left quite a black eye on the university."

But the words that left the biggest bruise on Notre Dame's reputation came from president Malloy, who actually said he was "embarrassed" by the chain of events. Less than a week after Willingham's December 1 news conference, Malloy spoke at the *Sports Business Journal*'s Intercollegiate Athletics Forum in New York. His criticism of his own institution quickly became national news.

"I thought we were going to abide by our precedent, which was a five-year window for a coach to display a capacity to be successful within our system," Malloy said. "The philosophical shift we have taken is a significant one. I am not happy about it, and I do not assume responsibility for it."

In short, Malloy all but admitted that his status as a lame duck president had been fatal. There had been a football coup d'etat.

"I think what Father Malloy said was one of the most courageous things I've heard in my 24 years as a university president," said Vanderbilt chancellor Gordon Gee in an interview with *The New York Times*. "What he basically said is that the value system of the university and value system of the athletic department have been totally disrupted."

Why hadn't Willingham been given five years at Notre Dame? His .583 winning percentage in three years (21–15) was exactly the same as that of his immediate predecessor, Bob Davie (35–25), who still got the traditional five. The university certainly had no reason to criticize Willingham's comportment during his three-year reign. He never sought to shift responsibility. He never questioned Notre Dame's high standards. He never questioned the academic restrictions. He never questioned Notre Dame's admissions policies. He offered zero excuses.

So it was no surprise that, in the end, Willingham took full responsibility for his fate. "To say that I am merely disappointed very much misses the mark," he said at the press conference. "But at the same time, I understand that I did not meet the expectations or standards that I set for myself. When you don't meet the expectations of yourself, you leave yourself vulnerable to the will of others. So today, I am no longer the head football coach at Notre Dame."

Asked what else he could have done to maintain his position with Notre Dame, Willingham answered simply and directly: "Win. That's it. That's the bottom line."

After winning the first eight games of the 2002 season, Willingham's first, with a defense that could score and an offense that couldn't, the Irish lost at home to Boston College, 14–7. Four weeks later, after Notre Dame victories over Navy and Rutgers, Pete Carroll's Southern California Trojans overwhelmed the Irish, 44–13. A month after that, North Carolina State defeated Notre Dame, 28–6, in the Gator Bowl.

What had begun as a promising, Bowl Championship Series-type season ended with 10 victories but also with three losses in the last five games. What would turn out to be Willingham's best season at Notre Dame had ended in disappointment and regression.

The following year, Fighting Irish losses came with greater frequency and startling one-sidedness: Michigan 38, Notre Dame 0; Michigan State 22, Notre Dame 16; Purdue 23, Notre Dame 10; USC 45, Notre Dame 14; Boston College 27, Notre Dame 25; Florida State 37, Notre Dame 0; Syracuse 38, Notre Dame 12.

The promise of a fresh start in 2004 quickly faded when the Irish and their anemic offense fell to an average Brigham Young team, 20–17. Three straight victories, including a stirring 28–20 win over Michigan in Notre Dame Stadium, were followed by a 41–16 shellacking from Purdue. Lackluster wins over Stanford and Navy were followed by a heartbreaking 24–23 loss at home to Boston College when kicker D.J. Fitzpatrick, virtually automatic all season, missed an extra point—his only botched PAT of the season. An unexpected victory on the road against Tennessee preceded another gut-wrenching home loss, this time to Pittsburgh,

41–38, as the Irish defense allowed a Notre Dame record-setting five touchdown passes. The USC Trojans then administered their annual 31–point whupping of the Irish as quarterback Matt Leinart tied the five-touchdown mark set by Pittsburgh's Tyler Palko two weeks earlier.

There was a disturbing lack of consistency all season long, and a feeling among a growing number of Irish supporters that the program had reverted back to the state in which Davie had left it.

After Willingham was fired, defensive coordinator Kent Baer took over as interim head coach for the December 28 Insight Bowl in Phoenix against Oregon State. A distracted, dispirited Notre Dame team lost, 38–21.

And yet, it wasn't the losses that made the 2004 season one of the lowest points in Notre Dame football history. The Irish had lost before and eventually risen again. What was happening inhouse, within the Notre Dame family and community, was the real tragedy.

The "will of others," as Willingham referred to it, certainly was divided in the immediate hours following Notre Dame's 41–10 loss to USC on November 27—its third straight 31–point loss to the Trojans under Willingham. As Kevin White met with the media outside the Notre Dame locker room in Los Angeles Memorial Coliseum, he gave no hint of what was to come within the next 72 hours. It appeared that White himself didn't even know.

Seven key players in the decision-making process convened on Monday, November 29: Malloy, White, president-elect Rev. John Jenkins (who would be replacing Malloy in the summer of 2005), university provost Dr. Nathan Hatch, executive vice president John Affleck-Graves, and trustees McCartan and Purcell.

They voted, 4–3, to fire Willingham.

After it was all over, there was no announcement of how the ballots were cast, but any close observer of Notre Dame football could make an educated guess about who took which side.

Malloy, in his final year as the university's president, was vehemently opposed to the firing. "In my 18 years," he would say later, "there have only been two days that I've been embarrassed to be president of Notre

Dame—Tuesday and Wednesday of last week." White and Hatch presumably sided with their boss. Jenkins, Affleck-Graves, and the two trustees must have cast the deciding votes to remove Willingham.

Despite his opposition to the firing, White remained loyal to the university. "All of us had great expectations when we sat here three years ago, and in a number of ways, Tyrone has been an excellent fit and a great representative of our program," White said after the deed was done. "He personally has displayed impeccable integrity and tremendous character, and his players have represented themselves off the field in a first-class manner. In addition, our football program under his watch has never been stronger in terms of its academic performance."

On the field, though, it was a different story: Notre Dame had lost 15 of its last 28 games, including eight by at least 22 points. "At the end of the day," said White, "we simply have not made the progress on the field that we need to make. From Sunday through Friday, our football program has exceeded all expectations in every way. Tyrone has done some wonderful things. But on Saturday, we have struggled. Nor have we been able to create the positive momentum necessary in our efforts to return the Notre Dame program to the elite level of the college football world. That's not a negotiable position at Notre Dame."

Nobody would come right out and say it, but Notre Dame football under Willingham was, well, boring. Not once in his three seasons did the Irish score 300 points or more. To put that in perspective, Lou Holtz (1986–1996), considered by most observers to be a conservative offensive strategist, had five teams that scored more than 400 points in a season and just one that scored fewer than 300 points—and that single instance came in 1986, Holtz' first year, when the Irish tallied 299 points.

The Irish running game, a staple of all great Notre Dame teams in years past, never materialized under Willingham. In the 20–17 loss to Brigham Young to open the 2004 season, Notre Dame managed a pathetic 11 yards on 21 carries—its lowest single-game rushing output in 39 years. The team's 127.4 yards per game rushing was the lowest in school history, almost a first down less than the 135.2-yard mark of 1959.

Still, why did Davie (but not Willingham) warrant the benefit of the doubt and get to serve the fourth and fifth years of his contract? After all, Davie's third team posted a 5–7 record, worse than Willingham's 6–5 in 2004.

One answer is that Davie's teams were much more competitive than Willingham's. Of Davie's 25 losses in five years, only four were by as many as three touchdowns. In addition, Davie seemed to be on the right path when he led the Irish to a BCS bid against Oregon State in the Fiesta Bowl during his fourth year. Willingham's teams were getting worse with each game.

In addition, Willingham's Irish teams were lousy at home. His three-year mark at South Bend was 11–7, including 7–7 in his last 14 home games. To put that home record in perspective, Willingham would have needed to win his next 13 games in Notre Dame Stadium—every home game in 2005 and 2006—just to equal Davie's 24–7 home record.

Willingham's plight was also made more difficult by the fact that he followed Davie. Most fans didn't look at Willingham as a coach in his third year, but rather, as the coach of a Notre Dame program that had been mediocre for eight seasons, including five seasons with at least six losses.

The national media raised the issue of race after Willingham's firing. In doing so, they used a simple formula: All the other Notre Dame head coaches, who were white, received at least five years; Willingham, who was black, received three. Therefore, racism must have been involved in the decision to end Willingham's tenure prematurely.

This made for an easy-to-follow story angle, but it was far too simple. And it overlooked the reality of Notre Dame football on the field. The Irish had played a steady brand of uninspired, inconsistent, and undisciplined football. Notre Dame had played like a poorly coached football team for the previous couple of seasons and had the record to show for it.

Had Willingham and his staff recruited well amid the strife on the field, perhaps the university power brokers would have shown a bit more patience. Davie, a proven defensive coach who showed the ability to make adjustments, had worked the recruiting trail hard, earning, for what they were worth, Top 5 rankings in both 1998 and 1999. Willingham, on the other hand, had earned a reputation from assorted recruiting gurus for their unwillingness to go the extra mile on the recruiting trail. Projections indicated that the Irish were on their way to a second straight substandard recruiting campaign, one that was expected to finish outside of the nation's Top 20 once again.

Three things were key in Willingham's life: his faith, his family, and football—in that order. Each received an allotted amount of time in his well-planned schedule. Anything beyond that was rare indeed. And there was the rub. Most football coaches who are known for their greatness are willing to sacrifice nearly everything in the pursuit of victory. Willingham drew a line in the turf: he refused to sacrifice his health and sanity for football. Besides, spending more time on preparation or recruiting would be an admission that he had somehow miscalculated, and that was something Willingham was not likely to do. It would be a sign of weakness, and Willingham never admitted to or showed weakness.

Notre Dame's recruiting efforts were becoming more sporadic and incomplete under Willingham. He usually brought in fewer than the 56 recruits the NCAA allows to visit a college campus per recruiting campaign. He was bringing in good kids, capable student-athletes who could make it in the classroom, but he wasn't bringing in kids who could make a difference on the field. Plus, significant gaps in the recruiting process were exposed. For example, just four offensive linemen were signed in two years, creating a shortage in both talent and depth. With Notre Dame's difficult schedule, Willingham's recruiting shortcomings were setting the Irish up for further problems down the road, particularly since adjusting on the fly within a game was not a staff strength.

Three of Willingham's top commitments in his final recruiting class decided to go elsewhere after he was fired. But with or without them, the class that was signed in February 2005 was not going to restore Notre Dame football to glory. The hard fact is that the Irish were no longer regularly competitive in recruiting with schools such as USC, Oklahoma, Miami, Ohio State, and Meyer's new employer, Florida.

Meanwhile, on the field, Willingham and his coaching staff provided few answers. Halftime adjustments were a rarity, based upon the results in the second half. In 2003, the Irish were outscored in the second half 21–0 by Michigan, 16–10 by Michigan State, 10–0 by Purdue, 17–0 by USC, 14–0 by Florida State, 14–13 by Navy and 28–9 by Syracuse. In 2004, Notre Dame was outscored in the second half by Michigan State (17–10), Purdue (21–13), Boston College (17–3), and USC (24–0).

And yet, one or two more victories in 2004 likely would have saved Willingham's job. At 6–5, on the heels of a 5–7 season, the university had some numerical justification for his dismissal. At 7–4 or 8–3—easily attainable in 2004—Willingham likely would have been retained.

Also, had Willingham been willing to make some changes to his coaching staff, the university might have been inclined to give him a fourth season. That would have displayed a willingness to be flexible and creatively solve the problems. Instead, Willingham chose loyalty to his assistant coaches over allegiance to the university. He announced late in the 2004 season that he expected all of his coaches to return in 2005, despite the obvious troubles with the offense.

Asked if replacing some of his assistant coaches had been an issue with the university, Willingham said, "I don't think that needs to be discussed." White offered a similar response: "Coach Willingham knows how to hire a staff and put together a staff, and he's a professional. We didn't spend a whole lot of time having those conversations."

Translation: It was an issue.

Something clearly had to be done with offensive coordinator Bill Diedrick, who, according to several players who would speak only with a promise of anonymity, was no favorite of the team. Diedrick had also grown surlier with the media with each passing week during the 2004 season. He usually managed to contain his anger while answering a question, but it was clear he had no patience for reporters who asked probing questions.

After Willingham was fired and Kent Baer was named interim head coach, Diedrick refused interview requests. The day before the Insight Bowl, a university employee observed Diedrick yelling in the direction of a reporter who had stumbled upon information pertaining to injuries that would keep several key players out of the game against Oregon State.

The day after Willingham's firing, running backs coach Buzz Preston, however, was easy to find in the football office—and more than willing to speak out. "It's sad that universities and presidents and boards of trustees, all of them, they talk two different things. They say one thing, but they really mean another," he said. "The bottom line is the dollar bill and wins and losses. They don't care about coaches and people; it's just about wins and losses.

"You would like to think that you'd get more than three years to run the program," he added. "There were times when we could have done a better job of coaching. But you don't give a guy three years and not get a senior class through."

Both Diedrick and Preston had experienced success with Willingham at Stanford. But the definition of success was different at Notre Dame. At South Bend, where spiritual, social, academic, and athletic success is expected, it wasn't enough to sign good kids, treat them with respect, and watch them graduate. Winning was important too. Striving for and attaining excellence came with the territory.

As he had been throughout his three-year tenure at Notre Dame, Willingham was succinct and to the point in his final news conference in South Bend. "My goals have always been to help our young people be absolutely the best they can be in all areas, and I believe I have been true to them," he said. "I'm appreciative of the opportunity. I'm appreciative of what we have done. I'm just disappointed in what I didn't do."

Toward the end of the 20-minute press conference, he began answering each question in single sentences or short phrases. In other words, he exited Notre Dame the same way he entered the Monogram Room in Notre Dame's Joyce Center on January 1, 2002, when he accepted the position.

When senior associate athletic director John Heisler announced that Willingham would take one more question and a reporter started to ask one, Willingham responded, "No, that was the last one. Thank you. My wish will be that this program has great success in the future, and that whoever the coach is, I hope he comes in and does a great job because I believe there are some great young men in this program."

And then, in seconds, he was gone.

The impact of Willingham's firing, however, wouldn't go away quite so quickly.

Chapter 4

••••••

THE NEW SHERIFF IN TOWN

CHARLIE WEIS MET WITH the media in South Bend for the second time on Friday, January 7, 2004. He had some free time because the Patriots had a first-round bye in the playoffs. Weis had been shuttling between Foxboro and the Notre Dame campus since being named Willingham's successor. But despite the hectic schedule, it was obvious he had somehow found time to analyze the many facets of the Notre Dame football program.

If anyone wondered how quickly Weis would assume total control of his new empire, this was the session that dispelled all doubts. The handful of reporters in the Joyce Center football auditorium expected to hear a rundown of Weis' schedule, a report on recruiting progress, and maybe a little something about the Patriots. Instead, they got a blunt lecture on how dreadfully the media had dealt with

Willingham's dismissal—and how they'd damned well better behave during his regime.

It was what they call in the South a Come-to-Jesus talk.

"I don't want *anyone* contacting a player or a coach on his or her own," Weis said sternly. "They're *all* off limits until I say otherwise. You want to interview a player or a coach? I'll be more than happy to give you permission to talk to them. I want all requests to go through our sports information department, *with* the subject. Not just *who* you want to talk to, okay? But the *subject* you want to talk about as well."

Weis had built his coaching career surrounded by the East Coast media, where combativeness was standard operating procedure and adversarial relationships between athletes and coaches and the press were common. Through the better part of a decade and a half, Weis had seen his former boss, Bill Parcels, lash out at the media more than a few times. It had worked pretty well for the Big Tuna; why wouldn't it work for his best student? Might as well establish the ground rules right now.

Plus, a certain degree of combativeness was part of Weis' nature.

Bill Belichick, a less outspoken but equally guarded man, had made his coaches off limits to the media. Weis would limit, though not totally restrict, his coaches' access during his first spring. But this was South Bend, not New York or Boston. More accurately, this was Notre Dame. A head coach lecturing the media and keeping them on a short leash had never been part of the Fighting Irish football experience.

Men's basketball under Digger Phelps? Different game, different story.

But not football. Not ever.

Until now.

Historically, the media covering the Fighting Irish football program had enjoyed—thanks in great measure to longtime sports information director Roger Valdiserri, who retired in 1995—a warm and fuzzy welcome at Notre Dame. (Read: access.) Valdiserri developed close relationships with reporters. The Chicago media were on good terms with Valdiserri and his staff, who believed dealing with the media was part of the educational experience of a Notre Dame football player.

"I used to tell the players, 'You can't just answer a question, yes or no.' I mean, that's no answer at all," said Valdiserri. "So you had to teach them what writers were looking for. I would talk to them individually, and I would talk to them as a group before the season. I just felt they had to develop and mature, and no matter where they went after they graduated, they had to learn how to deal with the media. If they went into pro football, they had to be equipped."

The head coach didn't dictate how the relationship between the football team and the media evolved; Valdiserri did. So revered and respected was Valdiserri that you can see his name on the back of a Notre Dame jersey worn by a football extra in the movie *Rudy*.

It was Valdiserri who taught former Irish great Chris Zorich a valuable lesson about dealing with the media. The No. 1 ranked Irish had just lost at home to Stanford, 36–31, in 1990. It was Notre Dame's second loss in 29 games. After the game, when Valdiserri told Zorich the media wanted to speak with him, Zorich said he didn't want to talk. "Whoa, wait a minute," Valdiserri replied. "If you're willing to talk with them when you win, you've got to be willing to talk when you lose."

Times have changed. The sheer volume of media today—network and cable television, newspapers, sports talk radio, the Internet—has forced schools to scale back on the athletes' accessibility. Under Willingham individual Notre Dame players could be interviewed just one day a week and following games.

Access to practices, which had been open to the media and followers of the program through the 1980s and early 1990s, was first limited, and then eventually closed except for a brief segment at the start of drills. The media were given 20 minutes to observe practice, which meant they were allowed to watch the players stretch and little else. Observing the performance and development of players on the practice field was now a thing of the past.

Willingham, for the most part, was cordial and accommodating with the media, although there were certain subjects—for instance, the personal lives of the coaches and players, as well as injuries—about which he would not speak. He was polite, yet it was obvious that he had little regard for the time spent with reporters, other than the distraction that it created.

Now, in just his second gathering with the media, Weis seemed hell-bent on setting the tone—make that laying down the law. And so, before he spoke about his itinerary and game plan for the next month or so, he made sure everybody knew who was boss.

And Weis had another commandment: Thou SHALT NOT DIVIDE THE TEAM.

"We have too many team spokespeople around here," he said. "The kids were put in a very uncomfortable situation"—he was talking about the aftermath of Willingham's firing—"with you guys asking about the past staff, about the present staff. I mean, you guys took total advantage of them. Those days are over. Let's get that straight first, because I'm not hanging the kids out to dry. I don't think that's right. Anyone you want to talk to, they're open to you. I just want to know what the topic of the conversation is, because if you want to talk about, Hey, tell me about the difference between Coach Willingham and Coach Weis, guess what? That interview is going to be rejected, declined, over before it starts."

(Had the media really taken advantage of the players after Willingham's dismissal? No. Questions were asked. Questions were answered. Had they wanted to, the players could have said the two magic words: "No comment.")

"We're more than happy to help you find out about any of the coaches here," Weis continued. "But right now, they can't talk about our players. They don't even know them yet. They're just getting in here, doing research on our players and getting involved in recruiting. Right now we're still in the information-gathering stage, not the information-passing-out stage."

Weis said the players weren't qualified to discuss the coaching transition, so that subject would be off limits. "Every time I turned around, we had another player giving you his opinion on the coaching situation," said Weis. "What do they know? They don't know anything.

They barely even know me. So I don't need them speaking for me. I think I can speak for myself."

Weis made it clear the same rules would apply to all members of the press. There would be no private "understandings."

"As far as interviews with me, I don't ever talk off the record," he added. "So don't say to me, 'Hey, this is off the record now.' You have a question for me? I'll answer it. And if I can't answer it or if I don't think it's appropriate, then I just won't answer it, okay?"

Weis said there would be a press conference every Sunday, the day after a game, basically to get the media out of the way. "Monday to me is a game-plan day and I don't want to be spending the whole game-plan day with you guys," he explained. "I want to be game planning so we have a chance to win on Saturdays. By Sunday, it will give me an opportunity to see the tape, to talk to the coaches, and then I will be available to you at length so that you guys can tell me how dumb or how stupid I am for something that happened during the game, or how brilliant I am, conversely, if something ended up going well."

In short, Weis would be media friendly — on his terms. "I understand the job you have to do, and I certainly will do everything I can to make your jobs easier," he said. "But we need to get this thing under control. I don't want to hang the sports information people out to dry. I don't want to hang the players out to dry. I don't want to hang the coaches out to dry. And I certainly don't want to hang you out to dry. So I'll make myself very available to you, but I need you to work with me."

Weis wasn't done. An anonymous quote from a Notre Dame player, printed in *Blue & Gold Illustrated* following the one-sided Insight Bowl loss to Oregon State, had been critical of the previous coaching regime. Weis said he didn't appreciate "anonymous quotes" from players. "If I start reading those anonymous quotes now, you're shut down," he told the assembled media. "I will never say another word to you. Let's understand that, too, because if I start seeing those anonymous quotes, not only will I try my best to find out who that anonymous player is, but you will be off limits to everyone in the program. So let's make sure we understand what the terms are walking in the door."

No one in the room doubted the new coach would keep his word.

As it turned out, Weis' bark was—probably intentionally—far worse than his bite. In the ensuing months, he would go out of his way to create a good relationship between his program and the media. Access to players and coaches, although controlled, was consistent and accommodating. Virtually any player could be reached over the course of a given week during the football season. Weis was relaxed and cordial—and accessible—throughout the spring. His responses to questions were cohesive, concrete, interesting.

The man who once dreamed of becoming a broadcast journalist was playing "the media game."

By his rules, of course.

Always by his rules.

......

Chapter 5

FAMILY FIRST

CHARLIE WEIS ARRIVED IN South Bend—make that returned home to South Bend—with a hard-wired understanding of what Notre Dame meant to Notre Dame people, for the simple reason that Notre Dame meant the same thing to him.

He was one of them.

For starters, he understood what buttons to push with the former players, including Chris Zorich, who returned to the campus to serve as an honorary captain of the annual Blue-Gold Game in the spring of 2005. Weis had heard about Zorich's stinging comments after Willingham was fired. He knew what he had to do.

"It's no secret that I was pissed off with the way the university handled the firing of Coach Willingham," Zorich said. "I was a huge fan of his. However, I got a phone call about a month ago from Coach

Weis, and we spent about a half-hour on the phone and he reminded me so much of what Lou Holtz talked about as far as bringing back an attitude, bringing back that winning desire. He talked about being mean and nasty, and that's something that, unfortunately, Notre Dame hasn't had in a very long time. All of a sudden you have a coach telling you that we need nasty players. I kind of got excited. So when he asked me to come, I was like, 'Coach, I'm ready to suit up!' "

Weis also persuaded larger-than-life former Golden Domers Joe Montana, Tim Brown, and Joe Theismann to return for the spring game. He wasn't simply rebuilding a football program. He was rebuilding a sense of order, and using the past to help ease the transition to the future.

"It's like a field of dreams," Theismann said. "If you build it, they will come. The fact of the matter is Charlie can bring back what we're looking for, and that's winning."

No former player is more revered in the Notre Dame universe than Joe Montana. When he spoke at the 2003 football banquet, it was as if Notre Dame were getting a visit from royalty. And how did the football program take advantage of Montana's presence? By bringing in four football recruits for the banquet. Four.

Perhaps schedules conflicted. Notre Dame had ended its regular season a week later than normal, which meant the team banquet was held a week later than usual. So perhaps timing played a role. But it also accentuated the inability of the Willingham regime to capitalize on the big picture of Notre Dame football, the magnitude of its tradition, and, most obviously, the cachet of Joe Montana. Or maybe Willingham's staff simply couldn't attract more than four recruits to the banquet.

"Many of the players from the past have moved further and further away from the program," Weis said. "One of the first things I'm trying to do is bring them back into the program so we can get everyone knowing what Notre Dame was when they were at the top."

When Montana returned to the campus for the 2005 spring game with the other former Irish greats, there were dozens of high school junior football players in attendance. Montana, Theismann, Zorich, and Brown mingled easily with the current players, eliciting a bunch of wide-eyed stares and excited conversations. By the time the four Irish greats left Notre Dame Stadium after the Blue-Gold Game, you could feel the family reforming. The rifts had been huge. Weis had set about repairing them, one by one.

Notre Dame still hadn't played a down under a Charlie Weis game plan, but the negative vibes lingering from the Willingham dismissal had dissipated. Weis had willed the Fighting Irish family back together, and inspired hopes that Notre Dame football could be a power again, as it had been under Ara Parseghian, Dan Devine, and Lou Holtz.

The staff was now newly charged with Notre Dame tradition. The defensive coordinator, Rick Minter, had coached under Lou Holtz at Notre Dame more than a decade earlier. Mike Haywood, a former Irish player and current coach who had declared the Notre Dame house "in a shambles" when Weis hired him, was the new offensive coordinator. The director of personnel development, Ron Powlus, entered the 2005 season holding many of the school's passing records. Peter Vaas, who had coached under Holtz before Minter did, would eventually replace quarterbacks coach David Cutcliffe when Cutcliffe developed heart problems.

Overseeing it all was Mr. Blue-and-Gold himself, Weis. While Bob Davie once said that Notre Dame relied too much on its past and tradition, Weis wrapped his arms around it and used it to his and the university's advantage. "I understand Notre Dame," Weis said. "Part of being successful at Notre Dame is really understanding the composition that makes Notre Dame, and I think that gives me a fighting chance."

CHARLIE AND MAURA WEIS' perspective on the role of family crystallized on April 7, 1992, the day their daughter, Hannah, was born. Actually, it was a perspective that began to hit home when Maura was seven months pregnant, when they were told that Hannah suffered from polycystic kidney disease and likely wouldn't live more than a few days.

After Hannah was born, polycystic kidney disease was ruled out, but her ureters—the ducts that carry urine to the bladder—did not open sufficiently. Both had to be surgically opened up and Hannah's non-functioning right kidney had to be removed. But Hannah lived. If doctors could just get at the root of Hannah's problems, perhaps everything would be okay.

Despite these health problems, Hannah was, according to Maura, a happy baby. She began talking at 18 months. But after awhile, she began talking less and less until, finally, she wasn't talking at all. Hannah "went into her own little world," Maura said. She would stare at the television set, get upset often, and rarely pick up her toys. "It was as if someone took her from us and we had no idea where she went," Maura said. Hannah had developmental disorders. She had delays in speech, motor skills, and social skills.

When the Weises realized Hannah had a hearing problem, they hoped surgery would have a domino effect on her other ailments. But the removal of her adenoids and a tonsillectomy had no effect.

"For a long time, I needed to know why it happened," Charlie said. "I felt sorry for Hannah. I felt sorry for myself. I still need to know, but for a different reason. I need to know so it doesn't happen to someone else's kid."

A few years later, when his weight ballooned to more than 300 pounds, Weis decided to have gastric bypass surgery. Complications arose from the surgery. Weis became gravely ill, slipped into a coma, and came close to death. The thought of staying alive for his wife and children saved him, he says. "I wouldn't let myself go to sleep at night because I was afraid I would never wake up. But every day Maura would come to the hospital in the morning, and she'd hold my hand and look into my eyes. And then I'd doze off. She was the only person I felt safe with. The only thing I remember throughout was fighting for my family."

Weis had met Maura 11 years earlier at his favorite spot on earth—the Jersey Shore—shortly after he collected his first Super Bowl ring as a member of Bill Parcells' New York Giants staff. Meeting her put his football successes into perspective. There was more to life than football, and now he had someone with whom to share it. The family soon grew to four, with the births of Hannah in 1992 and Charlie Jr. a year later. Hannah's ailments brought the family closer together. Charlie's full recovery from surgery further strengthened the family's unity.

In a press conference with Weis in May 2005, reporters wanted to focus on his late-spring recruiting trips. But the conversation inevitably kept returning to the importance of family and how he had stressed that idea to recruits and their respective families. "I always start with education and family, long before I get to football," said Weis of his recruiting approach. "I openly talk about my family, my wife and my kids, my love for them, and how important they are to me. I try to explain this to the recruits and their parents. I try to look at these kids as if they were my kids. I say to myself, 'How would they like to be treated?' "

Yes, Weis was a football coach with a reputation for being blunt. Not every situation on the gridiron would be a loving experience. "I have to explain to them that I'm not always the nicest guy, that things aren't always a bowl of cherries," he said. But at the same time, Weis understood how important it was to know "when to pull off of somebody or pat somebody on the back."

Weis practiced what he preached when it came to his family, especially now that he was at Notre Dame. The pro game, particularly in an assistant's role, is uncompromising. The game and the team take absolute precedence at all times. There are four exhibition games, 16 regular-season games and—for a perennial playoff team like the Patriots of recent years—usually about another month of football to follow.

The college game and its time commitments are a little more forgiving, and Weis' family benefited. "I've probably spent more time with my family in the last week than I have the past 15 years, other than vacations," said Weis when May recruiting had concluded. "My son said to me, 'Dad, I'm seeing you every day.' They know that when I'm not working, I'm doing something with them. They know I'm not on the golf course unless I'm doing something for work. I don't go fishing. I don't go out with the guys. When I'm not at work, I'm with Maura, Charlie, or Hannah. They know I will give them every second I can that's not work related."

For Weis, particularly at Notre Dame, it was family first.

NO ONE WAS A bigger Notre Dame football fan as an undergraduate student than Charlie Weis. Not only did he attend every home game, but he was always up for a road trip. When the Irish played in the Cotton Bowl his senior year, he and a carload of friends made the trek down to Dallas to watch fifth-ranked Notre Dame upset No. 1 Texas and claim the national championship.

During his first extended weekend at Notre Dame as its new head coach—the weekend of January 8, when the Irish basketball team hosted Villanova—Weis addressed the relatively small, Christmas-break crowd at halftime. He told them how important a role they played in Notre Dame's success on the field. He also said he hoped the historic Fighting Irish nemesis, USC, would be undefeated when it visited Notre Dame for the October 15 football game. The fans loved the bravado.

And maybe it was just a coincidence, but Notre Dame beat Villanova that day, 78–72.

Five weeks later, with another Super Bowl ring on his finger and his move to Notre Dame completed, Weis invited the student body to join him for a Valentine's Day meeting at the Joyce Center football auditorium—at 6 a.m. It was a brilliant gesture. He was making himself accessible to the entire student body, but he was also asking them to make a sacrifice, just as Fighting Irish players were in their winter conditioning workouts. You want to be part of the team? Then set the alarm for 5:30 and drag yourself to the Joyce Center in the dead of winter.

And hundreds did. When it became obvious that the 72-seat room booked for the occasion couldn't accommodate the 200–plus students who showed up, the group moved to the basketball arena, where Weis held court.

Wearing slacks, long-sleeve shirt, and tie, and sipping a cup of coffee, Weis appeared relaxed at his new home. He was back on his old campus with his Notre Dame family, and he wasn't going anywhere anytime soon. "I have a kid who is going to be in the seventh grade next year," Weis said, "and I'm definitely going to be here until he graduates."

Weis laid out a surprisingly uncomplicated 10-year plan: "My goal is to be able to leave this campus on my own terms about a decade from now with everyone saying, 'God, I'm glad we hired that guy!' Because if that's the feeling you have, and that's the feeling the people after you have, and that's the feeling the people who went to school before you have, then I did something right."

Weis did lots of things right as the session continued. He knew he had to give the students a reason to be optimistic about the upcoming season. They'd done their part by rolling out of bed at the crack of dawn. Now Weis did his part. "I've never been at a program that has lost," he said. "I'm 48 years old, and everywhere I've been we've won. And I've been part of the reason why we've won."

He admitted how disappointed he was when he lost out to Tom Coughlin for the New York Giants' head-coaching job. And he said he briefly considered pursuing the vacant Miami Dolphins' head coaching position. "I went to my wife and said, 'South Beach or South Bend? What's the difference?' In reality, when you think about it, if you're a family guy, do you want your kids growing up in a college town or in a city?" said Weis. "I'd pick a college town 10 out of 10 times."

Weis stressed the importance of having the players he recruited fit in with the rest of the student body. "I don't want prima donnas," he said. "I don't want guys who think they're better than the rest of you, because they're not. I went to school here and didn't play varsity sports, but I roomed with football players my whole time here, and they're still some of my closest friends."

Weis guaranteed the students that they would be proud of the team he would put on the field. "One promise you do have from me is you'll have a team every week that's ready to go and that's prepared," he said. "You won't have to worry about lackluster efforts. That's not going to happen, because that sideline is not going to be a pleasant sight if there's a lackluster effort. Don't stand too close, and don't read my lips. I might have gone to school here, but I've also been in the NFL for 15 years. We talk a tad different sometimes."

If Weis had kept going much longer, he might have had 200–plus new recruits clamoring to "get nasty," but he brought his little Valentine Day's message to an end with an old Boy Scout slogan: Be Prepared.

"Preparation is *the* reason why you win or lose," Weis said. "Football has become a very intellectual game. The most important thing when you're putting the offense and defense together is to be able to understand what your players can handle mentally. You don't ask them to do more than they're mentally capable of handling. At the same time, if you have them totally prepared, both mentally and physically, that's what gives you the best chance of winning."

When the nearly hour-long Q&A session ended, the students gave Weis a standing O.

Throughout the spring, Weis visited the Notre Dame dorms to speak with the students in a more intimate setting. A couple of times he grumbled that perhaps he'd taken on too much of a responsibility by talking to so many students, but it was his way of trying to pull the Notre Dame family together. This was his chance to reach out to the student body, to recruit them.

Some certainly had favored Urban Meyer, the former assistant to Lou Holtz and Bob Davie, who'd done big things at Utah and Bowling Green. Weis had been relatively unknown outside the NFL just a few months earlier. But as the students listened to him share his philosophy and provide a glimpse into his personality, they liked what they heard and saw.

Even in this very informal setting—a football coach chatting casually with students—the straight-shooting Weis made it clear he wasn't interested in discussing the Willingham Era, or "Error," as some critics called it. "A kid asked a question about last year, and Weis told him to shut up," laughed Keough Hall resident Steven Humphrey from Racine, Wisconsin. "It was really fun to listen to him because you could just tell he knew what he was talking about. He just seemed like a brutally honest guy, which was refreshing."

"I respected that he wouldn't talk about the previous coach," said Rick King, a Dillon Hall resident from Hatboro, Pennsylvania. "Even though he knew how we all felt about Willingham, he had respect for the former coach and the class to move on."

Weis wasn't motivated simply by his respect for Willingham. He knew that if the Weis Era was going to succeed, it needed to make a clean break from the acrimony and controversy caused by the firing. The halftime basketball speech, the 6 a.m. gathering, the dorm meetings—they all helped serve his purpose. Months before he would make his own coaching debut, Weis was putting distance between the past and the present.

He was doing what he had done with Zorich and the other alums.

He was pressing all the right buttons.

Chapter 6

......

CHEMISTRY CLASS

CHARLIE WEIS UNDERSTOOD HIS strengths. He could game-plan with the best of them, and he had the Super Bowl rings to prove it. His play-call lists were suitable for framing. His strategies and tactics were studied and copied by other coaches—the ultimate compliment.

But Weis also understood his weaknesses, or at least the areas in his game that might not be quite as well developed. This was his first time as CEO of his own program. He had never before hired or overseen an entire staff. And he was an NFL guy, accustomed to dealing with grown men who didn't have to maintain a 2.0 GPA.

Job No. 1, of course, was to assemble a coaching staff—and do it fast. Every day Notre Dame was without a full staff meant another day a competitor—USC, Michigan, Texas, Ohio State, Florida, and the other usual suspects—could gain an advantage.

"We've already started that process," he said the day he accepted the job. "That ball is already rolling, because I'm well aware that the sooner you can get those things in place, the easier my job is going to be in the short time frame I'm wearing two hats."

Not only did Weis have to build a staff fast, he had to build it well. With his attention divided between Notre Dame and the Patriots, Weis knew he had to put together a staff that could hit the ground running and begin the uphill climb in a recruiting season that had only seven weeks remaining. He had a very specific, very concrete wish list.

First, he wanted a solid Domer base—that is, former players who once represented the Irish on the field and coaches who had served at Notre Dame in the past. He wanted at least a sprinkling of assistants with head coaching experience to compensate, perhaps, for his having none above the high school level. He wanted youth, especially out on the recruiting trail. He wanted experience, men with a wealth of coaching knowledge he could tap. He wanted at least a few assistants who had coached in the NFL, as he had, to ensure that Notre Dame would be on the cutting edge in the X's and O's department. And he wanted coaches who were willing to set aside their own personal agendas—professional and personal differences can poison a staff—for the greater good of Notre Dame football. He wanted chemistry.

Weis wanted a lot.

And he got it all.

The nine-man staff Weis landed offered a mixture of all these traits, with an extra shot of experience. The 214 combined years of football coaching on Weis' first staff ranked second among the 11 teams on Notre Dame's 2005 schedule, behind only the 225 combined years of Joe Tiller's staff at Purdue. (In case you were wondering, Pete Carroll's USC staff, on the heels of back-to-back national titles, was last on that list, with just 109 combined years of coaching experience heading into the 2005 season.) Weis' staff included assistants with a combined 61 bowl appearances, 31 bowl victories, and lots of face time in the Associated Press final rankings (45 Top 25 finishes during their tenures with other teams).

Here are the nine men who made Weis' first starting lineup:

THE LINCHPIN

FORMER NOTRE DAME WIDE receiver and defensive back Mike Haywood, 40, had earned a reputation as one of the up-and-coming stars among the bright young assistant coaches in college football, most recently at Texas under Mack Brown and before that under Nick Saban at LSU.

The book on Haywood: excellent running backs coach, top recruiter, Domer from head to toe.

By the time he left South Bend in 1986 with a BA in government, Haywood knew in his heart he would someday return to his alma mater.

Four years earlier, though, it was a different story. All set to play wide receiver for the Irish, he was struck by a common freshman malady: acute homesickness. In fact, he was bit so hard by the hometown bug that he returned to Houston and stayed there for two weeks before Notre Dame coaches convinced him to come back. He returned to South Bend, switched to the defensive secondary, and made 18 career starts for the Irish.

After assistant coaching stints at Army, Ohio University, and Ball State, Haywood joined former Irish offensive lineman and then-LSU head coach Gerry DiNardo in 1995, where he served for eight years. Texas' Brown then lured Haywood to coach running backs for his home-state Longhorns in 2003.

Three previous times in Haywood's coaching career he had been offered a job at Notre Dame. The timing had never been right, he said. Neither were the dollars and cents, until Weis came on board. Notre Dame's pay scale for assistant coaches had lagged well behind those of top schools in the major conferences, something athletic director Kevin White would acknowledge publicly in May 2006. Plus, none of Notre Dame's previous offers to Haywood had been for a coordinator's job. It wasn't until Weis was hired that the university agreed to loosen the purse strings to lure some of the nation's top assistant coaches to South Bend.

Weis was certain Haywood was the right man for the job. "Michael is one of those sound, fundamental coaches, plus he's a Domer, and he's a recruiting machine. He's everything you're looking for in a coordinator. I wanted somebody who could be in charge of the offense when I wasn't involved in the offense. Our personalities mesh together very well together."

Among the running backs Haywood developed over the years were NFL draft picks LaBrandon Toefield, Domanick Davis, Kevin Faulk (who eventually played for Weis in New England), and Rondell Mealey. When Haywood went to Texas, he helped turn Cedric Benson into the NCAA's sixth all-time leading rusher and the fourth overall selection (by the Chicago Bears) in the 2005 NFL draft.

"He relates well to the kids," said Haywood's former Irish teammate, Allen Pinkett, who is number two on Notre Dame's all-time rushing list and an analyst for Westwood One's national radio broadcasts of Irish games. "He has a sense for what type of player is going to come to Notre Dame. He's honest. He doesn't make any promises, because if you're good enough to play as a freshman, you're going to play."

For Haywood, the chance to return to his alma mater was a dream come true. "When you sell something that's near to your heart, it's a lot easier," he said. "Sure, when you go into the home of a young man, you talk about the Notre Dame education, the high graduation rate, and the academics in the business school, what with more than half of the team in the business school. You give them all the facts."

But Haywood had more than facts when he went into a recruit's home. "When you talk about walking across campus, going to Sacred Heart Church, visiting the Grotto, seeing the snow embankments… When you can give them life experiences, it means a lot more. Unless you've walked across that campus and lived on that campus, you don't understand how special this university is."

The title of offensive coordinator, a hefty salary (estimated to be above $200,000), and the chance to work for Weis convinced Haywood that the time finally was right.

"I look at Charlie as a source of knowledge," Haywood said at the time. "I can pick his brain and learn more about offensive play, because when you get onto the professional level and you're playing teams two and three times a year, it becomes a little more technical. They tell me he's an unbelievable gamecaller. A man who has four championship rings is doing something right."

Upon his arrival, Haywood visited a place on campus that had served as an inspiration to him during his undergraduate days. "The first place I stopped was the Grotto," Haywood said, referring to the Notre Dame campus version of the shrine to the Virgin Mary in Lourdes. "I gave thanks for the opportunity to be here again."

He also recalled with fondness his playing days at Notre Dame: "Coming out of the tunnel, I looked over at Charlie and I said, 'This brings back chills. There are so many memories that come back with it. I'm looking forward to it.' And he said, 'Not as much as I am.' "

THE MOTIVATOR

WHEN RICK MINTER WAS Lou Holtz' defensive coordinator in 1992 – 1993, he liked to use little inspirational catchphrases with the players, and he even convinced Holtz to allow him to place outdoor signs — like political ads in the yard of a registered voter — that the players passed each time they walked out to the Cartier Field practice facility.

But Minter was the first to admit that it was talent, not rah-rah, that led the Notre Dame defense to be ranked ninth nationally against the run in 1992 and fourth in 1993. Among the players on those units were three NFL first-round draft picks (cornerback Tom Carter, defensive tackle Bryant Young, free safety Jeff Burris); a second-rounder (linebacker Demetrius DuBose); and two third-rounders (defensive tackle Jim Flanigan, cornerback Willie Clark).

Minter wouldn't have nearly as much talent on tap for his return engagement. "There was no doubt when I came in before that Notre Dame was in the midst of a run of players that may not ever be paralleled again," Minter said. "This program is in a little different stage right now. We're not saying we're horrible or good. We don't know. We'll declare that as time goes on."

In between his stints at Notre Dame, Minter fashioned a 53–63–1 record during 10 seasons (1994 – 2003) as head coach of the

Cincinnati Bearcats. He took four of his squads to bowl games and had three straight seven-victory seasons (2000 through 2002.) It was a decent run for Cincinnati, who'd had just one winning season in the 11 years before Minter arrived. But a 5–7 record (after a 3–0 start), declining attendance, and growing concerns about Minter's ability to lead the program once it made its scheduled move from Conference USA to the Big East conference in 2005 cost him his job. He was fired with three years remaining on his contract.

Minter was then reunited with Holtz at South Carolina in 2004 as the Gamecocks defensive coordinator and linebackers coach. Weis offered him the same job at Notre Dame.

"It's fun to be back," said Minter on his return. "It's been 11 long years. I left here with a lot of enthusiasm to be a head coach. Then I went with Lou last year, and things worked out to be back here at Notre Dame. I'm happy to be here and I appreciate working with Coach Weis. I'm looking forward to getting this defense on track, continuing what we did against the run game last year"—the Irish ranked fourth nationally against the run in 2004—"and trying to pick things up a little with the pass defense."

The longer an offense stays on the field, the fewer yards a defense surrenders. Weis knew how to keep an offense on the field—a fact not lost on Minter. "I'll be coaching defense for a guy who is on the cutting edge offensively, and that's exciting," Minter said. "As a defensive coach, I'm saying, 'Yeah, this could be pretty cool.'"

Even when he was at Cincinnati, Minter had kept an eye on his old employer. "Once you're Irish, you're always Irish," he said. "I watched them when they were on TV. You bleed with them a little bit when they're not doing well, and you cheer for them when they are. So you always have that spirit in you. It's a special place to be, and I'm just happy to be a part of that now."

For Minter, who'd just turned 50, a top job would remain his goal. Yet he'd be just fine if his career path stopped at Notre Dame. "I want to be a head coach again," Minter said. "But if I'm not, I can be content with that because I'm at Notre Dame. I want to be around high caliber people, high caliber student-athletes. I'm very happy to be back at Notre Dame."

The landscape of the campus had changed, but the essence of Notre Dame—to Minter, at least—had not. "I know how to deal with the Notre Dame spirit, the fans, and the expectations," he said. "All that hasn't changed. I just look forward to getting a new era going here. We've got some new faces and a lot of work to do to upgrade ourselves, but I think we're well on our way to doing that."

THE FIELD GENERAL

DAVID CUTCLIFFE, JUST FIRED after six years as head coach at Mississippi, had put together a respectable 44–29 record in the always competitive, talent-loaded Southeastern Conference. Now 50, Cutcliffe learned at the knee of the legendary Bear Bryant as a student assistant for the Alabama football team during his undergraduate days in Tuscaloosa.

Like Weis, Cutcliffe hadn't played college football. But "Coach Bryant had a huge impact on me," Cutcliffe said when he was introduced as Notre Dame's new assistant head coach and quarterbacks coach. "He was a hero. He gave me the desire to want to coach."

After a high school coaching stint, Cutcliffe joined Johnny Major's staff at Tennessee, where he served for 17 years, including the final six as assistant head coach, quarterbacks coach, and offensive coordinator for Phillip Fulmer. In Knoxville, he groomed top-notch college signal-callers such as Andy Kelly, Heath Shuler, Tee Martin, and, of course, Peyton Manning, an eventual two-time NFL MVP. And at Ole Miss, he taught a few moves to Peyton's kid brother, Eli, who led the Rebels to a 10–victory season in 2003, including a Cotton Bowl win.

Cutcliffe was at Notre Dame because he knew how to run an offense, because he knew how to refine a quarterback, and because he eventually wanted to be a head coach again. If the Fighting Irish were successful—and Cutcliffe was confident they would be—then his chances of running his own program in a few years would increase.

THE DISCIPLE

THE NOTRE DAME LINK, even when indirect, is powerful. New offensive line coach John Latina, who'd held that job at the University of Mississippi for one year before taking over there as offensive coordinator for five seasons (1999–2004), had no formal ties to Notre Dame. He hadn't played there, coached there, or gone to school there. But he did spend time at Temple (1986–1987) working with Owls assistant coach Joe Moore, who was hired by Lou Holtz the following year and went on to develop some of Notre Dame's best offensive lines ever during his nine seasons in South Bend.

Anyone who was a disciple of Moore's, even for just two seasons nearly two decades ago, was placed in a special group by devout Irish fans. (Some of that luster wore off when Moore won an age discrimination case against Notre Dame after Holtz' successor, Bob Davie, fired him following the 1996 season.)

"I was a very young line coach at the time," said Latina of his time with Moore. "It was a great way for me to continue to grow, to have him in the same office, to be able to run things by him, and to be on the field with him. He was my mentor. Even after he left to go to Notre Dame, I stayed in touch with him, sent him videotapes of my line, and asked him to critique it. When our games were on TV, he'd watch and then give me a call to talk about line play. Joe Moore was as good a line coach as there ever was. A lot of the techniques I've taught over the years come from things he did. That's where I learned."

Latina grew up Catholic, in New Castle, Pennsylvania. For him, Notre Dame was the mecca of college football. "I came here to visit several times when Joe was the line coach," he said. "Every time I would come up here, I just knew that if I was ever given the chance to be a part of this football program, I would jump at it."

In his six seasons at Mississippi, Latina coached 10 offensive linemen who eventually signed NFL contracts. Twice the Rebels allowed the fewest sacks in the SEC. His work with Mississippi's offensive line caught the attention of new South Carolina head coach Steve Spurrier, who hired him in December 2004, shortly after Cutcliffe and his staff were fired at Ole Miss. Latina's tenure with the Gamecocks can be measured in days. When Weis asked if it was too late for Latina to change his mind, Latina immediately contacted Spurrier and told him he was bypassing Columbia, South Carolina for South Bend.

It was nothing personal; it was Notre Dame.

"I felt very bad about the timing," Latina said. "When I took the job at South Carolina, I didn't know that Notre Dame was a possibility. I was excited about the opportunity to work with Coach Spurrier, but Notre Dame is a dream job. Nobody likes to accept a job somewhere and then change two weeks later. But this opportunity was too strong."

By the time fall camp opened, Weis was absolutely certain Latina was exactly the right man for the job. "I like the fact that he's a get-in-your-face coach," said Weis, the little bit o' nasty coach. "I don't have to be there to be on them all the time. It helps when you have a guy that you know is going to send the same message you're sending."

THE OLD PRO

BILL LEWIS, 63, BROUGHT more than four decades of coaching experience to his new post as Irish secondary coach. Over the years, the past nine of which he'd spent with the Miami Dolphins, Lewis had worked with such college coaching luminaries as Vince Dooley and Frank Broyles, as well as with the architect of the Pittsburgh Steelers' Steel Curtain defense, Bud Carson. Like Minter and Cutcliffe, Lewis had been a head coach—three years at Wyoming (1977–79), three at East Carolina (1989–91), and three at Georgia Tech (1992–94).

The bottom line: Lewis had forgotten more about football than most coaches will ever know.

"Notre Dame is one of the special programs," said Lewis. "For many years they had the highest winning percentage, and now they've dropped down a bit behind Michigan. For me, it would be unbelievable to be a part of the program that gets this thing back where it belongs."

Lewis had long carried a torch for Notre Dame. "Whenever I was involved in recruiting, if a guy ever told me he was going to Notre Dame, the only thing I did was shake his hand and wish him luck," he said. "You couldn't argue the decision. Now, I get to go to my office at Notre Dame. It doesn't get much better than that."

Nobody on the new staff had a longer history with Weis than Lewis. "I knew Charlie back when he was still coaching high school ball," said Lewis. "But our friendship really developed during the nine years that we competed against each other in the NFL. Having gotten to know him, I know that Charlie cares about people. That's important to me. He'll care about the people who work for him, and he'll care about the players. He's very kind, and he's the type of person I feel comfortable being associated with."

Weis, in turn, had learned through twice-a-year encounters with the Dolphins over nine seasons in the same AFC East how difficult it was to throw against a Bill Lewis-coached secondary. "It didn't hurt that he'd been a head coach at three different places in college ball," Weis said, "but the bottom line was I had trouble beating Miami's scheme, so I figured I might as well go get him rather than go against him."

THE SPECIALIST

BERNIE PARMALEE, 37, AN NFL running back for nine seasons, had been on the Dolphins staff with Lewis, but he left Miami after Dave Wannstedt was fired as head coach to accept a job under Weis at Notre Dame as special teams coach. The coaching change in Miami had something to do with it. But so did Weis' thoroughness and attention to detail.

"Once you reach major college or the pros, everyone's talented, but what edge are you going to have?" asked Parmalee, like Weis, a Jersey guy. "Do you understand what your opponent is trying to do? Do you understand how to run a route correctly? Do you understand the little details that can give you the edge on game day? That's what Coach Weis teaches, and that's why everyone in his system has been successful."

THE STOPPER

JEROME "JAPPY" OLIVER WAS the defensive line coach for the Air Force Academy in 1996 when the Falcons upset the Irish, 20–17, at Notre Dame Stadium. It was after that game that Holtz privately began leaning toward stepping down as Notre Dame's head coach. Seven years later, Oliver was coaching Holtz' defensive line at South Carolina, where he spent two seasons before joining Weis' staff.

"I haven't been allowed to talk about that 1996 game the past two years because I was working for Lou," Oliver laughed when talking to a reporter in early January 2005. "Being at Air Force for eight years, from 1995 through 2002, we were often giant-killers. Our kids played like gangbusters that day. That game was a highlight of my career."

Oliver was a senior wideout for Purdue when the Boilermakers held a 24–14 fourth-quarter advantage over the Irish in Notre Dame Stadium in 1977. Little did he realize that day that he was about to witness the emergence of a college football legend. Irish coach Dan Devine, desperately looking to spark his offense, sent out a third-string quarterback named Joe Montana, who propelled the Irish to a 31–24 victory and then proceeded to march them on to the national championship.

Seeking employment following Holtz' retirement after the 2004 season, Oliver jumped at the offer from Weis. "As soon as I got the Notre Dame job, I called Lou," Oliver said. "His first comment was, 'You're a class individual going to a class place.' That stuck with me. He had nothing but great, great thoughts about this place."

Oliver's background, particularly his stint with the Air Force Academy, was a good testing ground for his position at Notre Dame. "There are a lot of similarities between Air Force and Notre Dame," he said. "It takes a special individual to come here and deal with the high expectations."

A native of Flint, Michigan, Oliver, 50, also had personal reasons for wanting to return to the Midwest: proximity to his parents, who still lived in Michigan. But, as with his new colleagues, there was that Notre Dame thing too. "The opportunity to work with Coach Weis and this staff and just being here at Notre Dame was too great to pass up," he said. "You hear a lot of great things about the school, but you don't know the inner workings and why the school is the way it is until you're actually a part of it, and that's what I've experienced."

THE SALES DIRECTOR

AFTER THE OFFENSIVE AND defensive coordinator positions, a quality recruiting coordinator is the most significant hire a new head coach must make. You need a strong, savvy, well-organized, and dynamic personality to tie the recruiting effort together. Without that kind of person running the show, the replenishment of the talent pool will become fractured and inconsistent. You can have the greatest coaches in the game, and the richest tradition, but if the talent pipeline runs dry, you're dead in the water — if not this year, then next.

Enter Rob Ianello, 39, who earned his recruiting stripes at Alabama, Wisconsin, and Arizona before returning to Wisconsin under former Irish defensive coordinator Barry Alvarez. Weis made on offer to Ianello even though their first face-to-face meeting didn't take place until after Ianello was already on board as Notre Dame's recruiting coordinator and receivers coach.

"I was out recruiting for Wisconsin, and Coach Alvarez called me and told me what was going on," said Ianello. "Anybody who's a football person knows who Charlie Weis is."

Leaving Wisconsin wasn't easy for Ianello. His wife, Denise, was assistant women's basketball coach for the Badgers. Plus, Ianello felt an allegiance to Alvarez, who had hired him as on-campus recruiting coordinator in 1990.

"I had a very good job with someone who brought me up into the coaching profession," he said. "Coach Alvarez was awesome. He advised me as a friend. He talked to me about the expectations in South Bend. He said, 'Be ready for them.' And I am."

After all, said Ianello, he couldn't ignore the opportunity "to help return Notre Dame to its rightful place in college football." As for his loyalty to Alvarez, that became a nonissue when the longtime Badgers head coach announced that the 2005 season would be his last on the sideline. Beginning in 2006, he would concentrate solely on his job as athletic director.

At Arizona, Ianello helped develop wideouts Bobby Wade (Chicago Bears) and Dennis Northcutt (Cleveland Browns) into NFL draft selections. Those credentials earned him the title of passing game coordinator following his nine-year stint at Arizona.

But before Ianello could begin instructing the Irish receivers on the field, he would have to help Weis and the rest of the staff salvage an abbreviated recruiting campaign. "I have a vision and a plan," Ianello said, as that campaign was getting under way. "I want to see how this vision and this plan will play out, because it has been successful in the past."

THE KID

THE YOUNGEST MEMBER OF the staff was special-teams coach and defensive backs assistant Brian Polian, 30, who landed his first full-time coaching position in 1998 at Buffalo University at the precocious age of 23—thanks, in great measure (and he'd be the first to admit it), to his last name. The son of former Buffalo Bills general manager (and current Indianapolis Colts president) Bill Polian, he had witnessed firsthand the significance of special teams as a kid during his father's tenure with Buffalo. Marv Levy, who had established a rep as a special-teams specialist before being hired by the Bills, made a big impression on the young Polian.

But along with the name, Polian the Younger had game. A contrib-uting author to the American Football Coaches Association's book, *A Complete Guide to Special Teams*, he had made special teams his spe-cialty at an age when most young assistant coaches were still fumbling with the keys to the locker room.

"I think Coach Weis recognized my last name," Polian laughed when he was introduced. "But I also think he understood that I've grown up in the business."

No kidding. From the sixth grade on, Polian spent his summers at the Bills training camp. "If I wanted to be around my dad," Polian recalled, "I had to be around his work, because he wasn't coming home at 6 o'clock."

When you grow up that way, Polian said, one of two things is going to happen: "You either say, 'I'll never get into that racket because my dad was never home and we moved a lot,' or you say, 'This is the family business and I absolutely love it.' I ended up getting bit by the bug."

In a twist of fate, Polian spent the 2004 season at Central Florida, where he worked under head coach George O'Leary, the infamous "for-mer Notre Dame head coach" who lasted a mere five days before he was fired for fabricating information on his résumé. Polian's connection with O'Leary gave him a taste of recruiting in Florida, once a talent pipeline for Holtz and the Fighting Irish, but no longer: just four Floridians had signed with Notre Dame in the previous four years. Polian would be expected to help the Irish unclog that Sunshine State pipeline.

HIS NINE-MAN COACHING STAFF complete, Weis turned his atten-tion to two support-staff job openings that were vital to Notre Dame's success: strength and conditioning coordinator, and director of person-nel development.

It wasn't exactly a secret that Weis thought the 2004 Irish hadn't been able to impose their will physically on other teams. They weren't soft; they just didn't have the strength to overpower anybody, espe-cially on the offensive and defensive lines.

So Weis hired Ruben Mendoza, a barrel-chested behemoth of a man who had spent four years at Mississippi with Cutcliffe and Latina in charge of strength and conditioning. Weis made it clear he wanted Notre Dame's players, particularly the linemen, to dominate the opposition.

Then Weis turned to former record-setting Irish quarterback Ron Powlus, whom ESPN college football analyst (and noted Notre Dame enthusiast) Beano Cook once predicted would win a pair of Heisman trophies. A salesman at the time for First Horizon Home Loans in Pittsburgh, Powlus would now be selling Notre Dame to Irish recruits.

"For the last year or so, I've been feeling like I've been denying myself what I want to be doing and what I'm really passionate about, and that's college football," Powlus said. "I got in touch with Coach Weis, like a lot of alumni did. I said, 'I want to help. Is there anything I can do to be a part of the great things to come?' "

Little could Powlus have realized when he accepted the position how much his duties would expand in the spring. That's because on March 9, before Weis' new staff could even run its first scrimmage, David Cutcliffe suffered a heart attack.

Cutcliffe underwent triple heart bypass surgery and was told his recovery would be lengthy. Weis petitioned the NCAA to allow Powlus to work as the quarterbacks coach in the spring. Meanwhile, Powlus continued in his role as a link to former players and as a shoulder for current players to lean on, particularly starting quarterback Brady Quinn.

By the end of spring practice, a still-convalescing Cutcliffe decided it was time to set aside his dream of coaching at Notre Dame and instead dedicate himself to rehab. And so, on May 31, 2005, he called Weis and resigned.

"I would never give any program less than the passion and energy it deserves," said Cutcliffe in a June 1 teleconference from his home in Mississippi. "To do so would unfairly penalize the Irish players, staff, students, alumni, and devoted friends. As anyone who knows me can attest, it's all or nothing with me. I'm to the point where I'm just now getting into the rehab and getting into the endurance. I'm not going to be ready to jump back into it. I'm trying to be fair to everyone, players and coaches included."

No one could relate to Cutcliffe's plight better than Weis. "Having had health problems myself in the past, I greatly appreciated how Bill Belichick handled it with me," Weis said. "I learned from that experience, and I thought I should give David his time to decide when he was ready to resume coaching. I wanted to make sure he wasn't making a rash decision. I let him know that I was going to give him all the opportunities I could to make that decision."

Weis, true to form, had a backup plan. "Once you hire coaches," he explained, "you need to revise that depth chart so you know who's waiting in the wings." And whom should Weis find waiting there but a veteran head coach from Europe with Notre Dame ties.

"For several years, Peter Vaas has been on our radar and was certainly on my short list when I took this job," Weis said. "After further research, the support for Peter from people I know and trust was overwhelming, making this move an easy one."

Vaas had been Holtz' quarterbacks coach in 1990–91, when he helped develop Irish standout Rick Mirer. He then left Notre Dame to become head coach at Holy Cross, his alma mater, where he compiled a 14–30 record over four seasons. From there he moved to the Canadian Football League as an offensive coordinator, before landing a job as an assistant coach in NFL Europe. Vaas was named head coach of the Berlin Thunder, where he spent four years, followed by a two-year stint with the Cologne Centurions. The Thunder won back-to-back World Bowls in 2001–02.

"In this business, you always leave a place with a heavy heart and some sadness, yet arrive at your new place with a smile on your face," said Vaas. "That certainly will be the case with this move. My last experience at Notre Dame was fabulous, something that had a great impact on my family and me. The chance to return to South Bend and to work with and learn from Charlie Weis is an amazing opportunity."

For Cutcliffe, a dream had passed him by. The surgery saved his life, but it was unlikely there would be any job openings at Notre Dame any time soon. "I hope I have the opportunity to come back to Notre

Dame, but you never know what the good Lord brings," he said. "I've got a good start on my rehab. I just wanted to finish it and reach the health level that I should be at. I can tell you this: I don't think many people are going to be leaving Notre Dame. It's going to be an exciting time there."

Cutcliffe knew. He knew the quality of the staff Weis had assembled. He knew Notre Dame still had enough talent to be competitive. And he knew Weis was no dummy.

Weis had surrounded himself with a bunch of strong, savvy, and, most of all, tough guys. "I wasn't looking just at guys to pat players on the back and say, 'That's okay,' because that's not the way I am," said Weis. "I wanted guys who were not only good teachers but who coached the guys tough."

Toughness? Check.

"I wanted to find the guys who had the best foundations in recruiting, and at the same time I wanted to find the guys who I respect the most with X's and O's," he said. "I was fortunate enough to come up with a nice combination of the two."

Recruiting ability? Check.

X's and O's? Check.

Weis had, in fact, surrounded himself with a well-rounded staff. Not yes-men, but football guys who could work as a team. He became certain of that after a January recruiting weekend, when the Notre Dame coaches had their first staff meeting.

"I flew in and literally met these guys face to face, all together, for the first time about 20 minutes before we took the recruits out for dinner," said Weis. "I'd been negotiating with each of them, of course, but it was the first time I'd ever seen them together. Then I sat there that night at dinner with 11 recruits, of whom 10 ended up coming to Notre Dame, and I watched these guys work, and I said to myself, 'This is the first time these guys have ever worked together?' "

Now all they had to do was build a football team.

Chapter 7

......

LET THE BEAT-DOWN BEGIN

IT WAS PITCH-DARK OUTSIDE—sunrise was still 10 minutes away—but Charlie Weis' mood was even darker. What made him unhappy was the way his new team was struggling through a winter conditioning workout inside the Loftus Center. The session had begun with stretching precisely at 6 o'clock on this February morning, and it wasn't long before Weis realized his players didn't know the difference between being in shape and being in football shape—that is, being strong enough and fit enough to dominate an opponent physically from first snap to last.

That would change, of course.

It had to.

There was no other way to play nasty.

Each morning for the next two weeks, the coach arrived at the predawn workout session dressed in a jacket and tie and carrying a clipboard. He looked like a pollster. And in a way, he was. Weis was conducting a personal poll to determine how hard he was going to step on his new team.

As his assistant coaches and strength and conditioning staff conducted the drills, Weis walked from station to station and jotted down notes. For the most part, he didn't know who the players were. But he knew what they weren't. They weren't in football shape.

It's not that the players were in horrible shape. But, in Weis' judgment, they weren't anywhere near being in the kind of physical shape required by a championship-caliber team. You didn't need to be Knute Rockne to understand why: 13 losses in two years. If you don't have confidence that you're going to win, then more often than not, you won't. And if you haven't pushed yourself far enough and you feel yourself fading in the fourth quarter, you won't have that confidence.

Weis was here to win, which meant pushing his players until they got the message.

The team Weis inherited had a mind-set warped by having lost those 13 games in the two preceding seasons. They fought hard at times, most notably in victories against No. 8-ranked Michigan in September 2004 and at Tennessee's Neyland Stadium two months later. But the losses were beginning to come more frequently and, even worse, more decisively. Southern California mauled the Irish by scores of 44–13, 45–14, and 41–10 during Willingham's three years. Beyond the triple whammy of back-to-back-to-back 31-point defeats, there was the disturbing fact that, in each game, there wasn't much fighting in the Irish as the game went on.

One-sided losses undermine a football team's belief that it has a chance to win the next game. In addition to the blowout defeats to USC, there were woodshed losses in 2003 to Michigan (38–0), Florida State (37–0), and Syracuse (38–12). The following season, Purdue handed the Irish a 25-point loss, and the regular season ended with the now-all-too-familiar 31-point debacle against USC, followed by a 17-point shellacking by Oregon State in the Insight Bowl. (Weis later consigned the trophy Notre Dame had received for playing in the Insight Bowl to storage.)

As Weis watched game tape of the 2004 season, it became clear why the Irish had finished a disappointing 6–6: his new team wasn't tough enough, mentally or physically. The players couldn't maintain a level of consistency, couldn't break out of the pattern of poor play and sloppy execution. A change had to be made, and that change started at the top.

Mickey Marotti, Notre Dame's highly acclaimed strength and conditioning coach, joined the Irish staff in February 1998, a little more than a year after Bob Davie took over as head coach. Marotti made the transition to the Willingham staff in 2002. In 2003, Marotti was certified as a master strength and conditioning coach at the Collegiate Strength & Conditioning Coaches Association's national conference. The title of master strength and conditioning coach represents professionalism, knowledge, experience, expertise, and longevity in the field. Marotti became one of just 36 people in the world to earn that title.

And yet, Weis wanted somebody else. Or, more accurately, somebody different.

There was no debate about Marotti's credentials; they were top shelf. But this was a matter of philosophy and fit. Weis wanted somebody who represented change.

That somebody was Ruben Mendoza, a 6'4", 350-pound former NFL guard with a chest the size of a beer keg. Mendoza was so physically imposing that when he stood next to the beefy Weis, he made the head coach look like a pip-squeak, no small feat.

Mendoza had been an NAIA All-American offensive guard at Wayne State (Nebraska) in the mid-1980s. Later, he worked with offensive line coach John Latina at Clemson and Mississippi. Latina was a big believer in Mendoza, and Weis liked what he had heard about the Crystal City, Texas, native. (Meanwhile, new Florida coach Urban Meyer quickly hired Marotti as the Gators, director of strength and conditioning.)

Most of the qualities Weis sought in a strength coach were standard: focus bordering on obsession, discipline, energy, ability to motivate—pretty much what you'd expect. But one quality was an absolute prerequisite: "I didn't want someone who would be their friend."

Bullet point No. 1 on Mendoza's job description: push them to the max physically—and then some. You don't do that to a friend.

Mendoza's philosophy was twofold: work your way into the best cardiovascular condition of your life, and implement a ground-based, triple-extension weight-lifting philosophy based on movements that mimic actions on a football field—that is, squats, power cleans, and cleans, power lifting movements that simulate the explosive actions needed to dominate your opponent.

"Triple extension involves the ankle, knee, and hip joints—the three joints that move in coordination in order to move as fast as you can from a dead stop," said Mendoza after he replaced Marotti in late January. "In football, when players get in a three-point stance, they are bending those joints. The cleans they do with weights simulate the same movements employed when extending into the opponent. So a lot of stuff we do is geared toward sports-specific type movements."

The starting point was an outstanding cardiovascular regimen. Strength and power were essential, but they depended on superior cardiovascular preparation, particularly for the offensive and defensive linemen, whose conditioning in the fourth quarter would be critical to the team's success.

"My philosophy is based on being in great shape," Mendoza said. "When you come into camp in great shape, you're focused on the things you're doing. At the same time, it builds confidence in what you're doing. With freshmen, I don't emphasize their strength gains; I tell them to report in shape. We send them a conditioning manual before we send them a strength manual."

The first part of the conditioning test in preseason camp was the 110-yard sprint. Each player was required to do 18 110-yard sprints, regardless of position. The various positions had different time requirements. For the linemen, it was a grueling 19 seconds apiece, with 30-second breaks in between. For the skill positions, it was 14 seconds. That set the tone for what followed—and what was going to be expected.

Irish linemen, particularly on the offensive side of the ball, displayed a stunning improvement in stamina when they reported to preseason practice the following August. After those winter workouts back in

February, the linemen were stronger, faster, quicker, and leaner. They were now built for Weis-style football.

And the beat-down—as Weis would later refer to it—rolled on.

"To build, you've got to tear down and *re*build," Mendoza said. "We were teaching a lot. The triple-extension movements are all about coaching. We threw a lot at them—the squats, the cleans, the bench—and demanded that they do each one the right way every single time. Toward the end of spring, I think these kids started to understand the importance of generating force off the ground and how it applied to football."

The team was working out at the state-of-the-art, nearly 96,000-square-foot Guglielmino Athletics Complex, which was completed in 2005. ("Best facility in the country," according to Mendoza.) The combination of new facilities and new training methods helped make the transition easier, but there was still work to be done.

Mendoza was shocked when he discovered that Irish players had not incorporated squats into their regimen prior to his arrival. "When I first got here, they struggled with 315 pounds," Mendoza said. "Now, most of these kids, especially the offensive linemen, are squatting about 550 pounds. When I left Ole Miss, we had three kids who squatted over 700 pounds. Not that that's what we need to work toward. I'd like to get these kids up to where they're squatting 600, 625, 650 pounds."

Mendoza also established a clear demarcation between the players and himself. Remember, Weis hadn't hired him to be their friend. He was in charge of the beat-down process, and that didn't mix with friendship. "There are a lot of relationships that I build where I keep in contact with the students after they leave," Mendoza said. "But they've got to understand that my job is to make them better athletes. There are a lot of things I'm going to throw at them that they're not going to like, and they've got to understand that."

Most conditioning coaches follow a maintenance program during the season, but Mendoza believes in a more active philosophy. "We don't maintain; we actually want to get stronger," he said. "We limit the number of exercises we do, but we'll still make sure they lift pretty heavy."

The equation was really pretty simple: more strength + better conditioning = more confidence.

Some players called it the most demanding experience of their lives. Some quit the team. Some discovered things about themselves that they didn't know were there.

"When you try to roll over and push yourself out of bed and your arms don't want to work, it's pretty hard not to get really frustrated," said center/guard Bob Morton. "It all kind of comes crashing down, and there are days when you're emotionally spent. No smiles, no tears—you're just kind of walking aimlessly through the day. That's when you know that there's no place to go but up."

But when their bodies started to respond under the Mendoza regimen, "All of a sudden, we'd get two days off, and when we'd come back, we could lift more weight than before," Morton said. "We could run a little faster, jump a little higher. We were fresher and more flexible."

Most of all, they were stronger.

"I've always been strong enough to manage on the field," Morton said, "but I've never been strong enough to blow people away. All of a sudden, I felt like I was getting stronger with every lift I was doing. Mendoza's coaching was very specific to different people. He knew people's strengths and weaknesses."

Nose guard Derek Landri, a blue-collar, get-your-work-done kind of player, recognized the value of Weis' tough-love conditioning program. "You learn your place, you buy into it, and you grow from there," he said. "If you don't, see you later. If you do, you're in for a good ride."

How did Landri endure the beat-down? "Will, all will—and the guy next to you," Landri said. "That's why it's great we have roommates. When you're having those bad days, when you don't want to get out of bed, your roommate's there helping you out, lifting you out of bed, and pushing you through it."

At some point during the physical and mental beat-down, the players figured out Weis' motives. This wasn't simply about being in condition. It was about making a statement, about separating yourself from those 13 losses, those blowout defeats to USC, and the embarrassment of the Insight Bowl rout.

"When I look back and think about the amount of work we put in, we realized we had to raise the bar as to how far we could push ourselves," said quarterback Brady Quinn. "I think Coach Weis wanted to get us to our limits and then push us a little further. At some point, he did back off when he saw us respond, because we started to realize that we shouldn't place limits on ourselves. Just keep driving, and just keep pushing. Now our mind-set is that we should be able to accomplish anything when we put our minds to it."

"I went through the process until about halfway through spring ball of beating them down—just beating them down!—like nothing they did was any good," Weis said. "Somewhere along the line, they turned on the switch, and when a team does that, so does the coach. They go hand in hand. You never can take the pressure off them altogether. But about halfway through spring ball, they started to see the light that maybe, just maybe, they had a chance. You could see that their confidence was growing."

The tag team of Weis and Mendoza didn't let up after winter conditioning and spring drills. The running over the summer was the biggest shocker. Eighteen 110-yard sprints—a football field plus a first down to accentuate the relationship between doing a little extra and being successful—felt like a staggering amount of work in the beginning.

"I was like, Oh, God, what are we going to do here?" recalled tight end Anthony Fasano. "Early in the summer, 12 sprints was about the breaking point for me. I got through each one, but 12 was about the breaking point."

Said Morton: "I looked at the workout and said to myself, No way! Looking at 110 yards down there is a scary thing for a guy my size. But every day, we got closer to hitting our target, and every day, I saw everybody making their times, and I knew something special was happening."

When Lou Holtz arrived at Notre Dame, in 1986, the offseason conditioning program became known as The Puke Fest. Nineteen years later, the shock to the system wasn't nearly as great—the Willingham program had been more thorough and organized than the Gerry Faust program. But the shock to the system that Mendoza put in place for Weis still led to some physical breakdowns.

"I wouldn't call it a Puke Fest exactly, but some guys definitely did throw up, especially early in the summer," Fasano said. "You saw huge improvement by the end of summer from guys who had big-time trouble in the beginning."

New/old Irish defensive coordinator Rick Minter sat back and viewed the off-season conditioning with amusement. This was about more than just the physical beat-down of bodies not yet ready for prime-time college football. This was about the transformation of the mind, which, in turn, would lead to the transformation of the body.

"Anytime you take over a new job in a situation that hasn't been working the way it should, you've got to change attitudes, and that's what we set out to do," Minter said. "Coach Weis knows how to do things, and we jumped on his coattails. The kids did a great job of adjusting, changing, and adapting their way of thinking. That's what a new program has to do: get people to think in a different way."

Weis' program, said Minter, gave the team exactly what they wanted—although they didn't know it: "You'd like to think any child, deep down, wants to be disciplined, wants to be led, wants to be reinforced, wants to be supported, wants to be put in the proper position to be successful, wants to be pushed to limits he's never gone to before."

Latina, who had seen Mendoza's work at Clemson and Mississippi, was looking for a particular kind of offensive lineman. He wanted blockers who could run all day and physically whip a defensive lineman, particularly in the fourth quarter of a game. Conditioning without strength wouldn't work. Strength without conditioning wasn't enough. The beat-down program was designed to do both—in mega-doses.

"We went into off-season conditioning wanting to challenge our players," Latina said. "Obviously, to play at a high level in Division I-A football, you have to be very physical, you have to be tough, you have to be tough-minded. You have to push your players beyond where they want to push themselves. For the most part, our kids responded. Because of that, we felt like we were getting better, and that's the whole key: feeling like you're getting better."

As the 2005 season began, the Irish players knew they were better conditioned than a year earlier. The proof came when Notre Dame opened against Pittsburgh on September 3. Several Pitt players succumbed to the late-summer heat and humidity. Cramps and exhaustion crippled them, especially in the second half. Meanwhile, the Irish remained remarkably fresh. Their endurance was noticeably better.

It wasn't just that Notre Dame won, 42–21; it was how they won. After trailing, 10–7, at the end of the first quarter, the Irish scored touchdowns on their next five drives. The key drive took place at the start of the second half, when Quinn led Notre Dame on a 20-play, 80-yard drive that took 7:01—and wore down an already tired Pitt defense.

The game plan for that victory, Weis' first as a head coach, had been written six months earlier during those February beat-down workouts.

......

Chapter 8

REBUILDING THE RECRUITING MACHINE

O NE OF THE PIONEERS of the mid-1970s of what has since exploded into a nationwide industry, an entrepreneur and college football super-fan named Joe Terranova sold his first recruiting reports—ranking college football programs on the basis of their recruiting classes—for $2. Except for Terranova and a handful of others, nobody back then thought much about recruiting. What today is commonly known as college football's "other season"—the 12-month recruiting season—was, back when Terranova got started, pretty much ignored by just about everyone except coaches, prep stars, and their parents.

Terranova, by ranking the recruiting classes of the major college programs, laid the groundwork for a national craze. What was supposed to be a diversion, a way to kill time until spring practices began, soon mushroomed into a national obsession. Terranova had tapped into a whole new species of college football fandom, a strain of pigskin-mania that required no actual games to make its constituent members stark-raving, off-the-charts bananas. Recruiting, among hardcore zealots, became the game within the game.

The beginnings of Recruiting Madness were modest. Shortly after signing day, Terranova published a fit-in-your-back-pocket pamphlet that ranked the top players and recruiting classes in the country. Sometimes he tried to put a humorous twist on his individual recaps. For example, 1980 Notre Dame defensive line recruit Tim Marshall was called "Darth Vader in cleats."

Okay, so maybe Terranova was no Jerry Seinfeld. No matter. Soon, recruiting fanatics, who hadn't known they were recruiting fanatics, were eating it up.

It was a far cry from the old days, when a school announced its signees, and their names were quickly forgotten until 18 months later, when they took the field for real as sophomores. That all changed in 1972, when freshmen became eligible to play. Suddenly, hundreds of high school players were becoming household names in football-crazy households during the "off" season. After all, the guy your school signed in February might—and often did—kick-start your team on its way to a bowl game in the fall.

Other so-called recruiting gurus quickly followed. Tom Lemming from Illinois, Max Emfinger from Texas, Bill Buchalter from Florida, and Allen Wallace from California were among the earliest members of the "recruiting media." Terranova's mom-and-pop-style publications were soon challenged by others that offered frequent mailings during the recruiting season, with hundreds of high school prospects listed by position and region. Top-100 lists popped up just about everywhere this side of *The Wall Street Journal*. Fax machines and 900 numbers delivered hot-off-the-press recruiting information to the growing masses of hungry college football fans seeking more, more, more information—now!

And then came the Internet.

Today, spreading recruiting information is a multimillion-dollar business. Web sites such as Rivals.com and Scout.com pull together far more recruiting information than a fan with a normal life could possibly read in a year, much less a single recruiting season. Message boards where any opinion, source and tact be damned, is welcome, boost the information flow exponentially.

Recruits are bullied to share their up-to-the-minute "lean" with men who are mailmen, cops, or insurance agents by day and "recruiting analysts" by night. The college football recruiting process has become a year-round buffet of information, some of it actually true, and the hungry never get full. Many fans now know as much about the recruiting process as your typical assistant coach does.

Or at least think they do.

Of course, there was a time when Notre Dame didn't have to mount a full-throttle recruiting campaign. The Irish could just play the Victory March or post a "Play Like a Champion Today" sign outside a recruit's home, and he would fall in line. The Irish didn't recruit; they gathered.

But that was then, when unlimited scholarships and relatively circumscribed national exposure allowed the college football "haves" to build dynasties. Everybody knew about Notre Dame. It was college football royalty.

Slowly but surely, with cable television boosting the exposure of college sports, the "have-nots" were becoming household names too. No longer could Notre Dame, USC, Alabama, Tennessee, Ohio State, Michigan, and Texas corner the market on the top talent. Those schools remained superattractive, of course, but the three main schools in Florida—Miami, Florida State, and Florida—were keeping plenty of prospects home in the talent-wealthy Sunshine State and winning with them.

Recruiting borders began to expand. A top-rated player from Pennsylvania was just as likely to land in Texas as a Californian was to sign with Michigan or Ohio State. There was a place in college football for thousands of talented players, and if it wasn't at one of the perennial powerhouses, it might be at Virginia Tech or Oregon or Louisville or even the losingest program of all at one time, Kansas State. All of these programs eventually became Top-10 teams, and they did so because the plate tectonics of college football had shifted dramatically.

When Gerry Faust was named Dan Devine's successor as head coach of the Fighting Irish after the 1980 season, *Parade* magazine's list of the top players in the country was brimming with Irish recruits. Faust snagged 13 *Parade* All-Americas to claim the nation's No. 1 rank in recruiting. In fact, from 1981 to 1983, Faust signed the consensus No. 1 class each year. When many of those players struggled to a 30–26–1 mark under Faust (1981–1985) but then went on to play successfully in the NFL, the truth about the Faust regime was revealed.

Lou Holtz replaced Faust in 1986 and hired Vinny Cerrato as his recruiting coordinator. From 1987 to 1990, the Irish reeled in some of their greatest talent in the program's history, including players such as Chris Zorich, Ricky Watters, Todd Lyght, and Tony Brooks. Not surprisingly, those classes were ranked No. 1 in the nation.

The 1990 class is still considered the gold standard for modern-day Irish recruiting. Of the 23 players, 13 were later chosen in the NFL draft, including an incredible five first-round picks: defensive lineman Bryant Young, offensive lineman Aaron Taylor, running back Jerome Bettis, and defensive backs Tom Carter and Jeff Burris. The influx of quality players helped transform the Irish into a national power again. From 1988, when Holtz' recruiting classes began to assert themselves on the field, to 1993, Notre Dame compiled a six-year record of 64–9–1. Those six seasons included a national title (1988), a pair of No. 2 rankings in the final Associated Press poll (1989 and 1993), and a No. 4 ranking (1992).

The transition from Holtz to Bob Davie in 1997 marked an unraveling of Notre Dame's recruiting prowess. Cerrato was long gone, and so was the admissions office's willingness to accept borderline prospects. And, as is always the case during a coaching change, some recruits went elsewhere because of the uncertainty of the new regime.

Although Davie rebounded by landing top-five classes in 1998 and 1999, the 2000 class began a string of five years in which the Irish fell out of the consensus top-10 rankings four times—even though some recruiting analysts still ranked the Irish in the top 20 more or less out of habit. (Some did it because it was good for business to include them.)

The inconsistent recruiting efforts, as well as the questionable coaching performances of Holtz' immediate successors, showed up on the field. From 1994 through 2004, Notre Dame had a 79–52–1 record. Good, but certainly not up to Notre Dame standards.

Tyrone Willingham's 2004 class numbered just 17 players, tying Faust's 1984 group for the fewest ever signed at Notre Dame to that point in the school's history. When Willingham was fired, he was in the process of signing another marginal class before Weis picked up the recruiting process in mid-December.

Recruiting had long since become a year-round endeavor, and even a master salesman like Weis couldn't make up for lost time. A flurry of phone calls and correspondence from Weis and his staff made an impact, but not enough to save the 2005 class from ranking outside of the nation's top 25. When three of the best recruits—wide receiver David Nelson, defensive end Lawrence Wilson, and defensive back Brandon Harrison—chose to back off from their Notre Dame commitments and go elsewhere following Willingham's firing, the Irish lost significant talent.

Despite the setbacks, Weis didn't panic. And he certainly didn't beg Nelson, Wilson, and Harrison to change their minds. He had accepted the Notre Dame job with the understanding that he would first complete his contractual obligation to the Patriots. When Nelson wanted a visit from Weis, regardless of whether the Patriots won or lost their upcoming playoff game, Weis pulled the plug. If the Patriots were victorious, Weis wouldn't be able to accommodate Nelson, and he wasn't about to give in to the player's demands. If Nelson couldn't make some allowances for Weis' hectic schedule, he could choose a different school.

Yet with Rob Ianello coordinating the recruiting efforts and with several top-notch recruiters on the staff—most notably Haywood—the Irish laid the groundwork for long-term recruiting success amid the short-term frustration of an abbreviated first campaign. And Weis had an extra edge: he was the first head coach since Hugh Devore in 1963 who could legitimately say to a recruit, "This is what it's like at Notre Dame. I went to school there."

Weis scoffed at whispers that he might not be able to recruit in college because he had spent the previous 15 years in the NFL. Recruiting was another way of competing, and Weis was all about competing.

The changing face of the professional game now requires free agents to be wooed. Among those influenced by Weis to join the Patriots was Marc Edwards, who just happened to be a former Irish fullback and co-captain of the 1996 team.

Bill Belichick knew better than anyone that Weis' transition from the NFL to college football would be seamless. "On every staff I was on with Charlie," Belichick said, "he was one of the strongest recruiters in terms of talking to free agent players, getting them to come, getting them to take the opportunity we had, whether it was the Giants, the Jets, or New England."

Belichick said Weis was especially adept in situations where other teams were offering more money: "He could sell them on the premise that it wasn't about the money, that it was about opportunity and the quality of the team and the development of the players. He had a good rapport with the players, especially young players. I'm sure that's part of the reason he got the job at Notre Dame."

With his dual commitments to the Patriots and his alma mater, Weis had to recruit almost exclusively by telephone during his seven-week window of opportunity. Face-to-face would have been better, of course, but recruiting analysts quickly began praising Weis for burning up the phone lines.

"I felt the only thing I could really do was spend the phone time to try to get us into contention," Weis said. "In some cases, it helped; in others, it didn't. But one thing that you're never going to get from Notre Dame is a lack of effort."

Indeed, in Notre Dame's efforts to keep Lawrence Wilson, Weis sent seven Irish coaches to his house to make one last push before the defensive end eventually chose Ohio State.

Effort, or rather a lack thereof, had been at the crux of Notre Dame's recruiting problems in previous years. Several analysts said that during the Willingham regime, the assistant coaches simply lacked the dog-gedness and determination necessary to consistently recruit well. Notre Dame often lagged behind when it came to detecting prospects early and being persistent with recruits.

"The previous regime left recruiting in a shambles," said Bobby Burton of Rivals.com. "Weis had to start from scratch, from ground zero. Let's just say the previous regime didn't have enough bullets in the chamber."

When Weis began recruiting Steve Quinn from St. Joseph's Prep in Philadelphia, the linebacker had already verbally committed to Penn State. Weis gave Quinn his best sales pitch on Notre Dame and eventu-ally wrested him away from the Nittany Lions.

"It's not even close," said Gil Brooks, Quinn's coach at St. Joseph's, when asked to compare the recruiting approaches of Weis and the pre-vious Irish coaching staff. "The old staff was slow, overly methodical, and not at all energetic. There wasn't a whole lot of excitement. There wasn't a sense of, 'Hey, we're Notre Dame!' "

Yet even defensive coordinator Rick Minter, who coached all of the defensive talent that arrived at Notre Dame in the late 1980s and early 1990s, admitted the Irish were fighting an uphill battle during that first, abbreviated recruiting season. "Right now, recruiting is tough," said Minter. "We don't have the glow we used to have. It has nothing to do with admissions. It's just that kids today are instantaneous. They lean on USC, Oklahoma, LSU, Florida, Miami of Florida, and Ohio State. Next year's pitch will be our record. But for now, we're trying to get kids to jump onboard based on faith without proof. That's a tough sell."

Ianello offered the essential recruiting truth: "When you come in late, it's not necessarily about selling your university as much as it is about selling yourself."

By the time Weis & Co. had finished signing the Class of 2009, they hadn't dramatically altered the group that Willingham originally recruit-ed. But they had begun to build a foundation for future classes. For the first time in several years, there was a buzz about the Notre Dame coaching staff on the recruiting trail. High school coaches and their players, as well as the recruiting gurus, couldn't help but notice it.

"Charlie Weis has shown that he is going to be a very formidable coach and recruiter at Notre Dame," said analyst Allen Wallace. "This isn't the kind of class that will bring Notre Dame a national championship. But if you can recruit a Top-15, Top-20 class every year, you can win the whole enchilada."

Willingham wasn't the type of person to make excuses, but the word was that some people on his staff suffered from the attitude that Notre Dame's "disadvantages" in recruiting limited the Irish competitively. "All I heard about were the kids that Notre Dame couldn't get because of weather, social life, and academics," Lemming said. "Those are ready-made excuses that the last two staffs took advantage of. Any assistant coach who says that is going to fail."

Weis approached recruiting with what he perceived to be a practical, up-to-date approach. If the Irish were going to compete on a national-championship level, they would have to pursue the nation's best prep prospects who were able to qualify academically. Those players could expect a blueprint for the path to riches in the NFL.

Any college recruiter of blue-chippers needs to sell the parents and families, but ultimately, it's the player who has to buy the pitch. "When you first talk to parents," Weis said, "they want to hear what's going to happen to their boy. They want to hear about academic support, graduation rate, job prospects, all those things. But when the dust settles, it's the kid's decision. It's a teenage kid making the first major decision he's ever had to make in his whole life. He has guidance, but it's his call. It all comes back to the kid."

Weis began cultivating a relationship with Dan Saracino, the university's director of admissions, who had worked with Irish head coaches Davie and Willingham. "Charlie is good about not saying anything negative about the previous regime, and that's my position too," Saracino said. "Ty Willingham and his staff were nice people. Not that they didn't get it, but I want to say, with capital letters, these coaches GET IT. Am I excited about the coaches Charlie brought in? As excited as I am about Charlie. In my mind, there's no doubt Notre Dame will win again. No doubt."

Weis and his staff were committed to going beyond merely shipping academic transcripts to the admissions department. The new Irish staff evaluated a recruit's transcript and provided the admissions department with an initial, educated evaluation of his academic prospects. In essence, they were working for the admissions department.

"Our coaches have been educated on what we're looking for in terms of transcripts," Weis said. "So before we even go over to Dan Saracino, we'll say to him, 'Look, we realize this kid is a bit of an academic risk, but he's on the rise. With four or five core courses going into his senior year and with an approved ACT, does this guy have a chance?' If Dan says he has no chance, we move on. That doesn't happen very often, because we try not to give him too many of those instances."

No longer would academics be used as a crutch for the failure to recruit good football players at Notre Dame. In fact, Weis embraced the high standards and intended to use them to Notre Dame's advantage.

"People overplay the downside of wanting kids with higher academics," said Weis. "I think it's important to understand that you can play that to your advantage by playing the upside of how much more mental pressure you're going to put on guys, and how quickly you can instill things due to how much they can mentally handle. Then you go into the houses of the kids, and you say, 'Look, this is what we're looking for. If you're looking for me to talk about football first, go somewhere else.' I openly tell recruits in the conversation that if they want to go somewhere not as tough academically, don't worry about me, just move on to somewhere else."

While Willingham eased off on pursuing recruits who had gained favor with the nation's heavyweight schools, Weis immediately raised the bar. The Irish would do battle with USC, Oklahoma, Florida, and anyone else for any blue-chipper who Weis & Co. thought could handle the academic and football pressure of Notre Dame.

The Irish would lose some of those battles, particularly during Weis' first recruiting campaign. But the standard had changed. Notre Dame would recruit the best players as long as the prospects qualified and were a good fit for the university.

A few defections aside, almost all of the players who had committed to Willingham soon jumped on the Charlie Weis bandwagon. "It's obvious he wants to win, he wants to end his career at Notre Dame, and that means that he wants to be successful," said quarterback Evan Sharpley from Marshall, Michigan, who had been recruited by Willingham. "I liked how he talked about changing the attitude of the team to get that nastiness in there. That's a great thing to have a coach say. Notre Dame needs to get that swagger back."

"I can tell the passion that he has for the game," said tight end Joey Hiben from Chaska, Minnesota, another Willingham recruit. "I can tell Coach Weis is going to make it exciting, and I'm sure he'll make it nasty, too, which is how football is supposed to be. That's what Notre Dame needed the last few years, because two different teams would show up for every game."

Weis' seven-week recruiting campaign ended as it began, with an unusual twist: he introduced the 15-man 2005 class via teleconference from a media tent near Jacksonville, Florida, four days before Super Bowl XXXIX.

The class ranked outside the nation's top 20 in all three major recruiting services—Rivals.com, Tom Lemming, and SuperPrep—for the second straight year. The 15-man class was also the smallest in Notre Dame history. The 22 visits—out of an NCAA-allowed 56—was also a record low at Notre Dame. According to Rivals.com, 64 of the 117 Division 1-A schools in 2005 signed more players than the Irish brought in for visits.

But of the 19 who made official visits to Notre Dame after Weis was named head coach, 15 signed with the Irish. Ten of the 11 visitors during Weis' first recruiting weekend, on January 7–8, eventually signed with Notre Dame.

The recruiting campaign may not have turned out quite the way Weis and his staff would have hoped. Weis figured the Irish could have given out more than 15 scholarships. But "we decided not to go to the limit because we didn't want to bring in the wrong type of kid," he said. "We could have brought in another four or five kids just to make everyone happy. But it's not the number of guys you sign; it's signing the right types of guys, and I'm happy with the guys we signed."

Notre Dame had generated enthusiasm and momentum. And at the conclusion of spring drills in April, Weis and his staff hit the road again for spring recruiting. Head coaches were seldom seen recruiting in May, but Weis couldn't take the chance of staying home.

"I think I better be out there all the time in May," Weis said. "I might not be out there every single day, but I better be out there every single week. Let's face it, when you walk into a school and you're the head coach, it's different. No disrespect to the assistants, but it's a different message that's being sent to those kids and those programs. This isn't about PR; this is about letting these young men know that we want to be in the game."

The aggressive approach paid dividends as the Irish staff took the first steps toward signing their second Notre Dame class in February 2006: seven verbal commitments by the end of May recruiting and 10 by the start of fall camp, on August 8. "They've done a great job," said Jeremy Crabtree, the national recruiting editor for Rivals.com, at the conclusion of May recruiting. "The staff has worked harder than maybe anybody in the country. They'll have some hits and misses. They won't be able to land everybody on their national list. But they're surprising people by the number of quality kids they've attracted. They've set themselves up to be a potential Top-15 class in 2006, and if things go well the rest of the recruiting process, it wouldn't surprise me at all to see them in the national Top 5 or Top 10."

Even if the Irish couldn't land a top-five class, they were significantly increasing their odds of success. "Above and beyond the commitments, what I look at is the volume of players Notre Dame is in on," Burton said. "They seem to have a deeper field of players that they're recruiting this year than they've had the last 10 years."

Weis was confident that his recruiting plan was working. "Every day, we get one day further ahead of knowing where we are," Weis said. "Some recruits go somewhere else, so you just move on. Or if you really don't think they'll end up where they say they're going, you just go ahead and drop 'em an e-mail saying, 'You'll be back.' "

Weis instituted a series of Junior Days to piggyback on the enthusiasm generated in the Joyce Center for men's basketball. He even tapped into the student body for assistance with his recruiting endeavors. With 86 high school junior football players in attendance for the Notre Dame-UCLA basketball game on Sunday, February 27, Weis asked students to assist in the recruiting process by talking to the visiting prep stars about the positives of coming to Notre Dame.

"One of the things we're trying to do is get a real head start on 2006 recruiting," Weis told the halftime crowd. "We can't talk about names or things like that, because that's an NCAA violation. But today, we brought some juniors in to come and share the Notre Dame experience, which we all know is kind of special. The image that you students present has a lot to do with whether or not these kids are coming here."

Earlier in the day, university president Rev. Edward Malloy had spoken with the visiting recruits. Now Weis summed up the impact of that meeting: "When Monk Malloy got up in front of these young men, I tell you what, after 15 minutes I would have signed up. There wouldn't have been any doubt in my mind. I would have said, 'Give me the letter of intent, let's go!' "

Nobody had to cue the audience to roar its approval.

"We want to tell the truth," Weis continued. "There are pros and cons everywhere you go. If you want to tell them it's not 90 degrees every day, I can live with that. But the bottom line is let's talk about the reasons why we did come to Notre Dame. Let's talk about what we expect to get after we graduate from Notre Dame. We're all in this together. This is about all being on the same team."

The team—Weis' recruiting team—was beginning to have an impact on how the nation's best high school players perceived Notre Dame. There was still a considerable distance to go before anyone compared a Weis recruiting class to those glory classes of Holtz'.

But it was a good start on Notre Dame's way back to the gold standard.

Chapter 9

······

SEEING WHAT STICKS

AT AN ESTABLISHED PROGRAM—say, the defending national champion USC—spring practice had become a time to experiment, refine, and reload. At Notre Dame in the spring of 2005, it was something altogether different. Charlie Weis and his staff had exactly 15 spring practice sessions to evaluate, reinvigorate, and rebuild. Their first goal would be a modest one: turn a team unsure of itself into a competitor.

It wouldn't be easy to achieve. For starters, everyone on both sides of the ball—including the respective coaching staffs—would have to maneuver their way through the new terminology of Weis' offense and Rick Minter's defense. The staff had come from so many different points on the football map that they were, in many respects, starting from scratch, just like the players.

Implementing Weis' offense would be the most intriguing aspect of the transition. It had been a while since Notre Dame mounted an offense that ranked among college football's best. But Weis' cachet was based on having created an offense that was greatly responsible for three Super Bowl championships in the past four years. He had been Tom Brady's mentor, and Brady was now considered one of the greatest clutch quarterbacks in NFL history.

Before diagramming the first play, however, Weis knew he had to boost his team's spirits and intensity. Fifteen losses in the previous 28 games were bad enough; how the Irish lost was even worse. The scores were more lopsided than a comb-over. Worse yet, it sometimes looked like the players were just going through the motions—the most damning indictment possible of a football team and its coaching staff.

During the eight seasons from 1997 through 2004, Notre Dame's best national ranking on offense was just 19th—in 1999, the first year of Kevin Rogers' three-year reign as offensive coordinator. But even that season, the Irish could do no better than a 5–7 record. The team won nine games in 1998 and 2000, and 10 in 2002. But during the other five years of the Davie and Willingham Eras, they were a combined 28–32, principally because of anemic offense.

On defense, Notre Dame played more like, well, Notre Dame. The Irish had a couple of excellent years, including 2001 and 2002, when they finished 14th and 13th in the nation, respectively, in yards surrendered per game. And while not every year was as good, clearly, it was the offense—and later, special teams under Willingham—that failed to pull its share of the load throughout the eight-year tailspin.

A greater emphasis on spread formations and the passing game over the previous decade had diminished the relative importance of the running game throughout college football. Yet there remained no greater indicator of dominance at the line than a team's rushing offense and rushing defense. Notre Dame's rushing defense had improved from 1997 to 2004, but the offensive ground game under Davie and Willingham was woefully inconsistent and, at times, as painful to watch as someone else's home movies.

In 2002, Willingham's 10–victory season, the Irish rushed for the school's fewest yards in 40 years. Two years later, Notre Dame set a record for the lowest rushing output — just 127.4 yards per game — since 1946, when statistics like these were first tracked. In an age when offense had moved to the forefront of the college game, Notre Dame used a Neanderthal game plan. The Irish gained fewer than 400 yards in 31 of their preceding 37 games before Weis' arrival (including the 2004 Insight Bowl) — and Willingham had arrived in South Bend with a reputation as an offensive mastermind.

Not surprisingly, scoring also nose-dived. The Irish ranked 99th in the country with a 19.4 points-per-game average in 2001, the last year of the Davie regime. The next three years, under Willingham, the Irish finished 91st, 93rd, and 72nd. The 2002 offense was so anemic that had the defense and special teams not scored nine touchdowns and recorded two safeties, Notre Dame would have averaged just 17.2 points per game.

Numbers like that help explain why Davie and Willingham were no longer at Notre Dame.

In just 15 spring practices, Weis had to get his players to think like Weis guys. He believed strongly in his system, but he needed them to believe in it too. Weis wanted to get his players to think in a whole new way. They were going to win. They had to believe that. If they didn't believe that, it didn't matter how good his system was.

"It's really important that the head coach's attitude permeates the team," Weis said. All they had to do was follow his lead, fine-tune their execution, and buy into a simple concept: *They ... Were ... Going ... To ... Win.*

"My basic philosophy is to have fewer plays but to run them from multiple looks," Weis said. "Give the defense a lot of different looks, but run your base plays and the defense won't know what you're going to do. If you're going to try to exploit defenses, you can't let them figure out what you're going to do by your formation every time you line up. Now, there are several ways to do that. But the first thing you need to do is get your players to understand that regardless of what personnel group is out there, you can run the same play."

It's a cliché, but Weis really did regard a football game as a chess match played on 120 yards of field. After whipping his players into the best shape of their lives off the field, the idea was to be prepared to outmaneuver the opposition on the field.

Weis' offensive philosophy was predicated on practicality. "First of all, you find out what your players can do," he said. "We have a very expansive offensive package, but you have to be able to use the personnel that you have available. If you have a team that has multiple tight ends that can play, or if you have a team that has multiple wide receivers that can play, use multiple tight ends or receivers."

During New England's 2001 Super Bowl season, Weis leaned toward using two tight end/two running back sets because the Patriots were playing behind an inexperienced quarterback in Tom Brady. Weis' play-calling put Brady in a position to manage games. The Patriots emphasized the ground game first. Three years and another Super Bowl title later, the Patriots passed first and ran second. Instead of using two-back sets, New England was more inclined to go with three wideouts. Weis learned and adjusted right along with the Patriots' offensive players, particularly Brady.

"Charlie doesn't impose his offense on his players, he adjusts to them," Edwards said. "A lot of coaches have a certain ego that their system is so smart that it will outsmart anybody. That's not necessarily the case."

This was the first time any of the offensive assistants had worked with Weis. It was an eye-opening experience. Assistant head coach and offensive line coach John Latina was impressed with Weis' ability to communicate concepts. "You might have 20 running plays, but five of them may be the same conceptually," he said. "To teach 20 plays is monumental, but to teach three concepts makes it a little bit easier."

Ron Powlus, filling in for the then-convalescing David Cutcliffe, marveled at the simplicity of the teaching process from a quarterback's perspective, and at the pressure Weis' offense put on opposing defenses. "I really like the ability the offense has to create options for the quarterback," Powlus said. "A great offense is one that can find some way to get to a good situation on every play, and that's what this offense does. Essentially, you wind up with hundreds and hundreds of plays from an opposing defensive perspective, because they're seeing something different every time."

Weis had a veteran offensive line to drive his first Notre Dame offense. "The most experienced offensive line in school history"—that's how preseason observers and analysts routinely described it. The unit was led by fifth-year seniors Dan Stevenson and Mark LeVoir, along with fourth-year senior Bob Morton, two-year starter Ryan Harris, 2004 starter John Sullivan, and veteran backup Dan Santucci.

Latina would periodically test the offensive linemen, not only at their own position, but on the duties of the rest of the offensive line, as well. If they understood the overall concept of the play, they would have a better understanding of how to make things work, even when the opposition adjusted.

With only 15 spring practices to get it all down, Weis didn't have time to spoon-feed his offense. Instead, he threw them into the deep end of the pool and forced them to swim. "We can always tone it back if it's too much," he said philosophically.

These were exciting times for Brady Quinn, who had taken a beating during his 2003 freshman year after replacing Carlyle Holiday as the starting quarterback in the fourth game of the season. He had shown marked improvement in his touchdown:interception ratio as a sophomore, but the team continued to struggle. With two full years of eligibility remaining, Quinn already had 21 starts to his credit. The Irish were a disappointing 10–11 in those 21 games, and Quinn wanted to take his game to the next level. Blessed with a sturdy 6'4" frame and above-average arm strength, Quinn should have been rounding into a future NFL draft prospect. But the previous offensive system had been stuck in a "one step forward, two steps back" mode. When Weis explained a nuance of the game to the quarterbacks—say, hot reads and sight adjustments at the line of scrimmage when it appeared that the defense was going to blitz—Quinn was surprised at how easy it was to understand it all. It was as if he had finally found the perfect football interpreter.

"It's probably the best experience I can have working through an offense with someone who *is* the offense," Quinn said of Weis. "He knows the ins and outs, and he knows the best way to teach it."

Yet Weis could also be unforgiving. He would bark loud and often if need be to get his point across. "He's never going to pat you on the back if you make a great play," Quinn said. "He might compliment you and say you should have done this or should have done this. No matter who's in there, he's going to push you."

Quinn wanted to be pushed. After all, he was already the starting quarterback at Notre Dame. He wanted more. He wanted a future in professional football.

Weis was pleasantly surprised by the quarterback he inherited. Not only did Quinn have the physical tools to succeed on the field, he also had an inherent toughness. Weis had seen the beating Quinn took during his first two years at Notre Dame, yet the kid kept pulling himself up off the turf and going back for more.

Now Weis was beginning to learn about Quinn's mental capacity, and he liked what he discovered—namely, that you couldn't oversaturate Quinn with football information. The more Weis gave him, the more voracious his appetite for knowledge became. "You try not to ask them to do more than they can handle," Weis said during spring practice. "But at this time of the year, you overexpose them, you push them, because you want to see what level you can get them to. I've been more than pleased with how Brady Quinn has mentally picked up the game. At this early stage I can say that I'm cautiously optimistic."

Running back Darius Walker, who turned in an impressive freshman season with 786 yards rushing and seven touchdowns, believed that Weis' lack of playing experience may actually have helped him be a better coach. It was an interesting theory, especially for someone who only had one year of collegiate experience himself. "He has a deeper knowledge and understanding of the game," said Walker. "By not actually being a player, he would have to think a little harder than people who played the game, and he seems to have benefited from that."

Thinking a little harder meant Weis could be unforgiving during tape study, even when a play was successful. He was exacting. He demanded efficiency of motion. During one film session, Weis watched in dismay as Walker scored on a running play. "You didn't have to make that cut to get into the end zone," Weis told Walker. The running back thought to himself, "Wow, I just did a good job and he's still going to bash me because I didn't have to go through what I went through to get to the end zone."

Walker loved some of the video sessions leading into spring drills. Instead of the usual cut-ups of different plays or practices, Weis showed them tape of the Patriots offense. *His* offense. "We're watching a pro team's cut-ups and we're going to be running the exact same plays the Patriots were running," said Walker. "In a sense, it gives us the experience of what it will be like at the next level, and it also helps us understand what the pros are doing and what it's like being in the pros."

Quinn had studied Patriots tape before Weis signed a contract with Notre Dame. He admired Tom Brady's game. "The biggest thing when you watch New England tape is how they adjust to certain situations on the field," Quinn said. Now he was being coached by the guy who had helped transform Brady from a sixth-round draft pick into a Super Bowl ring machine.

Of course, the transformation wouldn't—couldn't—happen overnight. The terminology was completely different. Although Weis had a knack for zeroing in on the essence of what they were trying to accomplish offensively, there would be some growing pains, even for the most experienced offensive line in Notre Dame history. "We're all rookies," Morton said. "We're all just trying to get a grasp of who's around us at different positions."

Plenty of doubt had been planted in their heads over the previous two seasons. Thirteen losses in two years, 15 losses in the last 28 games, will do that. But young, talented athletes are resilient. They have good imaginations. They can picture success just around the corner, and with a head coach like Weis, it seemed within their grasp.

"For the past couple of years I think you've seen the offensive line grow and develop, take its bumps and bruises, but at the same time learn from it," Stevenson said. "We have so much talent and so much experience, there are no excuses. We can be one of the top lines in the nation."

Weis also was intrigued by his receiving corps: Maurice Stovall and Jeff Samardzija, dual 6'5" targets; veteran wideout Rhema McKnight, with 98 career catches and six touchdowns; and smallish fifth-year senior Matt Shelton, who spent the spring recovering from a late-season knee injury. Shelton had speed and a 25.5-yards-per-catch career average. "We have great size at receiver," Weis said. "I'm used to coaching a bunch of midgets. The last tall one I had was Keyshawn Johnson with the Jets."

Following the fifth practice of the spring, however, Weis was unhappy with what he had just witnessed. "If the offense played the defense today, it would have been a blowout for the defense," Weis declared.

Ah, the defense. It was a transition year for all the Irish, of course, but for the Notre Dame defense it was a whole new way of looking at things. The change in coordinators from Kent Baer to Minter was a huge adjustment. There was a major overhaul in personnel, too. Defensive end Justin Tuck, Notre Dame's all-time sack leader, had bypassed a final year of eligibility to turn pro. Defensive tackle Greg Pauly and defensive end Kyle Budinscak also were gone. That left nose guard Derek Landri as the only returning starter on the defensive line. And at linebacker, Derek Curry and team co-captain Mike Goolsby, two players who led by word and deed, had graduated.

Even more than his predecessor, Minter steered clear of high-risk, high-reward schemes. He preferred to stay in a base alignment. And he had his defensive line coach, Jappy Oliver, teach his players assignment football. In other words, instead of just shooting off the snap and going hell-bent for the football, they would play the gaps, close off the running avenues, and set up the inside linebackers to make tackles.

For fifth-year senior linebacker Brandon Hoyte, Minter was his third defensive coordinator since his arrival at Notre Dame in 2001. Hoyte had taken Willingham's firing hard. A bit more introspective than most of his teammates—Hoyte wrote poetry in his spare time—he nonetheless understood that change happens, and that as a team leader, he would have to make the adjustment.

"It was tough," said Hoyte. "But then there's a period where you have to understand that you have to move on. Then there's a period of excitement. I'm flourishing right now in the period of excitement."

The defensive front seven would be fine. Highly touted Victor Abiamiri and Trevor Laws would move into the starting lineup. Curry's intelligence would be missed, as would Goolsby's passion for contact. But talented sophomore Maurice Crum Jr., the son of the former Miami Hurricanes standout, and fifth-year senior Corey Mays were joining the starting lineup.

The greatest concern was in the Irish secondary, which had been torched for 14 touchdown passes in the final three games of the 2004 season. That was precisely why Weis tabbed Lewis to take charge. "There are so many inexperienced players in the secondary that there was no thought of starting out with a depth chart," Lewis said just before spring practice began. "I'm not concerned about that. I'm concerned about trying to find who our best four guys are and the positions they fit into within our defensive system. One of the keys to coaching is to get the right people on the bus. Then you worry about getting them in the right seats."

Among the would-be passengers were Tom Zbikowski, Mike Richardson, and a whole bunch of young players who had yet to make a mark, including converted receivers Chinedum Ndukwe and Ambrose Wooden. "One thing I can say about the secondary is that there are several athletes with a lot of speed," Weis said. "Now, how good of football players they are, I can't tell you. But usually when you have athletes and you have speed, you have a chance."

Added Minter, "We don't have much experience back there, so we'll use it as an asset and say, 'Hey, you guys don't have a whole lot to forget.' The one thing about young guys is they haven't been here long enough to judge whether they can or cannot become great players."

Weis was determined to excel on special teams as a way to help a defense in transition. And on special teams, the key to success had more to do with discipline and pedal-to-the-metal effort than complex schemes and nuanced tactical football.

Weis placed Brian Polian in charge, with Bernie Parmalee assisting. When necessary, half a practice would be devoted to special teams. This was serious business, not an afterthought. "If you don't practice special teams full speed, you never get any good at it," Weis said. "It's not something where you can go out there and just kind of jog down the field. You need to see whether cover guys running down the field can make somebody miss, whether they're going to run in their lanes, whether they're going to have discipline. You want to see how the guys are going to do under pressure. You want to see returners fielding kicks. You don't make any judgment until you get there and get a chance to watch all those things."

Everyone, with the exception of Quinn, was a candidate to play special teams. "If we can find eight to 10 guys who can be our hard-core special teams maniacs—those guys who just make a living in the kicking game—we would be thrilled," Polian said. About 20 players volunteered to return punts and kicks. "We essentially said, 'Who wants to try it? This is an open dress rehearsal,'" Polian said. "We want to find guys who can catch the ball first and will go up the field north and south."

The tryout produced a few surprises, among them Zbikowski on punt returns and speedy walk-on Brandon Harris on kickoff returns.

The Irish wrapped up spring drills on April 23 with the annual Blue-Gold Game, in which Weis pitted the No. 1 unit against the No. 2. Not surprisingly, the projected starters came out on top, 28–6. A crowd of 23,324 endured snow and bone-chilling cold to get a sneak preview of Weis' new team. Quinn (8-for-12, for 120 yards) was voted the most valuable player. Walker rushed for 83 yards on 10 carries. Rashon Powers-Neal gained 51 yards on seven carries and scored two touchdowns. Travis Thomas picked up 63 yards on 14 carries with a backup offensive line leading the way. Defensive end Chris Frome, who was competing for the defensive end spot vacated by Tuck, paced the Blue defense with 2.5 sacks.

Particularly striking about Quinn's performance were his decisiveness and quick release. "That's completely Coach Weis," Quinn said after the game. "By the time I'm on my fifth step, I have to know if I'm throwing to the first guy or not, and right on down the line in the next couple of split seconds."

Over the course of spring practice, the Weis offensive scheme received a grade of A+ from the guy who would be throwing the ball. He sounded very much like a quarterback who couldn't wait for the September 3 opener against Pittsburgh.

To thank hardcore Notre Dame fans who braved the cold to see their new and improved Irish, Weis arranged for guest appearances by Joe Montana, Joe Theismann, Chris Zorich, and Tim Brown. The four Irish legends served as honorary captains of the two squads: Montana and Zorich worked with the No. 1 unit, Theismann and Brown the No. 2. Asked what he thought when he saw the lopsided score, Theismann said, "Montana was cheating."

Of the four, Brown could best relate to what the current Irish players were experiencing with a new head coach. He played for Gerry Faust for two years, and then Lou Holtz during his junior and senior seasons. In Brown's senior year (1987), the Irish were ranked as high as fourth. The following year, they won the national title.

"In 1986, when Lou came in, he was talking about all these great things we were going to do, but we had to believe in him," Brown said. "It started that year, and a couple of years later we won the championship."

When Weis asked Brown to speak to the team, the Hall of Famer-to-be stressed a single point. It would be some of the smartest advice the Irish heard all year. "You've got to pay attention to this guy," said Brown, glancing at Weis. "Believe in what he says because he can take you to a new level. It may not be this year, it may not be next year, but certainly in the future he'll take this program to the very top."

Spring practice was finished. May recruiting was done. Now there would be the long, frustrating, clock-watching wait—June, July, August—until Weis and his team would assemble for fall training camp. The new coach believed the Irish had made significant progress since the start of spring drills. But there was still a long way to go, and Weis wasn't used to spending his summers playing golf and mowing the lawn.

"I don't like the fact that I'm not going to be hands-on again until August," he said. "What concerns me is how much retention we have two months from now when we crank it up again."

That wouldn't be a problem.

Fifteen practices had proven to the players that Charlie Weis' system was worth the effort.

They would remember it all.

Chapter 10

......

THE MARATHON BEGINS

FROM THE OUTSIDE, THE just-completed Guglielmino Athletics Complex looked more like a modern monastery than it did the new $22 million home of Notre Dame football. Nicknamed the Gug (as in "Goog"), it had every convenience, from an auditorium with specially designed seats for larger athletes, to shoe warmers/driers for wet cleats, to a players lounge — some of the cushioned chairs were still encased in plastic wrap as the Irish moved in — with its very own Gatorade station. For the first time in Notre Dame's football history, the program was housed all in one place.

Before the Gug, the Irish coaching staff worked in the Joyce Center. But because of space limitations, some of the meeting rooms were located across the street at Notre Dame Stadium. And the only suitable locker room was also at the stadium. Not an ideal setup.

The new facility was as impressive as anything Weis had seen during his NFL coaching career. Now it was all his. He could wow recruits here. He could oversee the Notre Dame football empire from the staff's 7,775 square feet of office space. He could use the building as a symbol, as a separation point between BC (Before Charlie) and DC (During Charlie).

Whereas access to the football offices at the Joyce Center under previous regimes had been casual and receptive, entering the conclave of offices at the Gug with Charlie Weis as head coach was like trying to break through a fortress.

From the day the staff moved into the Gug, the football offices were treated as an inner sanctum. Visitors—even Irish football alums—couldn't get beyond the reception room without prior arrangements. As he had with most issues pertaining to the Notre Dame football program, Weis had assumed the role of judge and jury when it came to interlopers, innocent and merely curious though they might be.

Now, as he stood behind the podium in front of the Gug's 150-seat auditorium, Weis readied himself for the inevitable questions about the state of mind of his team as his first season fast approached. It was August 8, and the opening game at Pittsburgh on September 3 was less than a month away. Not since the early 1990s, when Holtz' teams were always a threat to win the national title, had there been this much anticipation about a Notre Dame football season.

Weis was accustomed to high expectations. Anything less than a Super Bowl championship was considered a down year for the Patriots. Anything less than a national championship, no matter how unrealistic those hopes might be, was considered a down year for the Irish. Or at least that's the way it had been after Holtz' final year at Notre Dame in 1996. Weis had been hired to boost those expectations back to where they had been under Holtz.

He began with Psychology 101. "The first message we're trying to teach the players is you have no chance of winning if you don't believe you're going to win," he told the reporters, repeating what he had told his team at the start of preseason camp. "If you go into games thinking, 'Well, this team is a lot better than us,' you really have no chance. So the sooner we can get more people thinking confidently, the better our chances are. There aren't any games on the schedule I've looked at and said, 'Well, we're losing that one.'"

With four of the first five games on the road, convincing his players they were going to win was no small task. When a reporter began reciting the early-season schedule and the difficulties it would present, Weis cut him off. "What's the biggest game of the year for me?" Weis asked. "September 3. Do you think I will have any trouble getting a team ready to play the first game of the year against Pittsburgh? Then we go to Michigan. Do you think the kids will be ready to play Michigan? Do you think I'm going to have any problem getting the team up to play the home opener against Michigan State? Do you think I'm going to have any trouble getting them ready for the Ty Bowl on September 24? At Washington? You know what it's going to be for them. It's going to be one big distraction the whole week. I'm already on top of that. How about going on the road to play Purdue, who whipped us pretty good last year, then coming home to play USC?"

By now, the reporter was wishing he'd never been born — and Weis wasn't done: "Give me a break! If you can't get the team up to play those teams, then you've got a problem. So let's just worry about being ready for the first one and let everything else take care of itself."

Yet there were some things that couldn't just take care of themselves. Weis rarely spoke publicly about the negative feeling that had enveloped much of the program after Willingham was fired. It would have sounded like an indictment of the previous regime, and Weis had been extra cautious not to offend his predecessor. But now he admitted that he had spent much of his time trying to repair the damage from the messy divorce.

Priority number one, before he could work on getting them to believe they were going to win, was earning the players' trust.

"I think the team was fractured after Coach Willingham left and I wasn't here yet," he observed. "There was that window in between where the players were kind of left on their own. I think a lot of little groups had formed that all had their own opinion."

The team had started coming apart even before Willingham's depar-ture. The frustration reached a tipping point at the end of the 17-point loss to Oregon State at the Insight Bowl. Defensive end Justin Tuck, Notre Dame's all-time sack leader, had to restrain running back Jeff Jenkins as the Irish trudged down the hallway to the Bank One Ballpark locker room after the game. Jenkins had failed to see action in the one-sided contest, and just exploded. "Things are going to change around here!" he yelled.

The frustration could be felt everywhere. The players were frus-trated. The fans were frustrated. The alums were frustrated. And the powers that be had obviously become frustrated enough to cut short the Willingham era.

"But you know something?" said Weis. "I think we got them back together, and I think the support seems to be pretty strong. It still comes down to how you play. But we've gotten past that other stage. Now we're just worrying about how we're going to play."

Weis was still a first-year head coach, and to completely discount his inexperience because of his confident approach would be foolish. In a couple of weeks, he would be making critical decisions that he hadn't made since his high school head coaching days back at Franklin Township High School in 1989. But he certainly had an edge that most first-year major college head coaches did not.

"The reason I don't feel like a first-year guy is because of the resources that I have to talk to," Weis said. "Like this morning, I'm sitting there at 5:30, and Bill Belichick called, and we talked for a half hour. I have guys like that I can bounce ideas off. Having links to guys who've been doing this at a high level for a long time really fills that void. When I wonder what I'm supposed to do in this or that situation, instead of guessing, I just call somebody who has done it. That way you can avoid making a rash or improper judgment."

Weis had other resources to call upon besides Belichick. He had left a message with Philadelphia Eagles head coach Andy Reid who, a day ear-lier, kicked temperamental wide receiver Terrell Owens out of camp for his insubordinate behavior. "I asked him if he threw anyone out of camp today," Weis laughed. "I'm sure he got a chuckle when he got it."

Weis also made phone calls to Carolina head coach John Fox and his old Patriots coordinating partner, Romeo Crennel, now the head coach of the Cleveland Browns. And on occasion, Weis would call the Big Tuna himself, Bill Parcells. "But he's a lot like me," said Weis. "He's usually in a very ornery mood during training camp. So I try to leave the man alone."

As promised, the first 20 minutes of the team's first practice was open to the press. As a whole, the assembled reporters agreed, the team was noticeably leaner and better conditioned. That was particularly true of the linemen. The prominent midsections of Bob Morton and Mark LeVoir and Dan Stevenson had been trimmed back. "They're in way better shape than when they left," Weis said. "They all passed the conditioning test, which is a modern miracle in its own right."

When a daily newspaper featured a picture of a scowling, incensed Weis dressing down freshman linebacker Steve Quinn, who was late for the start of practice after being sent back inside to retrieve ankle supports that he already should have had on, the public got a glimpse of life at Camp Weis. Asked about the picture, Weis replied, "I'm on a mission to get things done a certain way, and most of you who've been around here have seen both sides of me, the ornery side and the side that isn't so ornery."

But even a my-way-or-the-highway guy like Weis knew that he wouldn't get through to all of the 100-plus players on the practice field. "At the end of this week, there will be 20 guys who will listen and swallow up everything we've said, and there are going to be 20 guys who don't want to listen to anything we've said," Weis acknowledged. "In between, there are going to be about 60 players. The question is which way are those 60 going to go, because when you go into a game, you need about half a hundred who buy into your program and do things the right way to have a legitimate chance at winning."

Already short on depth along the offensive line, Weis received an unpleasant surprise as camp opened. Sophomore Chauncey Incarnato, a promising offensive tackle, had decided to quit the team. Weis couldn't understand the decision. How could a player go through the entire summer conditioning program and pass the preseason conditioning test, only to leave the team a few days later? Ultimately, however, it didn't matter. If Incarnato didn't want to be a part of it, said Weis, then it was on to the next guy.

Incarnato's departure meant that both the offensive linemen brought in during the previous recruiting class (John Kadous was the other) were now out of the program. Six offensive line recruits in three years had been reduced to four. Yet even with a mere 10 scholarship offensive linemen, Weis insisted there was no need to panic. None of the defensive linemen would be shifted to offense: "You have 14 guys, counting the walk-ons, who are out there practicing, and a lot of guys are playing multiple positions. Depth is something that can be built inherently by having guys able to play multiple positions."

Weis had studied the tapes of Notre Dame's 2004 season. He had seen how minor errors had become blowout losses. The Irish had become experts at hanging close early, only to commit a handful of mistakes, lose their composure, and get beat by double digits. It was the hallmark of a mediocre football program.

During Day 3 of training camp, Weis witnessed firsthand the warning signs of a team conditioned to fail. There was a botched drill, followed by another mistake, followed by more breakdowns in concentration. So he stopped practice and delivered a short lecture on the importance of composure.

"Sometimes you have a game where one side of the ball is really taking it to the other side of the ball," Weis said. "Guys on the side that's not doing too well have to learn how to stop the bleeding. Sometimes players lose their composure. Sometimes it snowballs and before you know it, you end up getting blown out."

That was preventable, he continued. Coaches could help control a game's tempo with conservative or aggressive calls. Up to a point. "But eventually," he said, "the guys on the field are going to have to step up and say, 'Okay, enough of that.' And it can't be that rah-rah stuff. That doesn't work in the real world. In the real world, somebody has to step up and say, 'Calm down, get your composure, and let's go.' So that was a valuable experience today. If you can't do that, all of a sudden you're getting blown out of games that you might have had a chance of winning."

Notre Dame's 15-man freshman class was acclimating quickly to their new team, due in great part to a new NCAA rule that allowed incoming freshmen football players to spend the summer taking classes, adapting to the new environment, and getting to know their older teammates. The coaches couldn't talk X's and O's with them during the summer, but the players could at least begin the process of blending in with their teammates.

"In the old days, when you were a freshman, you got razzed pretty good," Weis said. "These guys have already settled in. It allows them a comfort level where a young guy can go to an older guy for a coaching point. It isn't like the old days when they would look down on a freshman. These guys have been around here for two months, so they're welcomed right into the mix. Which, from our standpoint, is imperative because it gets them involved, into the depth chart, and into the flow of things."

Sophomore running back Justin Hoskins was just getting back into the flow of things after an injury-plagued freshman season, followed by his suspension from the squad during spring drills. Hoskins was back in uniform, wearing number 33, and impressing Weis enough to get yelled at—a lot. This was a good sign for the Grand Rapids, Mich., native. If Weis took the time to berate a player in practice, it meant he thought he was worth the effort.

Sarcasm is a powerful weapon for a coach, and Weis was the type to lean heavily on its benefits. Early in preseason drills, the defense, which had been hit significantly by graduation, was a frequent target for Weis. When the defense failed to pursue a play down the sideline, Weis was right there. "That's okay," he said, loud enough for the entire unit to hear. "Everyone says you aren't going to be any good anyway!"

In reality, Weis was optimistic about Minter's defense. The defensive line, led by highly touted Victor Abiamiri at end and talented interior linemen Derek Landri and Trevor Laws, was a good starting point. Two of the three linebackers—sophomore Maurice Crum Jr. and fifth-year senior

Corey Mays—had virtually no starting experience. (Mays had started just one game at linebacker in his previous four years.) But Mays was a veteran of special-teams play, and Weis couldn't ask for a better leader than senior Brandon Hoyte at linebacker. The secondary was the biggest question mark. It had been torched for 14 touchdown passes in the final three games of the 2004 season. Three of the starters were gone, leaving junior Tom Zbikowski to head up the unit coached by Bill Lewis.

Weis remained hopeful that the Irish could compensate for the lack of defensive experience with aggressiveness. "I can tell you this: they're going to be flying to the ball," he said. "No matter what level of football you play, if you've got 11 guys flying to the ball, you've got a chance. Because even if you make a mistake, if you're making it full speed, that's a lot better than when you're out there not knowing what you're doing and playing passively."

Projected first-time regulars included end Chris Frome, linebackers Mays and Crum, free safety Chinedum Ndukwe, and cornerback Ambrose Wooden who, like Ndukwe, was a former receiver. But there were no promises, except this one from Weis: "Whoever performs the best will end up being out there."

On offense, the gap between starting quarterback Quinn and backups David Wolke, Evan Sharpley, Dan Gorski, and Marty Mooney had become a chasm. The overwhelming amount of information was not an overload for Quinn, who had those 21 career college starts in his back pocket. The others were having more difficulty digesting Weis' system.

Clearly, it was imperative to keep Quinn on the field. Quinn suffered a "minor" concussion late in the Stanford game in 2004. He was reluctant to admit it at the time, but he had been knocked silly by the Cardinal defense and didn't remember much of what happened down the stretch of that game. Fortunately, he recovered quickly and was able to lead the Irish to a 27–9 victory against Navy the following week.

The battle for No. 2 was between Wolke and Sharpley. Wolke took what had amounted to a few meaningless snaps in the 35-point victory over Washington in 2004. He had not attempted a pass in live competition. Sharpley displayed a nice delivery and strong arm in practice. But when Weis was asked about the possibility of Sharpley doubling as a third baseman on Paul Mainieri's team, he said Sharpley needed to worry about calling the right play at the line of scrimmage before giving any consideration to fielding ground balls at the hot corner.

One drill that came early in most practices emphasized the importance Weis placed on his quarterbacks' ability to run the football, particularly Quinn. The wide receivers, tight ends, and quarterbacks joined the running backs in working through a gauntlet of football bags strategically placed on the ground. Weis wanted his quarterbacks to learn how to feel and accept the pursuit of a defender, and then adjust. Rather than force a pass or bolt out of the pocket, Weis preferred his quarterbacks to slide-step away from the pressure and maintain vision of his downfield receivers.

Weis had quarterbacks coach Peter Vaas charting every play every day as he broke down the practice tape. "Sometimes a guy might have a good day or a bad day, but we're going to make objective decisions," Weis explained. "We're not going to say, 'I like this kid, I don't like this kid.' We're going to look at the facts. The facts don't lie when you chart everything."

If Quinn could stay healthy, the Irish offense would be in good shape, especially with its veteran receiving corps. Led by Rhema McKnight (98 career catches heading into the 2005 season), Maurice Stovall (61 receptions), the intriguing Jeff Samardzija, playmaker Matt Shelton, who had set a Notre Dame single-season mark for yards per catch (25.8), and a strong tight end corps headed by Anthony Fasano (45 career receptions), the Irish had some legitimate weapons on offense. Now Weis had to decide how best to use them.

Both Stovall and Samardzija are 6'5", and that offered some intriguing possibilities. "It's a different kind of group than I've ever had, because I've never had that kind of size at wide receiver," Weis said. "You're looking at one side with Stovall and you're looking at the other side with Samardzija. That's two big men. There aren't too many teams playing with receivers that size."

Size wasn't everything, though. Stovall, a stout 235 pounds in the spring, didn't fit the mold Weis had in mind for his wideouts. "I told him in the off-season that the only fat guy around here was going to be me," Weis said. "I told him he was too heavy. I've been around big receivers before that thought bigger was better. There is not a big receiver alive who doesn't benefit from trimming down." Stovall got the message. He reported to camp at a lean and hard 220.

Beyond the top four, Notre Dame's receiving corps wasn't the most talented in the country. But Weis believed he could get production out of anyone, as long as he had the time to "coach him up."

Adding to the team depth was Notre Dame's embrace of the process of red-shirting or fifth-year seniors. Nearly two decades earlier, when Holtz had arrived, the university was sometimes reluctant to keep freshmen on the bench to preserve a fifth year of eligibility. But in order to compete on a national scale, the university eventually relaxed its policy. As long as a player completed his undergraduate degree in four years with a respectable grade-point average, he could be granted a fifth year of eligibility. This was particularly important with linemen, who needed that extra time in the weight room to off-set the physical edge their counterparts at schools with a fifth-year policy would otherwise have. By the time Holtz had completed his 11-year tenure at Notre Dame and the Davie and Willingham Eras rolled around, it was common for a half-dozen to a dozen players to be granted a fifth year of eligibility.

But a fifth year isn't for everyone. "We had one guy this year who asked me if he could have a fifth year and I said yes," Weis said. "Then he got into medical school and he sat down with me and asked me what I thought. I said, 'If I were you, I'd go to med school. If you want to be a doctor, go be a doctor.'"

Fifth-year players on the 2005 roster included Shelton, LeVoir, Hoyte, Mays, fullback Rashon Powers-Neal, Stevenson, LeVoir, defensive tackle Brian Beidatsch, and kicker D.J. Fitzpatrick.

With nearly a week of preseason camp completed, it was time to pick up the pace. On Saturday, August 13, the coaching staff stepped back and began allowing the players on both sides of the ball to fend for themselves a bit more. At that night's practice, plays were called without a script. Officials were brought in to call penalties. "I want to see how the players respond when they're on their own and without the coaches spoon-feeding them and telling them what to do," Weis said.

As promised, Weis set aside additional time—a full 45 minutes—to tend to special teams. It would be interesting to see how many offensive and defensive starters Weis would be willing to commit to the special units. The last thing a coach wants to do is lose a front-line player to an injury on special teams. And yet, special teams could often make the difference in a close game. For the Irish, who had seen so many games slip away from them in 2004, the new emphasis on the kicking, punting, and return games could be decisive.

"Everyone will be involved in special teams, but you have to be smart," Weis said. "I'm not going to take Tommy Zbikowski and play him on four special teams, but he's going to have a role, so maybe he'll be on one team; whatever team we need him on the most."

And, as Weis pointed out, not all special teams are created equal: "You've always got to be concerned about the punt team because they can get you beat the quickest. If you can't protect, you can lose. If you can't long snap, you can lose. If you punt it crummy, you can lose. And then if you can't tackle after you punt it, you can lose. So both coverage teams, on punts and kickoffs, are areas of concern. The flip side of that—punt return and kickoff return—is all about field position. Every 10 yards more you can get, that's one less first down that the offense has to get."

Whoever did the job would get the job, regardless of class rank. "The easiest way for a freshman to get on the field is special teams," Weis said. "So if a coach sees him as a backup defensive back but he can be a mainstay on special teams, on September 3 he's going to be on ABC under the lights. He won't just be standing on the sidelines waving to his family."

(Asked if he were actually going to permit freshmen to stand on the sideline and wave to their families on TV, Weis just smiled: "Once.")

The media noticed, at least during the 20 minutes they were allowed to observe practice, that Weis spent the majority of his time on the offensive side of the ball. Minter ran the defense. Weis would then turn his attention to the defense as soon as practice was over. "I watch all the tape from practice," Weis said. "Just because I'm not over there doesn't mean I miss anything. That's why we tape everything. The first thing I watch after practice is defensive tape. I'll go back and watch the offensive tape again to see what I missed, because you don't see everything. But I know from going against the defense that they're presenting some problems to us. Then again, there are other times where I'll go up to Rick and say, 'If you do this, this is what I'm going to do and you're going to have a problem.' That lets the defensive coaches understand how an offensive mind is going to attack what they're doing."

When the Irish were forced inside by bad weather on Monday, August 15, the media found Weis relaxing in a golf cart. A couple of photographers approached him with cameras, and someone suggested that he could conduct the postpractice interview while sitting in the cart, á la Florida State's Bobby Bowden. Weis wasn't having any of that. He got up and walked to the foyer outside the doors leading to the football field, where he had given an interview a day earlier. He clearly didn't want the cameras to catch him looking too relaxed: "I haven't done anything yet."

But he was getting there. Not all of the offense and defense had been installed, but both were mostly in place. After a sluggish start, the players were picking up the pace. The intelligence advantage Weis claimed the Irish possessed also was becoming apparent. Each day they were becoming more comfortable with the new schemes and the new coach.

"Parcells used to preach that you have to view your season like a marathon," Weis said. "Bill said there were going to be peaks and valleys, and the coach's job was to keep everyone on an even keel."

As marathons go, the Irish were just leaving the starting line.

......

Chapter 11

SWEATING THE DETAILS

A S THE IRISH HEADED into their second week of pre-season camp, the depth chart was slowly beginning to take shape. Some players, such as Quinn, had guaranteed themselves starting spots, but a depth chart goes three to four deep, which means there was still much to be decided. Who would be the backups, the guys just a twisted ankle away from a starting position? Who would play on special teams? Who would be candidates for a redshirt season? Who would find themselves as roster afterthoughts? Who would be the surprises of the camp?

"There's still plenty of room for guys to slide up or down," said Weis. "It's sort of like the stock market. We look at a player and say, 'Buy! Buy!' or 'Sell! Sell!' Not to be dehumanizing, but all of a sudden, a guy has three good days and you're like, 'Where have you been?'"

The media took notice when freshman David Bruton began working with the first unit at free safety alongside junior Tom Zbikowski. Bruton hadn't really emerged as a frontrunner for a starting spot. Weis was simply trying to get everybody involved, especially a bright prospect like Bruton.

"A lot of times, there are communication problems when you play inexperienced guys only with inexperienced guys," Weis said. "Putting Bruton with the first team is a way to mix and match so that we have the younger guys playing with the older guys to help with the communication on the field. I don't like taking the younger guys and just throwing them down on the other end of the field. If you do that, they're not being coached anymore, and they don't ever develop. So I have blocks of periods during the day when they are being coached by their position coaches. We also have blocks of time that are team-related periods where we set up the basic Pittsburgh offense, defense, and special teams. It's not about first team; it's about knowing what you're doing."

In addition, Weis was looking for ways to take advantage of any specialized skill a young player might have, even if his overall game still needed work. For example, if a freshman had a knack for being able to sprint around the corner and pressure a field-goal kicker, then Weis wanted the freshman on the field for those exact situations. An edge is an edge, no matter how small.

Like most coaches, Weis believed in piping in noise at practice to simulate a game situation. But even this was fine-tuned. "Communication is a key element in football," Weis said, "and it's toughest for a defensive player when you're at home. Hopefully, it's very loud when the opponent is on offense, so therefore you have to learn how to communicate defensively without being able to hear." So Weis designated one day a week as a "sound day," when speakers blared crowd noise when the Irish defense was on the field. It was unusual to prepare a defensive unit for crowd noise, but Weis wanted his entire team prepared for everything.

After about 10 days of camp, the Irish moved their practice sessions from outside O'Neill Hall, on the west side of campus, to Cartier Field. Before Notre Dame Stadium was opened in 1930, the football team played games in 30,000-seat Cartier Field. Only the practice fields remained from those days, and the actual field the Irish used to play their games on was now the home field for the Notre Dame soccer teams. The Gug would assist in the transition.

"Before, we had a bunch of 310-pound guys riding bicycles from the stadium over here to practice," said Weis. "It was refreshing that they could walk out through the mud room, put their shoes on, and walk a short distance to the practice field."

On August 17, less than three weeks before the season opener at Pittsburgh, Weis began introducing the Panthers offensive and defensive schemes to the players. He had a pretty good idea of what the Irish would see from the Panthers, because Weis had observed Pittsburgh's new coach, Dave Wannstedt, when he was the defensive coordinator of the Dallas Cowboys under Jimmy Johnson. Weis also was familiar with Wannstedt's new offensive coordinator, Matt Cavanaugh, who had recently been involved in the Baltimore Ravens' offensive scheme. At least from a preparation standpoint, Weis had things figured out pretty well. He wasn't afraid to say it, either.

"I think it's significantly easier in college," Weis said. "Every school has the same time restraints, so it's actually easier to figure out what they're doing. Now, whether you can successfully attack what they're doing, that's another story. But it doesn't take a brain surgeon to figure out what Pittsburgh is going to do. I've studied Pittsburgh's defensive scheme, and we're in for a blitzathon. Matt Cavanaugh has been in a West Coast offense, but he's also been in that two tight-end offense in Baltimore, so what's it going to be? When you haven't played a game yet, you've got to be ready for everything."

First and foremost, though, Weis had to make sure the Irish were at their peak offensively. That's partly why he had been hired: to revive an offense that was predictable, unproductive, and just plain boring. In his NFL days, Weis had witnessed the demise of a program, the Washington Redskins, under offensive guru Steve Spurrier, who had shredded defenses on the collegiate level but struggled in his transition to the pro game. Weis was making the easier transition from pro to college.

"Steve is a great coach, but the defenses in the NFL will figure you out in a hurry," Weis said. "If every time you blitz you're going to throw a slip screen, which is what he did, everyone in the league knows it. It's a little different in college, when you don't have as much time to prepare. In the pros, that's all those guys do. It's football 24 hours a day."

The weeding-out process on the Notre Dame squad continued. Sophomore defensive tackle Brandon Nicolas had decided Notre Dame was not the place for him. He packed his bags and departed about a week after offensive tackle Chauncey Incarnato left the program. If Nicolas wanted to leave, that was fine by Weis. But he wasn't going to release a player to an immediate competitor.

"We'll let them out of their scholarship as long as it's to a school we're not going to play," Weis said. "If a guy wants to play at the University of Texas, go play there. But if he wants to play at Michigan, I'm not going to let him. Why would I do anything that would make one of the teams we play better?"

As the Irish completed their second week of drills, Weis was still adapting to the pace and nuances of coaching on the college level. Friday, August 19, was the start of a three-day freshman orientation. For the first time in nearly two weeks, Weis sensed that he was losing the focus of his players. When Friday's evening practice ended, Weis said it marked his first "bad day" with the team. And bad days come with a price.

As usual, the Irish ran sprints at practice's end. But on Friday, Weis instructed each player in charge of a position—Quinn, for example, was in charge of the quarterbacks—to add as many sprints as he thought necessary. It was up to the players now, not the coaches. Weis was forcing them to take ownership of the team and of the workout.

As Weis and the assistants watched from the sideline, the position captains actually ran the players harder and longer than the coaches would have. This was exactly what Weis had hoped would happen.

As the players dragged their weary bodies from the practice field, it was obvious Weis had accomplished one of his preseason goals. He had physically challenged the Notre Dame players in a way they had never

been challenged before. Three-hour practices weren't unusual anymore. Two-a-days weren't uncommon. Nor were postpractice sprints,
especially if the players had failed to concentrate during the workouts.
Nobody was spared.

"I'm feeling it all over," said wideout Rhema McKnight. "My mind's
tired, my body's more than tired. I can't even describe it."

The intensity was paying off, not only physically but also mentally.
In a short period of time, the Irish offense had begun to grasp the
big picture. They understood how to run Weis' plays; now they were
beginning to understand why those plays would work against certain
personnel and defensive schemes.

By Week 3, the Irish concluded each practice (before the sprints, that
is) with a live offense-defense drill designed to help prepare them for
the pressure of a close game. Weis called it the four-minute offense.
The setup: the offense was up by three points and trying to run out the
clock, and the defense had three timeouts. The players were instructed to be alert as to when the head coach might want to use one of
those timeouts.

Once again, Weis was trying to teach his players specific game-
management skills. He had taught them plays. Now he was showing
them how the plays meant nothing if they didn't know how to manage
the beginning, the middle, and especially the end of a game. The intent
of the drill was to get them thinking like a head coach would think in
crucial situations.

The players handled it well. They were tired, and yet they didn't lose
their composure in those make-believe final minutes of a game. Weis
was pleased, and said so.

The last day of preseason training camp, August 22, ended on an
upbeat note when Weis announced that three walk-ons would be getting
scholarships: senior cornerback/kick returner Brandon Harris from
New Orleans; senior wide receiver Rob Woods from Atlantic, Iowa;
and junior defensive lineman Casey Cullen from Victoria, Texas.

Weis had reserved one scholarship for a walk-on, but when Incarnato
and Nicolas left camp, it opened up two more. To determine the scholarship winners, Weis had considered the individual player's character, his

grade-point average the previous semester, and how he was received by his teammates, as well as his potential for helping the team.

Harris, who had come to Notre Dame on a partial music scholarship, impressed Weis with his speed. "I told him he could throw that music scholarship away because I was picking up the tab this year," Weis said.

Woods, who had racked up a remarkable 3.95 grade-point average in mechanical engineering, was on the two-deep chart on every one of the special teams. "How many plays will he play in a game?" Weis asked. "I don't know. But in life you want to surround yourself with guys who are winners, and this kid is a winner. When I talked to the team, I said, 'He may not be the greatest athlete in the world, but if you get a bunch of these guys on your team with that type of heart, that type of intelligence, and that type of work ethic... well, that's the kind of guy you want on your team.'"

Cullen had led his high school to a state championship. Until now, however, he was best known for being the great-grandson of two-time Notre Dame All-America halfback Christie Flanagan. "This was a long shot," said Weis. "Trust me, you know how important special teams are to me and I've been looking. But one guy, day in and day out, who's been impossible for anyone to block or stop in the special teams is a junior named Casey Cullen. Right now he's just a third-team defensive end. He's not going to play much on defense unless there are a lot of injuries. But he's going to be on three or four of our special teams and has become a core special teams player for us."

Particularly gratifying to Weis was the reaction of the team as he revealed the names of the three scholarship winners. "When I said 'Brandon Harris,' they were fired up," Weis said. "When I said 'Rob Woods,' they were fired up. When I said 'Casey Cullen,' they were as shocked as me and they were even more fired up."

By handing out scholarships to hardworking walk-ons, Weis had provided tangible evidence that busting your butt and being committed to the cause paid dividends. Ultimately, these guys weren't likely to make much of a difference in Weis' first-year record. But the reaction of the team was great. It showed a wonderful camaraderie, even for the walk-ons who often were little more than unidentifiable numbers to the scholarship players.

On August 23, Weis faced his biggest personal adjustment so far: the beginning of classes. Weis was used to coaching professional football players morning, noon, and night. With classes going on, Weis and his staff had plenty of time to plan games, but they were allowed just 20 hours per week with the players. Every available minute would have to be used wisely.

This meant the staff had to set up a game plan for coaching. Out of those 20 hours, how much time would be devoted to special teams? To meetings? To walk-throughs? It was a barter system of sorts, trading one priority for another.

Of course, Weis didn't share many of those details with the media. Maybe that's why reporters were stunned to walk into the Loftus Center at 9 in the morning during the third week of camp and find themselves watching something other than the Irish doing their usual prepractice stretching or position drills. Instead, the Notre Dame offense was working its way down the field with the ball precisely spotted after each play.

Was Weis throwing the media a little "bonus footage" for the cameras? No way. The truth? A mistake had been made. The media were supposed to be directed onto the field at 9:20.

When Weis spotted several camera crews shooting the practice, he went bonkers. Unfortunately for football sports information assistant Doug Walker, he became Weis' target of opportunity. Several members of the media immediately began walking briskly toward the door as Weis barked at Walker, "Why don't you just give them our playbook?"

Moments later, a reporter's cell phone rang. It was Walker. Walker said that Weis, who was not scheduled to speak with the media following the morning practice session, now wanted to speak with everybody for a couple of minutes. Could the reporter spread the word?

Great. Another lecture, this time blaming the television crews for compromising Notre Dame's preparation for the Pittsburgh game. It wouldn't be the first time a football coach had been so paranoid.

Instead, Weis apologized to the media, including the cameraman he had yelled at. It had been a miscommunication between Weis and the sports information department. Weis said he was accountable, and he was sorry for the incident. He said he didn't want the same kind of relationship that sometimes existed between the media and Davie (contentious) or Willingham (standoffish). As a Notre Dame student, he had dreamed about a career in broadcasting. He understood the needs of the media and would do everything to maintain a good working relationship with them.

He had made a mistake and he was sorry.

Jaws dropped.

Heads shook.

He said he was *what*?

It had been three years since a Notre Dame head football coach had treated the media like anything but a necessary nuisance, much less apologized to them. There really was a new sheriff in town.

As the preseason practices continued, so did the process of recruiting the Class of 2010. Notre Dame's commitment list had reached 12 with verbal pledges from North Carolina cornerback Raeshon McNeil and Top-100 player Demetrius Jones, a quarterback out of Chicago. These were two huge catches for the Irish. McNeil was the first defensive prospect among the 12 to commit, and Jones completed Notre Dame's quarterback recruiting for the year. Pennsylvania quarterback Zach Frazer had been the first to jump on board, and with Jones' commitment, it meant the Irish were no longer in the running for prized Arkansas prep quarterback Mitch Mustain.

Weis very much wanted Mustain, considered one of the top prospects in the entire country, but the Notre Dame coach had made it clear that the program only had two quarterback openings. Frazer and Jones had made their decisions; Mustain hadn't. End of discussion.

Recruiting was a part of the coaching staff's 18-hour days during preseason camp. After the conclusion of a Saturday night practice session, Weis returned to his office and text-messaged recruits. It wasn't the same as talking on the phone or in person, but it did allow a coach to keep in contact with a prospect while staying within the guidelines of NCAA rules. "If you're working from 5 o'clock in the morning until late, there's plenty of time to recruit at night," Weis said. "You can't call them until September, and that's only once a week. So right now you sit down with your phone and start texting away. That counts as an electronic message and doesn't count as a phone call."

Weis didn't care how much work it took to land one of the nation's top classes. "I just want to get 'em," he said.

With about a dozen days before the opener against Pittsburgh, Weis was confident his team was on target for the start of the season. "We have the foundation set where we can game-plan and put ourselves in a position to win," he said. "We have enough offense and defense in. We understand who our personnel are. There is still some jockeying between a second or third guy. There are a couple of first positions with people in the hunt, as far as how we will rotate players. But otherwise, we're pretty well set to go."

For longtime Notre Dame football observers, it sure seemed like the Irish were tending to details that had either been swept under the carpet in the recent past or simply not addressed. During the August 23 practice, for example, Weis had his players practice end-of-game plays and jump ball situations. "You might practice a situation one time in training camp, and it might be the only time you practice it before the next time it comes up in a game," Weis said. "So it's important to explain to the team, 'Now men, it might not be until the eighth game of the season that this comes up. But this is what we're going to do when this happens.'"

Putting the team to the test applied to the coaches as well. "I put the pressure on the staff, too, because I want them to have to react the same way the players have to react," Weis said.

Weis was pleased with the way things were taking shape. When asked about the most pleasant surprise of camp, he said, "The minimal amount of problems I've had off the field. They've been few and far between. We've had leadership from the players, accountability by the players, and the coaching staff has done a good job of spreading the message. Give the credit to the players. I've been very content to this point. I haven't had hardly anyone come into my office for anything.

With school starting, they better be going to class because that's a whole new set of encyclopedias."

Exactly two weeks before the opener, Weis gave the players Saturday night and Sunday morning off. Before dismissing them, he said, "If I hear you're in a bar, you're off the team."

To his delight, those kinds of boundaries didn't always have to come from his office. Members of the team's leadership committee had come to Weis and asked if they could place a curfew on the players two days before a game. "*They* asked *me*," said Weis. "It's a self-imposed curfew. This way, 48 hours before the game, they're starting to get ready to go instead of turning Thursday night into a college party night with people carousing all over the place. Now, we negotiated the hours of that curfew. Their hours and my hours are a little different. But I've been pretty pleased with that."

With the arrival of the rest of the student body and the start of classes, the Notre Dame campus was bustling. The energy level was on the rise, not just because of the start of school, but because of the excitement the football program was creating among the student body. Some of that excitement had been lost in recent years. The Irish had played 97 games in the previous eight years and lost 41 times, an average of five per season, with 14 of those losses coming at home.

But now, at the beginning of the 2005 school year, there was a palpable difference in the air, a buzz of anticipation. The cause of that buzz could be summed up in two words: Charlie Weis.

As at a lot of schools that play big-time football, it's a tradition at Notre Dame for the head coach to meet and greet the incoming freshman class. So on August 21, the Class of '09 and their parents jammed the Joyce Center, where they were treated to a few minutes of vintage Charlie Weis.

Asked if there were any Cinderella stories in the Class of 2009, where a regular student might one day grow up to be the head football coach at Notre Dame, Weis said, "I hope none of you is sick enough to go into the coaching profession."

He spoke about his passion for South Bend, the campus, and the tradition that they would soon be contributing to.

He told them they were here to get an education, of course, but they were also at Notre Dame to learn how to stretch themselves, to grow up, make good decisions.

"Of course, when I was here," he smiled, "all the decisions I made were good."

As the man had been saying for the past nine months, you can't win unless you have confidence.

......

Chapter 12

FRESH LEGS, FAST START

IF YOU WATCHED EVEN the first 20 minutes of a Weis preseason practice in 2005—and that's all reporters were ever allowed to see—you couldn't help but notice a change in the volume level from 2004.

The year before, under Ty Willingham, the stretching drill was relaxed, almost playful time. Assistant Buzz Preston, who coached the running backs and special teams, would play a verbal game with the players' names. He'd call linebacker Maurice Crum Jr. "Crumb Cake." Defensive tackle Greg Pauly was "Pauly Want a Cracker." Preston loved coming up with new twists on player names, and the players loved hearing them. Stretching was a time when players and coaches bonded, a time for keeping things light until the serious contact in practice began.

No such warm and fuzzy time was to be found in a single Weis practice in August 2005. The head coach might walk among the rows of players, often with a smile on his face, but happy chatter was neither encouraged nor forthcoming.

The silence could be attributed to one factor: conservation of energy. The players, you see, knew what was coming. Barely recovered from the preceding day's ordeal, they were going to have to plead with their exhausted muscles to get them through another practice. At this point, the players were simply trying to survive another day.

Pauly want a cracker? Had the graduated Pauly still been around, he would have needed a hot tub and a nap.

What Weis wanted was for his players to understand what it took to get stronger and tougher, both mentally and physically. That was the only way they would get better.

Weis continued to marvel at how much time he had on his hands. The college coaching schedule provided him with bonus hours to examine every facet of the Notre Dame program. And he did. Weis was in his office by 5:30 a.m. and in a staff meeting by 7.

As he explained, "It's not a Club Med program around here."

But it wasn't the New England Patriots, either. Pro players begin their workday first thing in the morning. The Fighting Irish players didn't report to the Gug until 2:30 p.m. That left Weis time for scouting, evaluating, recruiting, game-planning—and staring at the clock. "I'm just not used to having this much time," he said. "When you get in here early in the morning and you don't have them until 2:30 in the afternoon, this is like, 'Okay, what can I do now?'"

One person who took full advantage of the extra time was offensive coordinator/running backs coach Mike Haywood. Haywood could have remained on Mack Brown's Texas staff for as long as he liked. He was close with Brown and his family. He was considered one of the premier assistants and recruiters in the country. And his hometown of Houston was only a three-and-a-half hour drive from Austin. Life was good.

But returning to Notre Dame as a member of Weis' staff was an offer he couldn't refuse. He admired Brown, and he also knew—better than anyone, because he'd recruited many of the key Longhorn players—that

Texas was talented enough to win the 2005 national championship. But while Texas had almost everything an assistant could want, it didn't have the emotional pull of one's alma mater.

Haywood was a Notre Dame man. The Irish needed him, and Haywood needed the Irish. Haywood had learned how to run a first-class program from Brown, but now it was time for a new lesson. Weis could provide that. If the Irish turned this program around, it would only enhance Haywood's chances of running his own team one day.

Although Haywood was the offensive coordinator, there was no question Weis would call the plays. That might change down the road, depending on how quickly the offense developed and how soon Haywood was ready to take on the duties. But for now, Weis would maintain firm control.

"We'll see how that goes." Weis said. "Ideally, somewhere down the line I'd like to just be the head coach and manage the team and be involved on both sides of the ball."

(Key words in that last sentence: "somewhere down the line.")

The players and coaches were learning the offense, and Weis was learning about the players and coaches. Weis had spent the better part of eight months making mental notes to himself. He had been through spring drills, summer conditioning, and now, with preseason camp wrapping up, Weis had a good feel for his roster. He also knew when it was time to take his foot off the accelerator.

"When I was younger, I only knew one way, and that was to be really hard on my players all the time," Weis said. "You have to understand which guys respond to that and which don't. That doesn't mean you don't push them all. You have to push everybody. But you have to realize that you can't afford to lose them by putting them in the tank. You have to coach them hard, but then push the right button for each one of those individuals."

He added, "I watched Parcells do that for years. You would think that all he did was hammer people all the time—which he did a pretty good job of, by the way. But I also watched how he worked the locker room and the training room and the weight room and how he worked the coaches. He knew everyone's button. He knew what was going to really get you. But he also knew when to back off. He knew what made everyone tick, and that's one of the reasons he's a great coach."

Weis had won the trust of his players without ever having coached them in an actual game—no small feat. His intelligence, organization, and commitment to the program had an impact on his players. Bob Morton, an affable, earnest guy who would be starting his third season in the interior of the offensive line, had returned to fall camp in superb condition. A bit flabby in the midsection during his first three years in the program, Morton, as much as any of the offensive linemen, had benefited from Ruben Mendoza's off-season conditioning program. He had made the effort because he could tell Weis was making a similar effort to rebuild Irish football.

"With this coaching staff, there's no way we can say we have to make up for a handicap in coaching the X's and O's," Morton said. "We haven't seen the offense in action, but I know I'm not going to be asking what Coach is thinking. I'm going to go out and do it because I know he sees something that I don't. That's why he's here. That's why he's had the success he's had in his career. He knows a lot more about this game than I do."

On August 25, President Jenkins and athletic director White attended the Thursday practice session. At Weis' invitation, Jenkins spoke to the team before the workout began. He told them he was there to express his support and his expectations. "Basically, he was there to show that he cares," said Weis.

True enough, Jenkins' appearance had another purpose. His decision to support the firing of Willingham hadn't been popular among Notre Dame players. By attending practice, Jenkins had reached out to the team.

Weis responded by asking the team to reach out to him. He invited Jenkins to join the Irish huddle. Then he asked him to break it—an honor for any outsider, even if the outsider is your school's president. By having Jenkins break the huddle, Weis made it clear where he stood. The gesture didn't go unnoticed by the team. (It certainly didn't go unnoticed by Jenkins, "It's one thing to talk to them," said Weis of his players, "but sometimes when they're all around you, it's not the greatest odor in the world.")

The final scrimmage of the preseason was scheduled for Friday evening, August 26, at precisely 8:07 p.m.—eight days to the minute before the season opener against Pittsburgh. Weis and his staff planned to use that time to determine the final depth chart. Realistically, the starters had been determined. The scrimmage would be used mainly to decide second- and third-teamers, as well as which players would be making the trip.

"I'm a very go-by-what-you-see guy," Weis said. "After tomorrow night, we'll come in as a coaching staff, we'll watch the tape, we'll meet with the players, we'll meet again on Sunday, and we'll say, 'Here's where we are and here's where we're going.' That's in fairness to the players. You have to give everyone an opportunity to not just compete for No. 1, but also compete for No. 2."

Weis did not take the effort of even the most inconsequential player lightly. "There are guys who will never play in a game or whose chances of playing in a game are very small," he said. "But if a guy busts his butt all week, he deserves to travel as much as guys who will be playing every down."

Among the other things Weis and his staff worked on during the final scrimmage, as they had done several times previously, was the actual game-day communication between the field and the press box.

On offense, quarterbacks coach Peter Vaas, receivers coach Rob Ianello, and offensive graduate assistant Shane Waldron would be stationed in the press box. Haywood, tight ends coach Bernie Parmalee, and offensive line coach John Latina would be on the field.

On defense, secondary coach Bill Lewis and defensive graduate assistant Jeff Burrow would be upstairs, while coordinator/linebackers coach Rick Minter, line coach Jappy Oliver, and special-teams coordinator/ assistant defensive backs coach Brian Polian would be on the field.

They all needed to be 100 percent confident that they would be able to communicate quickly and effectively.

Satisfied with the final scrimmage, Weis knew it was time to make the practices less physical. The opener against Pittsburgh was five days away, and Weis had learned years ago that fresh legs are better than tired ones. It is a remarkably simple concept that football coaches often overlook. The temptation to try to squeeze in one more drill, one more sprint, one more scrimmage play—all in the name of preparation—is sometimes more powerful than common sense.

The Irish weren't shutting down, but in the final five days before taking on the Panthers in Pittsburgh, they'd be in full pads only once. "I want them to be flying around out there at Heinz Field," he said. "I don't want there to be any excuses."

The media continued to encourage Weis to make comparisons to the 2004 team, but he remained diplomatic. Behind closed doors, Weis might have prodded his team to rise above the substandard play of a year ago. Publicly, however, when asked if he was coaching a dramatically improved football team, he said, "I just like the way they've responded to our coaching. It's a different style. Every coach has his own style, so when you're in charge, you're going to do it according to your style."

He also reminded NBC network officials (NBC has carried broadcasts of Notre Dame's home games since 1991) that he preferred the cameras to be pointed anywhere but at him. "I've already had this gripe with them," he said. "I told them they spend way too much time putting the head coach on TV. I think it would be time better spent showing players and the fans and all that other stuff instead of spending it on the head coach, waiting for him to mess up."

Weis had treated a few of the NBC executives to a gathering on his balcony outside his new office at the Gug. When they asked if they could film a few segments to be played during the game, Weis suggested they tape some segments with the players instead.

Weis reserved Sunday, August 28, to announce the depth chart for the opening game. There were a handful of surprises, mainly involving freshmen. David Grimes, a small wide receiver, was listed at the top of the punt return chart. Several other freshmen appeared in second- or third-team roles, including Michael Turkovich and Paul Duncan at offensive tackle, Asaph Schwapp at fullback, David Bruton and Kyle McCarthy at safety, Pat Kuntz at defensive tackle, and Steve Quinn at outside linebacker.

Junior center John Sullivan, who started 12 games in 2004, had been displaced by senior Bob Morton, with Dan Santucci at guard. Weis explained that four players, right guard Dan Stevenson included, would play the three interior spots. Only five seniors would be in the starting lineup on defense.

Finally, game week arrived, and one could sense the excitement building in Weis' voice. He had waited a long time for this opportunity. A year earlier, he had been preparing the Patriots for another Super Bowl run. He wasn't even on the Notre Dame fans' radar. Most didn't know who Charlie Weis was, much less that he was a Notre Dame graduate. Now here he was, less than a week from his debut, expected by the Notre Dame faithful to lead their cherished Irish back to national prominence.

"There are always uncertainties at this point because you have two sets of expectations out there," Weis said. "On the one hand, the players hear from the Notre Dame alums that they're going to win every game. On the other hand, they hear from the national broadcasters that they're going to lose every game. So somewhere in between lies the truth."

But he believed he had converted his players to the Weis way of doing things. When he was first introduced to the team, there had to be some doubt among the players. Willingham had been all about composure and keeping his cool. Rarely were the players subjected to verbal outbursts. He was patient, unflappable. There was no fear factor with Willingham.

Weis was much more combustible, a ticking time bomb when things didn't go his way. The loss of seven players from the program since spring practice—some at Weis' suggestion—was evidence of the stresses that accompanied the transition from Willingham's approach to Weis'. Eight months of settling those issues had led Weis to find a comfort zone with his players.

Two weeks earlier, Weis had eaten breakfast with Lou Holtz. He would see Joe Theismann in Pittsburgh. But the evening he treasured most was the one he had recently spent with Ara Parseghian, the legendary Irish coach from 1964 to 1974. For three hours Weis and his wife sat spellbound as Parseghian talked about all things Notre Dame. Weis just listened.

"I'm 0–0," said Weis. "He's won a few games, the last time I checked. Just hearing his approach from his first year right through his last year was a very educational experience. You could see how he approached the game and how he approached all the sidebars that go with being the head coach."

Soon Weis would experience firsthand what it meant to follow in Parseghian's—and Rockne's, and Leahy's, and Holtz'—footsteps.

Pittsburgh Week had finally arrived.

Chapter 13

......

THE DEBUT

HURRICANE KATRINA HIT THE Gulf Coast on August 29, 2005, displacing thousands of people from their homes in Mississippi and Louisiana. As terrible as the destruction was, it seemed a long way from South Bend, where the Irish prepared for the Labor Day weekend trip to Pittsburgh that would mark the beginning of the Charlie Weis Era. But the disaster *had* hit close to home: the family of reserve defensive back Brandon Harris had been forced to evacuate their New Orleans home. Fortunately, they were safe and planned to make the trip to Pittsburgh for the September 3 game.

Although the physical workouts were getting lighter, the mental ones were not. Every day of practice was Football Philosophy 101 with Professor Weis. The course covered virtually everything you could possibly want to know about the physical, mental, and emotional approach of the Irish, and how it all matched up with the Pitt Panthers.

The Wednesday before the Pittsburgh game, the traveling squad of about 70 was set. By then, Weis was focusing on the opening sequence of offensive plays he would call. "As a playcaller, when you're not sure what your opponent is going to do, you'd better be prepared to have an answer," he said. "That's where all my energies the last couple of days have been geared: setting up the call sheet so I have enough ammunition to attack what they do."

Former NFL coaching great Bill Walsh, who, like Weis, enjoyed talking about the game with the media, was also known for scripting plays ahead of time. Weis had the same philosophy, but his script was a bit shorter. "I don't script 25 because I don't think you can stick to 25 plays," Weis said. "It doesn't give you a chance to react to what they're doing. All of a sudden it's halftime, and you haven't made any adjustments. You're just calling plays to run down the list. That's why I try to keep it to 15, and there are times when, if they're not working, I won't get to those 15."

And those 15 were to be a carefully guarded secret, even from his players. "I won't tell them until late, so they won't tell anyone else," Weis said. "There have been times when we told players on Saturday morning, 'Here's what we're going to do,' and all of a sudden you see a replay of the game and the announcer says, 'They might take a shot here on the first play.' I mean, hello!"

One player Weis did feel comfortable sharing everything with was his junior quarterback, Brady Quinn. Weis' praise of Quinn had been effusive since he began working with him in the spring. Quinn had paid his dues. He had taken a pounding during his first two years as Notre Dame's starting quarterback, particularly as a freshman in 2003, when the offensive line was talented but inexperienced. But he had proven his toughness time and again, both in game competition and under the watchful eye of Weis in practice situations. With the exception of the concussion he suffered in 2004 in a game against Stanford, Quinn had fought through every hard knock. (As it was, Quinn was back in the lineup the week after the concussion.)

Weis not only had a physically capable quarterback to run his offense, but a smart, mentally tough one. "Brady's the closest player we have to being in tune with the coaching staff, and that's what he's supposed to be," said Weis. "I think he knows more than any other player on this team in terms of what the coaching staff is expecting. That's the position you're in when you're the quarterback. I have a lot of respect for him and I think he'll play well. For his sake I hope he does, because he deserves it."

Quinn admitted during the 2004 season that he sometimes had too much nervous energy before games. But Weis had a plan to keep his talented but hyper quarterback calm. "I tell him not to think," Weis said. "I tell him, 'I'll do the thinking, you just run the plays.' To be honest with you, that's what I used to tell the last guy I worked with."

(That "last guy" was, of course, Tom Brady.)

With an intelligent quarterback and a veteran offense, a coach can put more on the offensive plate. Recognizing that he would have only 20 hours a week to practice with his team once the season started, Weis installed a core set of plays that wouldn't need a lot of practice every week but would remain a part of the weekly play selections. "I put in about 50 plays in camp that are in whether we practice them or not," he explained. "The players get handouts every week, but there are some plays we laminate that are permanent fixtures of their playbook."

The Irish practiced under the lights inside Notre Dame Stadium on Thursday night. Weis said he had one final thought for Notre Dame fans everywhere as he addressed the media for the final time before the opening kickoff:

"I appreciate how everyone, including the media, has rolled with the punches since I've been here. It's time now to focus on the players and not the coach. These guys were beaten down last year. They ended up getting their clocks cleaned in the bowl game and then went through a coaching change. I came in, and there was all the pomp and circumstance that goes with a new coach. But I really think the game should be about the players. I hope for their sake the game goes the way I expect it to, because they deserve it more than I do."

Weis bristled at the notion that his players might be investing too much emotional energy in the first game of the year. "I don't think you can ever invest too much in one game," he said. "You invest everything you've got in one game and then you start it all over again. As long as you understand that it's a marathon and not a sprint, that there are peaks and valleys in the season, you have to give everything you've got each time out. If you don't put it all into Pittsburgh, then when are you going to put it all into it? What are you going to do, save it for Michigan or save it for Michigan State? You're supposed to put it all on the line every week. That's what players do."

With the kickoff at 7:07 South Bend time Saturday night, Weis insisted the players attend all their Friday classes before boarding a bus that would take them to their charter flight at the South Bend Regional Airport. When the traveling squad arrived in Pittsburgh, there would be no walk-through at Heinz Field, the field where, eight months earlier, Weis had helped the Patriots win the AFC Championship. Weis said his team didn't need it.

"When we get to the hotel Friday night, we'll eat dinner, have a special-teams meeting, a religious service, a snack, and we'll go to bed," Weis said. "Saturday will be offensive and defensive meetings, our team meeting, a team Mass, and then we'll hop on a bus. This is very meticulously laid out. Even when we're home on Fridays, I'll have a walk-through but we're not practicing. Anyone who has been around football long enough realizes Friday has to be mental, not physical. Friday is not a day you wear them out. Friday is a day you're saving their legs, hydrating them, and getting them ready to go, so there are no excuses on Saturday."

THE MATCHUP BETWEEN CHARLIE Weis and Pittsburgh head coach Dave Wannstedt had all the components of a Hollywood screenplay. Two pro football coaches going head-to-head—one who had thrived as an offensive coordinator, one who had reached the highest level as a defensive coordinator and then a head coach (Bears, Dolphins). Both were returning to their alma maters. (Wannstedt was a three-year letter winner and captain of the 1973 Panthers football team.) Both had achieved success in the NFL. They had competed against each other in the AFC East for years.

Just as Notre Dame had heralded Weis' appointment by bringing home illustrious graduates, Pittsburgh celebrated its storied history by bringing back former players such as Dan Marino, Mike Ditka, and Tony Dorsett for the season-opening game.

After recording five straight winning seasons under Walt Harris, Pittsburgh picked Wannstedt to bring back the glory from the national title that Dorsett and his teammates had snagged in 1976.

Weis knew Pittsburgh's coaches well. Wannstedt knew some of Weis' coaches too, and had actually employed two of them, secondary coach Bill Lewis and tight ends coach Bernie Parmalee. Weis had coached against Pittsburgh offensive coordinator Matt Cavanaugh, and he had coached Cavanaugh during his days as a backup quarterback with the New York Giants.

So Weis knew what he was up against. He had devised offensive schemes against Wannstedt before. He had watched Cavanaugh's game-planning and play-calling with the Baltimore Ravens as well as the Dolphins. Wannstedt had retained Panthers defensive coordinator Paul Rhoads, an aggressive signal-caller whose defense Weis referred to as a "blitzathon." With Wannstedt, a conservative play-caller by nature, Weis might be able to exploit him with an aggressive approach.

Weis had been warned by pro coaches he knew that they had received phone calls inquiring about him and his style. But Weis had a deal with Bill Belichick: You don't help anyone beat Notre Dame and I won't help anyone beat the Patriots.

Make no mistake, Wannstedt knew Weis too. He knew Weis' play-calling tendencies, which is to say, he knew the new Notre Dame coach could be innovative and unpredictable. That was his tendency: to not have a tendency.

Weis realized he would have to be prepared to adjust on the fly. That was an ability that had eluded the previous Irish coaching staff, which is partly why so many two-touchdown deficits turned into four-touchdown holes in 2003 and 2004. Pittsburgh quarterback Tyler

Palko, who had shredded the Irish for a record five touchdown passes the previous November, was back and primed for a big season.

But Weis believed he was holding a couple of pocket aces: Bill Lewis and Bernie Parmalee. Both had worked on Wannstedt's staff—one on offense, one on defense—and that would help eliminate some of the guesswork as the Irish prepared for the Panthers.

One striking difference between Wannstedt and Weis became apparent in the days leading up to the game. Wannstedt said he would have liked another week, or at least another day, to prepare for Notre Dame. Weis said he had more time than he knew what to do with.

While Weis preached confidence to the fans and players, Wannstedt pleaded caution. The Panthers had two first-time starters on the interior of their offensive line, and their defensive front had two players making the transition from a different position, one of whom was also coming back from an injury.

ESPN'S LEE CORSO HAD speculated during the preseason and even on the day of the game that the Irish might well lose all of their first six games. He cited the inexperience Notre Dame had on defense, with just three starters returning: noseguard Derek Landri, linebacker Brandon Hoyte, and safety Tom Zbikowski. What Corso and many other analysts weren't taking into adequate account was the star potential of junior defensive end Victor Abiamiri and tackle Trevor Laws, the veteran status of fifth-year senior linebacker Corey Mays, the lessons learned by Mike Richardson at cornerback, and the high hopes for end Chris Frome, linebacker Maurice Crum Jr., safety Chinedum Ndukwe, and cornerback Ambrose Wooden.

"Senior leadership is significant," Weis later insisted. "Even though Corey hasn't played a whole bunch in his career, I think he brings senior leadership. A lot of these guys, starting with Brandon, took it personally when everyone said, 'Well, they're only returning three guys, the defense isn't going to be any good.' "

The media also focused on the Panthers' veteran secondary, led by free safety Tez Morris, and cornerbacks Bernard "Josh" Lay and Darrelle

Revis. Weis believed he had devised a game plan that would exclude the talented defensive backs from the equation. "That secondary could have not even been out there as far as I was concerned, because that's not where we were going," he said. "Their front seven was inexperienced, and I thought that was where the game should be won."

Or lost. Just 4:02 into the first quarter, the Pitt quarterback connected on a 39-yard TD pass to Greg Lee. But what could have been a disaster turned out to be just a little bit of the jitters. After the touchdown, the Irish defense settled in and limited the Panthers to just 250 yards. Pittsburgh went 43:03 before they scored another touchdown. The Irish offense didn't have to wait nearly as long.

Trailing 7–0, the Irish tied the game on a 51-yard screen pass to Darius Walker. It was the second screen in a row to Walker. Two screens in a row? A bit unorthodox, sure, but when Weis diagnosed the Panthers defense, he knew which calls would work. He had quickly determined that he was seeing Wannstedt's defensive approach, not coordinator Paul Rhoads' philosophy. "As I said all along, I was going to make adjustments as to which defense they were playing," Weis said later. "That screen was designed to go against a team that played four across, and fortunately, we got a couple of blocks, Darius made a nice run and it turned into a big play."

By the end of the first quarter, Pittsburgh held a 10–7 lead. That didn't last. The Irish scored 28 points in the second quarter to take a 35–13 halftime lead.

Notre Dame didn't dominate on special teams, but at least they didn't "stink"—the word Weis used to describe the 2004 not-so-special teams. And against Pittsburgh, they did make the decisive play, a forced fumble on a kickoff midway through the second quarter that helped turn a 21–10 Irish lead into a 28–10 advantage.

A former walk-on caused the fumble. Casey Cullen, one of the surprise scholarship recipients at the end of preseason camp, stripped the ball. (Cullen's overall performance earned him the right to join Quinn and Hoyte at the center of the field for the coin flip the following week in Ann Arbor.)

By halftime, the score was 35–13. Through 30 minutes, the Irish had more yards—319—than they had racked up *in total* in five of their 12 games in 2004. The 35 points were the most scored since Notre Dame put up the same score in the first 30 minutes against Rutgers on November 23, 1996, a 62–0 victory in Lou Holtz' last game at Notre Dame Stadium.

The Irish started the second half a little sloppy. Three times Notre Dame was whistled for a penalty on the opening drive of the third period, but they overcame the mistakes. And when Quinn ran on third down and fell well short of a first down, the Irish caught a break. A personal foul on Pittsburgh kept the drive alive. Rashon Powers-Neal capped a 20-play, 80-yard drive that chewed up the first 7:01 of the third quarter to give Notre Dame their largest margin of the evening, 42–13.

By the fourth quarter, Weis substituted liberally. Several freshmen made their debuts, including offensive tackles Michael Turkovich and Paul Duncan. Being able to play two true freshmen on the offensive line in the first game of the season was a rare blessing, especially for a team that needed to get inexperienced backup linemen some playing time.

When it was all over, Notre Dame had rushed and passed for 502 yards on the way to a 42–21 blowout. Only two of Quinn's 18 completions accounted for more than 20 yards. But Notre Dame piled up first downs (33 to Pitt's 20) and converted on six straight red zone opportunities. (The clock ran out with the Irish in there again.) In the end, Notre Dame rushed for 275 yards against Pitt, accentuating one of the significant Irish advantages: a veteran offensive line going up against an unproven Panthers defensive line.

So dominant was the Irish offense that D.J. Fitzpatrick didn't attempt his first punt until the 14:55 mark of the fourth quarter. Notre Dame's 502 yards marked just the second time in five years that the Irish gained at least 500 yards in a game. The 42 points scored were the most in a non-interim head-coaching debut at Notre Dame since Jesse Harper's squad started the 1913 season with an 87–0 victory over Ohio Northern and interim coach Ed McKeever's outfit beat Pittsburgh 58–0 in 1944.

Like Willingham and Davie, Weis had won his first game as Notre Dame head coach. But after the game, Weis tried to deflect attention away from himself and onto his team. Deep down, Weis loved being considered an offensive mastermind, and he knew he had a significant edge in a battle of wits with Wannstedt. But this was a time to pass the credit on to his players.

"You can point at me all you want," he said, "but Brady Quinn and Darius Walker are the ones. I think at one time Brady completed 11 in a row. Other than the interception and the one incompletion in the first half, everything else was complete. It wasn't as good in the second half, obviously, but the good part of that is that it gives you a chance to offer constructive criticism, and I'm looking forward to that."

Quinn finished 18-for-27 for 227 yards, with two touchdowns and one interception, after completing 14-for-16 for 197 yards in the first half. He expressed his thanks to the coaches who had decided to follow Weis to South Bend: "All these coaches made career jumps to come here and work with us and help this team to become what it's capable of being. We wanted to win one for Coach Weis and the rest of the coaching staff."

Walker, who notched his third career 100-yard game—exactly 100 yards on 20 carries—had also learned to put his trust in the Irish coaching staff. "It doesn't come as too much of a surprise to us," said Walker. "Coming into a new system, you've got to believe in what the coaches are saying, especially with the type of coaches we have now. They've had a lot of success, so they obviously know what they're doing. If we follow them, we should be all right."

Seven different receivers caught passes from Quinn, including eight by wide receivers and flankers, six by the tight ends, and four by the running backs. Jeff Samardzija's diving 19-yard grab for a second-quarter TD was an instant highlight, and Powers-Neal's three touchdowns equaled his total for the three previous years combined.

In essence, Pittsburgh's defense couldn't get Notre Dame's offense off the field. The Irish scored on six of their first seven possessions, including five in a row. Samardzija's TD catch came after Pittsburgh fumbled a kickoff, as Weis' emphasis on special teams had paid its first dividend.

On the other side of the ball, Weis was especially pleased with the way his defense had performed. There was a letdown following the opening drive of the second half, when the Panthers snapped off a 55-yard run. But for the most part, Rick Minter's defense had done a credible job against Palko, who had shredded the Irish a season earlier. Notre Dame sacked Palko five times, but this statistic was somewhat misleading. Palko actually had time to throw most of the night, but this wasn't the same Notre Dame secondary he had picked apart the previous November. This time it gave up just one touchdown pass. Lewis' unit had played with more confidence, although three catchable interceptions—one each by Richardson, Wooden, and Ndukwe—fell incomplete.

"We weren't exactly killing him, but I thought Palko was under duress most of the evening," Weis said. "That is a tough kid, because he took a licking but kept on ticking." Palko finished 20-of-35 for 220 yards and had to battle through a right hand injury inflicted by Irish co-captain Hoyte.

In fact, the linemen on both sides of the ball had made Weis proud: "I would say we won the line of scrimmage. It was a very physical game and our players played very physically. We're looking to play tough and rough and physical, and I think it showed up out there. The offensive line played like they wanted to be the ones delivering the punches, not the ones taking them."

Deliver the punches. That's exactly what Weis and conditioning coach Ruben Mendoza had been preaching since February. Now the players could see the results for themselves.

As it turned out, Notre Dame's first victory under Weis came so easily that his biggest problem all evening was getting used to the headphones that connected him to both his offensive and defensive coaches. As the offensive coordinator of the Patriots, Weis didn't have to deal with switching the headphones to the defense. Getting used to the new technology proved to be a bit of a challenge: "I was hammering somebody on the offensive staff and I hear through the headphones, 'You're on defense, Coach.'"

Longtime observers of Notre Dame football knew they had just seen a different kind of Irish team and a different kind of victory. This bunch was more confident, more self-assured. "You only get 11 opportunities to go out there and play in the regular season," Weis said, "and each one of those is special. It's been a long time since there were that many smiles in the locker room. I wanted to let them go ahead and savor it a little tonight."

The savoring ended the next day, when the Irish came together to review the Pittsburgh game and move on to prepping for Michigan. Weis wanted them to enjoy what they had achieved, but there were way too many mistakes, including 10 penalties, to bask beyond Sunday. The Wolverines were just six days away.

If Weis needed his own reality check, all he had to do was remember what his son, Charlie Jr., had said to him as he walked off Heinz Field moments after his first victory as the head coach of Notre Dame:

"Congratulations, Dad. Sloppy second half, huh?"

......

Chapter 14

ROLLER-COASTER RIDE

OVER THE YEARS, THE Notre Dame football schedule has been applauded, questioned, ripped, and ridiculed. It has been called too tough, too imbalanced, even too military (Army, Navy, Air Force). Now, as the 2005 schedule unfolded, there was one thing it couldn't be called: too boring.

Four of the first five games were on the road, but it was the middle three—at Michigan on September 10, home against Michigan State on September 17, and at Washington on September 24—that presented a delicious collision of fate and coincidence.

Michigan and Michigan State were not newcomers to the schedule. This would be the 33rd meeting between Notre Dame and the Wolverines, and the 69th between the Irish and the Spartans. In fact, the tag team of Michigan-Michigan State had been back-to-back early season opponents since 2002.

But no one could have imagined the perfect storm of firings and hir-ings that would produce Notre Dame at Washington, starring Charlie Weis and Tyrone Willingham, in ... the Ty Bowl.

BIG DAY IN THE BIG HOUSE

THE TRAMPLING OF PITTSBURGH lifted Notre Dame to No. 20 in the Associated Press poll and No. 23 in the *USA Today*/Coaches Poll. The Irish would undoubtedly leap into the Top 10 if they beat number-three Michigan at Michigan Stadium.

Wait.

Beat Michigan at Michigan?

How likely was that?

Lloyd Carr, now in his 11th year as head coach, had a 59–6 mark in Michigan Stadium, a.k.a. the Big House, which accommodates 107,501 rabid Maize and Blue fans capable of reducing visitors to mush. Carr lost to Davie's Irish in 1998, and to Willingham's teams in 2002 and 2004, but those three Notre Dame victories had been at South Bend. Carr was 3–0 against the Irish in the Big House, including a 38–0 romp in 2003.

Now Michigan was fresh off a double-digit win against Northern Illinois and counting the days until it could seek revenge against a Notre Dame team that had beaten the then-No. 8 Wolverines a year earlier.

Irish coaches seemed to welcome the idea. "We enjoy going to the Big House," said Rick Minter. "You coach in college football to play in college football's best venues, and Michigan Stadium is one of the game's greatest venues." Carr, on the other hand, had never been a big fan of the Notre Dame-Michigan rivalry, openly complaining about it on several occasions. The gist of his argument? If you want to play us, join the Big Ten.

It just added to the intensity of the rivalry, which had resumed in 1978 after a 35-year hiatus. Since then, the Irish and Wolverines had played 21 times, with the Irish winning 11, losing nine, and tying one. Over the last quarter century, Notre Dame vs. Michigan had become one of the nation's greatest matchups. But while the Irish were holding their own against the Wolverines, they were struggling mightily against the rest of their schedule. Michigan had won at least eight games every season since 1985; Notre Dame had lost six times or more in five of the previous eight seasons. By the start of the 2005 season, one of Notre Dame's most sacred records—the all-time highest winning percentage—had been eclipsed by Michigan. The Wolverines concluded the 2004 season with an all-time record of 842–275–36 for a 74.588 winning percentage. Notre Dame was 802–263–42 for a 74.345 winning percentage.

In the college football world, things like that matter—a lot.

For the Wolverines, it likely would be another nine- or 10-victory season; for the Irish, six or seven wins would be considered a good first year under Weis. That was the line of thinking before Notre Dame manhandled Pittsburgh and Michigan struggled a bit against Northern Illinois in their respective season openers. Michigan had given up 211 yards rushing against the Huskies. More striking was the 6.6 yards per rush allowed in 32 attempts. Throw in another 200 yards through the air, and one thing seemed clear: Michigan had some defensive problems, including an iffy Wolverine linebacking corps. Suddenly the Irish had confidence and the Wolverines had questions.

Weis was intent on avoiding an Irish letdown after an impressive performance against Pittsburgh. He talked to the team about it after the victory, then again on Sunday, Monday, and Tuesday. The message was always the same: "You can't rest on your laurels and feel good about yourself because you played a good opener. You've got to be worrying about Michigan. If you don't, you'll get your butt kicked."

At the regular Tuesday press conference, Weis also offered a little soliloquy on existential angst that he did not deliver to his team. "Football coaches really don't enjoy the wins, and they are miserable after the losses, because rather than feeling good about the win, we're already worried about the next game. Usually when you lose a game you spend too much time worrying about that game, and you're not worrying about the next game."

Before Tuesday's practice, nine-time Stanley Cup-winning coach Scotty Bowman spoke to the team. (Three of those nine Stanley Cups came as head coach of the Detroit Red Wings, whose headquarters are less than an hour's drive east of the Ann Arbor campus.) Bowman was as blunt as Weis, telling the Irish, "Your last game doesn't mean much. You're only as good as your next game."

Added Weis: "I have no emotions at all about Notre Dame vs. Michigan. None."

Believe him or believe him not, his goal was transparent: to teach his players how to treat each game the same.

"You understand the significance of rivalries between schools," Weis explained, "but if you ever treat any team differently, you're just setting yourself up for a fall. That would be like saying, 'We'll get up for Michigan, but we're not going to get up for somebody else.' It's disrespectful to the other opponent, and you're setting yourself up for emotional highs and lows. If you're going to be a consistent football team, you must treat every week the same."

Yes, Michigan was a rival. But there were a lot of teams on Notre Dame's schedule that were going to play the Irish like it was a rivalry game. That comes with wearing the golden helmet; you get everybody's best punch. Better that the players focus on how to defeat the upcoming opponent, rather than on *who* the upcoming opponent was.

For Carr, the game may have been a bit more personal. As a Michigan assistant and as head coach, he had been on the sidelines for 19 previous games against Notre Dame and his record wasn't pretty: 8–10–1 overall, 3–3 as a head coach.

The pressure was also mounting on Jim Herrmann, Michigan's defensive coordinator since 1997. In 2002, the Wolverine defense gave up 265 points, the second-most allowed in school history until 2004, when Herrmann's defense yielded 279. The last four opponents of 2004—Michigan State, Northwestern, Ohio State, and Texas—scored an average of 33 points against the Wolverines.

The poor defensive showing even prompted legendary Michigan head coach Bo Schembechler to sound off about the state of the Wolverines. Not surprisingly, Carr had grown irritable about questions pertaining to the poor play of the defense. Now Northern Illinois had exposed more defensive soft spots.

On the other side of the ball, though, Michigan fans had little to complain about. When the Irish defeated the Wolverines a year earlier, Michigan quarterback Chad Henne and running back Mike Hart were true freshmen. It was Henne's first career road start, and Hart had carried just five times for 17 yards. Henne went on to start all 12 games in 2004, completing 60.2 percent of his passes and throwing for 2,743 yards and a school-record-tying 25 touchdowns. Hart rushed for 1,455 yards and nine touchdowns en route to being named the 2004 Big Ten Freshman of the Year.

"Even though Hart's not the biggest person, he runs inside and outside, and he has quickness and speed," Weis said of Michigan's top ground threat. "That's a lethal combination. On top of that, he never fumbles."

Henne had lost his number one target, wide receiver Braylon Edwards, who became the number three overall pick in the NFL draft, but he still had Jason Avant, Steve Breaston, and tight end Tim Massaquoi. And if Hart needed a break, the Wolverines could turn to true freshman Kevin Grady, the all-time leading prep rusher in the state's history with 8,431 yards, 151 touchdowns, and an incredible 24 straight 100-yard rushing games.

Leading the way for the Wolverines was another typically huge, experienced offensive front. Three fifth-year seniors—left tackle Adam Stenavich, left guard Leo Henige, and right guard Matt Lentz—anchored a Michigan line that averaged almost 320 pounds per man.

Adding to Michigan's ability to move the ball was special-teams ace Breaston, in line to become the first player in Big Ten history to gain more than 1,000 yards as a receiver, punt returner, and kick returner.

The huge crowd at Wolverine home games presented another problem. Heinz Field in Pittsburgh held only 66,451, including a decent-size Notre Dame contingent. The Big House was the Big House for a reason. Weis piped blaring music into the Loftus Center to help simulate the wall of sound produced by the crowd of more than 100,000. Being a New Jersey guy, he went with a couple of Garden State guys—Bruce Springsteen and Jon Bon Jovi.

"It's not something where you just say, 'Okay, we're going to handle the noise.' It's something you have to practice," he explained. "You have to try to make sure the players concentrate so you don't have false start penalties. You don't want runaway rushers outside the tackles because they didn't hear the snap count."

As an exhausted-looking Weis trudged up the steps of the Guglielmino Auditorium early Thursday evening, intent on honing in on the Wolverines, he did admit that he would take a peek at the Patriots-Oakland Raiders game that kicked off the start of the 2005 NFL season. "I'll enjoy it because I have nothing to do with it," he told reporters with a smile. "If they score 50, I can cheer for them; if they don't score 50, I can say, 'What are they doing?'"

Weis still kept in touch with Tom Brady, his former Patriots quarterback. Brady, a member of Michigan's 1997 National Championship team, made a bet with Weis. If the Irish won, Brady would wear a Notre Dame hat at his next press conference. And if Michigan won? Weis refused to name the other half of the bet. (It was later revealed to be a case of beer.)

Never one to be ruled by conventional thinking, Weis instructed his game-day captains that if the Irish won the coin toss, they should elect to receive. (Usually a coach who wins the toss will defer so his team can receive the ball to start the second half.) The players did a double take. "You mean if we win the toss we want the ball?" one of them asked.

"Why *wouldn't* we want the ball?" responded Weis.

And sure enough, the Irish offense scored on its opening drive. A big reason for the early success was Weis' strategy to combat the noise from the Michigan Stadium crowd. The plan was to come out in a no-huddle offense. Quinn would look to the sideline for a number, look it up on his wristband, and call the play at the line of scrimmage. As a result, when the crowd was its loudest—during Notre Dame's opening possession—the Irish responded with a mouth-closing, 12-play, 76-yard drive that took just 2:58 to get them into the end zone.

By halftime Notre Dame was leading, 14–3. While the Irish were racking up 14 first downs and another 12-play, 72-yard drive for a second touchdown, Michigan netted just five first downs. Hart left the game after just three carries for 4 yards when a hit by Corey Mays aggravated a hamstring injury. His backup, the freshman Grady, managed 79 yards on the ground.

In the second half, what was billed as a potential shootout became more of a defensive struggle. Notre Dame was aided by the fact that Michigan's starting right tackle and his back-up were out with injuries. So was their tight end, Massaquoi. One of Michigan's guards also went down with an injury during the game.

"Hard-nosed games always come down to defense, whether it's the last five minutes in a 42–40 game or the last five minutes in a 17–10 game," said Irish center Bob Morton. "We have that hard-nosed mentality. We just got it sooner than other people expected."

The first three times the Wolverines penetrated the red zone in the second half the Irish came away with a stop. A 14-play, 69-yard drive to start the second half was squelched when Notre Dame's Tom Zbikowski intercepted a Henne pass at the 1. Another Michigan drive ended at the Irish 5-yard line as Henne threw incomplete to Jason Avant on fourth down.

The Irish also were aided by two calls that were reversed by instant replay, one of which resulted in a Michigan turnover. As Henne tried to sneak the ball in from the 1-yard line with 5:21 remaining, the ball squirted out of his hands and into the pile of players stacked up at the goal line. Notre Dame safety Chinedum Ndukwe looked down, saw the football peeking out at the back end of the pile, picked it up, and waved it around to show the officials. After review, the officials ruled it a fumble and gave possession to the Irish at the 20-yard line. Moments later, Quinn was ruled down by contact, negating what originally was called a fumble.

Weis had focused heavily on special-teams play in an attempt to bottle up the dangerous Breaston. Punter D.J. Fitzpatrick and kickoff man Carl Gioia either forced Breaston to catch the ball on the run, or Notre Dame's coverage units blanketed him before he had a chance to hit full stride. Breaston finished with six punt returns for 31 yards and two kickoff returns for 30 yards.

The Wolverines made it interesting with a touchdown with 3:47 left in the game. But the Irish defense held on downs on Michigan's final drive to claim the 17–10 victory.

Minter's defense bent but didn't break. Michigan outgained the Irish, 337–244, but scored only one touchdown, and it didn't come until late in the fourth quarter. Weis and his staff had also noticed a flaw in Henne's delivery, which the defensive front exploited by batting down five passes. All told, the Irish broke up nine passes. Due in great part to the steady Irish pressure, the sophomore quarterback managed to complete just 19 of 44 passes. "Their quarterback is very good, but his release is more at three-quarters, and any time you release the ball from a lower trajectory, the better chance there is of knocking some balls down," Weis later explained.

Darius Walker rushed for 104 yards, most of them in the first half when the Irish were building an 11-point lead. "We like being the underdog," Walker said. "If people want to make us the underdog, we'll keep showing up and show them what we can do."

It wasn't a smooth game offensively for the Irish. The offensive front didn't handle several of Michigan's "vanilla" blitzes, as Weis called them. And Quinn looked more like the quarterback with the 10–11 career record than the guy who had dissected the Pittsburgh defense in the first half of the previous week. "It wasn't perfect, but he didn't turn the ball over, and he threw two touchdown passes and managed the no-huddle operation with 111,000 people yelling," Weis said. "I, like anyone else, can talk about all the things that went wrong in the game and start singling people out, which I'd never do anyway. But the kid came out there the first time we had the ball and went on a 12-play drive and threw a touchdown pass. That tells me more about the kid than anything anyone can write about."

Still, the offense had struggled, particularly in the second half when it managed just 56 yards. To make matters worse, Quinn lost his No. 1 target, Rhema McKnight, to a knee injury shortly after McKnight gave the Irish an early lead with a five-yard touchdown reception.

Two games into his coaching regime, Weis had seen the offense, defense, and special teams play championship football at varying points of the first eight quarters of the season. "Now the important thing is to get all three in sync," he said. "That's easier said than done. But because there is evidence that it can be done, now my expectations go up." In other words, he wanted—no, expected—all three to play well at the same time, for a full 60 minutes.

"This one feels really good, mainly because everyone had this game pegged as an offensive team versus an offensive team," he continued. "Like I told the team this morning, you never know how the game is going to be played. I'm really happy for our kids. They're starting to figure it out. That's two weeks in a row. That's a really happy locker room, and they deserve it."

The victory catapulted the Irish from No. 20 to the No. 10 spot in the AP poll. It was the first time they had been in the top 10 since 2002. A little more than a week earlier, most media outlets had the Irish pegged as a Top 50 team, but certainly not in the Top 25. In the initial AP poll, the Irish had earned exactly one point. Now they were within striking distance of teams such as Florida State, Georgia, Florida, Tennessee, Virginia Tech, LSU, and Texas.

The day after the victory, when asked whether the Irish deserved the ranking, Weis wasn't about to discount his football team. "All I know is we just beat the No. 3-ranked team in the country and we're 2–0," he said. "Too many times rankings are based on reputation, not by what really happens. There are some teams that are unranked that maybe should be ranked. But maybe if you go by what you see, maybe the answer is yes, we do deserve the No. 10 ranking."

How good were the 2–0 Irish? "Good enough to compete to win every week," Weis said. "That's what they should be shooting for, to compete to win every week. That doesn't guarantee they're going to win every week, but they're good enough to compete to win."

When Quinn was asked what message the victory sent to the college football world, he wasn't prepared to respond. "I don't know what kind of message it sends. We've got Michigan State next weekend. We just want to be 1–0 again."

Ah, 1–0. Treat each week as if it were an individual season. Message received, computed, and implemented.

Weis had one more bit of business to deal with: By the time he met with the media at 12:30 p.m. the next day, he had already spoken with Bill Belichick and Patriots quarterbacks coach Josh McDaniels about making sure Brady wore that Notre Dame hat.

HOME, (BITTER) SWEET HOME

FOR JUST THE SECOND time since Lou Holtz' departure, the Irish had opened 2–0. Now came the home opener against Michigan State, and the South Bend campus and Greater Michiana (southern Michigan/ northern Indiana) was thumping with excitement. The Spartans were unbeaten as well, with comfortable victories against Kent State (49–14) and Hawaii (42–14), both in Spartan Stadium.

Homefield advantage didn't seem to be a factor when it came to the Notre Dame-Michigan State series. The Spartans hadn't lost to the Irish on the road since 1993. Most of the current Spartan upperclassmen were in grade school the last time Michigan State had lost to the Irish in South Bend. And overall, MSU was 6–2 in its last eight games against Notre Dame.

Even Notre Dame's most beloved images held no fear for the Spartans. "I was looking for Touchdown Jesus," said MSU junior defensive lineman Clifton Ryan. "Once I saw it, I realized it wasn't all it's cracked up to be. I'm 1–0 down there, and I'm looking forward to making it 2–0."

Spartans head coach John L. Smith, who had been successful at Idaho (53–21), Utah State (16–18, but with two Big West Conference titles), and Louisville (41–21), was similarly fearless. "It's not that we're unimpressed with Notre Dame," he said. "We respect their guys. But you have to put everything in perspective. Hey, we think we're okay too. We're not going to look down our nose at those guys, but we're not going to go around saying, 'Wow, we're playing Notre Dame!'"

And who could blame him? Michigan State's 11 total victories in Notre Dame Stadium were the most by any Irish opponent in history. With four consecutive wins at South Bend, there didn't appear to be anything to fear.

Except that Weis' team had just beaten two ranked teams on the road. A year earlier, under Willingham, Notre Dame had beaten the Spartans at East Lansing. So the Irish had some confidence on their side too. Maybe too much. "This would be a perfect opportunity for our guys to feel so good about themselves that they forget to show up to play a team that has been beating them regularly," Weis said. "I need to make them understand that we have to play our best game if we're going to beat Michigan State."

Weis had his staff splice together 15 minutes of clips from the previous four visits by the Spartans and sat his team down to watch it. "I really didn't have to say much to the players because after 15 minutes of watching that tape, I think they got the picture loud and clear," he said. "It was ugly."

The cause of Weis' uneasiness was MSU quarterback Drew Stanton, who was rapidly developing into one of the nation's top quarterbacks. Rated No. 4 in the nation in passing efficiency, Stanton had completed 43 of 55 passes against Kent State and Hawaii—an absurd 78 percent—for 598 yards, five touchdowns, and just one interception. True, those numbers had come against weak teams, but Michigan State averaged 515.6 yards total offense and 34.9 points per game in Stanton's nine career starts, which included Iowa and Michigan in 2004. If the Spartans continued to win, Stanton would almost certainly emerge as a legitimate Heisman Trophy candidate. He was that good.

The demand for a seat inside Notre Dame Stadium and the excitement around campus were both on the rise as the undefeated Fighting Irish prepared to take on the undefeated Spartans. Everything was at a premium during a home game weekend: tickets, restaurant reservations, hotel rooms.

"We're getting 50 phone calls per day," said Rona Brenner, general manager of the Jamison Inn, a 49-room bed-and-breakfast on the east edge of the campus. "They had faltered in the last couple of years. But after these two wins and with a home game coming up, everybody is calling to find out if there are any openings. Everywhere in South Bend, the place is abuzz."

Rooms at the Jamison Inn had long ago been sold out. But that didn't stop the steady stream of calls from people who claimed to be an old classmate of Weis' or a distant relative of the new head coach. One caller even suggested a family link to Knute Rockne. "Sold out is sold out," Brenner smiled.

Barb Mickow, the manager of the Irish Import Shop, had spent her life in South Bend. She recalled Notre Dame football from the Ara Parseghian era. She could see strong similarities to Weis' program. "People sense that he's playing old-fashioned Notre Dame football, the way it used to be," she said. "People in the know come in and say, 'I've stopped by practice,' or 'I talked with someone at practice, and those boys are getting whipped into shape.' He's no nonsense...and he's a little bit of a character."

If there's one thing South Bend has always been well prepared for, it's the hype that surrounds a big home game. Certainly, 41 losses in the past eight years had curtailed the enthusiasm somewhat. But things had changed. In a community starved for a winner and a coach they could rally behind, demand for tickets was way up even before the Irish opened with a pair of victories.

There was something about Weis' everyman persona that resonated with the fans. Plus, it looked like he could coach. "His personality is one thing, but add the intelligence factor that he brings and I think that's why you saw the optimism generated before he had even coached a game," said Chuck Lennon, executive director of Notre Dame's alumni association. "People see his track record and believe he knows what he's doing."

Each year approximately 32,000 of the 80,795 seats in Notre Dame Stadium are up for grabs among alumni who enter Notre Dame's ticket lottery. For the Michigan State game, 49,521 people applied for seats. Only Notre Dame's showdown with No. 1 USC on October 15 drew more interest—more than 54,000 applicants. A record $5.2 million was refunded to alumni who lost out in the lottery for the six home games.

Weis looked forward to his first pep rally as the Irish head coach, not for himself as much as for the team. "It's an opportunity to get everyone a little fired up, but really, it's about connecting the football team with the student body," he said. "A lot of times the athletes are put on a pedestal, and that's not really the Notre Dame way. The Notre Dame way is for these players to be a part of the student body, not to be above and beyond the student body."

While Weis didn't want to do anything to stifle the excitement around campus, he was acutely aware of the stumbling blocks awaiting a football team that succumbs to its own hype. On the bus trip back from Ann Arbor, he carefully combed through the Notre Dame media guide, gathering facts on the Irish-Michigan State series. Before he would even talk to the players about the Michigan game they had just won, he began his Sunday meeting with a stern warning about the abilities of the Spartans.

And while playing inside Notre Dame Stadium could have its benefits, the Irish hadn't taken advantage of homefield advantage in recent years. Willingham's teams each lost three times in Notre Dame Stadium in 2003 and 2004, finishing with a 6–6 record in his final 12 games on Irish turf. "There are more distractions when you're at home than when you're away," Weis said. "When you're away, it's us against the world. Now you're coming home and the families start coming in for the games, and the dog-and-pony show arrives for the pep rally on Friday. It can be quite a distraction."

Weis, much like Holtz before him, placed great significance on the way the team practiced during the week. They shared a conviction that a poor week of practice usually leads to a poor game, while a good week usually leads to a well-played game. So dogs and ponies were not allowed as the Irish readied for Michigan State.

The players were responding, he believed, because they were beginning to see the rewards of playing the game the right way. They were walking with a bit of a swagger. At this point, they had earned it. "Expectations by the media were extremely low," Weis said. "My expectations were always high. I thought maybe I was delusional there for a while. But the fact that the team is playing more to my expectations than to everyone else's expectations hasn't surprised me; it's validated what my thoughts were."

For Brandon Hoyte and other Notre Dame veterans, their time had come. "We've been through a lot, and we're tired of it," Hoyte said. "We've been really fortunate because Coach Weis and the staff have instilled in us what needs to be done to get to that next level. A lot of people call it a cliché, but when you can take a whole football team and get such focus on a game-by-game basis, that's a credit not only to the coaching staff, but to the mental focus of that team."

As for the fans, Weis had but one requirement: "Just be loud." Notre Dame Stadium crowds had earned a reputation for being quieter than a cat's purr. They had been spoiled for so many years. Then they had been bored for three out of the past four seasons. Now there were no more excuses. He wanted them to make some noise.

Weis coaching his first game in Notre Dame Stadium sparked an outpouring of sartorial creativity among the Irish student body. Women could be seen wearing blue and gold "Charlie's Angels" T-shirts. Also popular were the navy blue T-shirts that said, "New Coach, New Pope, New Era" on the front, and "Same Old Jesus" with a picture of a smiling redeemer on the back. Another shirt played on Weis' nasty theme: "You can't spell dynasty without the nasty."

But in the end, it was Michigan State 44, Notre Dame 41—again— only this time in overtime.

Stanton, as expected, played brilliantly on a sun-drenched afternoon. Fourteen of Michigan State's plays accounted for 347 of the 488 total yards gained by the Spartans. Meanwhile, Quinn set a Notre Dame single-game record with five touchdown passes—including three to Jeff Samardzija—while completing 33 of 60 for 487 yards. But his interception on the second play of the second half was returned by SirDarean Adams for a touchdown and a 31–17 MSU lead.

The deficit grew to 38–17 with 5:07 left in the third quarter. Notre Dame put on a furious rally that tied the game with 2:31 remaining. And then they had a chance to win the game in regulation when Zbikowski forced a fumble near midfield. But the Irish failed to capitalize.

When the game went into overtime, the Irish couldn't move the ball and had to settle for a 44-yard field goal by Fitzpatrick. The Spartans responded with a 19-yard touchdown run by running back Jason Teague. You could hear the Irish bubble burst from miles away.

After the game, about a dozen Michigan State players accompanied the school's flag onto the field. Then several players planted the flagpole into the Notre Dame Stadium turf, proudly suggesting that Michigan State owned the Irish in their own house. And they did. No other school except Purdue had ever beaten Notre Dame at home five consecutive times.

It had not been a good performance by the defense. They stiffened in the second half, allowing the offense to make the dramatic comeback when Michigan State got conservative with the big lead. But after opening the season with back-to-back victories over ranked teams, nobody was interested in almosts. Notre Dame's defense had been overwhelmed by Stanton.

Quinn led the Irish comeback with several remarkable throws, particularly to wide receiver Maurice Stovall, who racked up a career-best 178 yards on eight receptions. But Quinn's accuracy had been streaky once again. The interception to start the second half was thrown well behind Samardzija. "Brady had a couple plays, like the interception, that he'd like to have back," said Weis, defending his quarterback. "But when you throw the ball 60 times and take 98 snaps, there are going to be some bad ones in there. He made a lot more plays than he missed. I'd rather lose by 50 than not try to win the game, so when we got down by 21, we were going to throw it on almost every down. That's the same guy who bounced back to tie the game, so overall I'd have to say there were a lot of things out there that I was happy about with Brady."

But he wasn't happy about the loss, even though the Irish had rallied from a 21-point late-third quarter deficit. "Sometimes you feel good about yourself because you come back," Weis said, "but guess what? That's just not good enough. I'm never satisfied losing a game."

For the first time in his brief tenure as head coach of the Irish, one of his tactical/personnel decisions came under question. It involved 6'2", 230-pound freshman fullback Asaph Schwapp, pound for pound one of the strongest players on the team. Schwapp played nearly 30 minutes a game in the first three games of his rookie season. Although he had some running skills, his presence in the lineup was due mainly to his blocking abilities. Three times in the second half against Michigan State, Schwapp was given the ball in short-yardage situations, and each time he came up short. His fumble on a first-and-goal from the MSU 1-yard line early in the third quarter was a devastating turnover.

Fifth-year senior Rashon Powers-Neal, who had scored three touchdowns in the season opener against Pittsburgh, did not carry the football once against the Spartans. He appeared to have been shaken up on a play in the first quarter. Weis also said Powers-Neal had been groomed to play halfback in the Michigan State game because of the match ups. When the Irish were forced into a pass mode because of the quick deficit, the playbook page with Powers-Neal's name on it was removed from the plan.

"It was not by design that Asaph was ahead of Powers-Neal," Weis said. "It was the fact that we intended to use him more at halfback in that game." But unless Powers-Neal was injured and Weis didn't want to reveal it, the comment came off as a somewhat lame excuse. Your veteran fullback, a fifth-year senior, couldn't be inserted at fullback because he had worked at halfback all week?

Still, Weis always preached accountability to his players, and he was the first man in line to accept responsibility for the loss. "I told you when I first got here that the first thing you would hear if and when we ever lost a game was the blame starts at the top, so let's start with things that definitely fall under the category of me," he said. "Although the team had a really good week of preparation physically and mentally, the one thing that happened in this game that I didn't do a very good job of was keeping focus through the distractions that come with playing at home."

Weis talked about the number of mental errors that occurred in the first half, which told him that he didn't have the team focused enough to start the game. He also questioned his time management at the end of each half.

Taking the loss as hard as anyone was Quinn, whose facial expressions and soft tones displayed his emotions. "When you come back like that, you have a lot of emotion that you're carrying," he said. "You feel pretty good about yourself, and when you can't come through with the victory, it's a big letdown."

When a reporter asked Quinn how the team would respond, a company line was expected. Instead, Quinn's answer was surprising and revealing. "I don't know; it's hard to tell right now," he said. "I think this team is pretty resilient, but at the same time a loss like this can do a lot of things. Hopefully, guys will come back with their heads up, make corrections, and move on."

Amid the dejection on the field, Charlie Weis Jr. watched the Michigan State players as they celebrated their victory. The flag-planting incident had bothered him. It was such a defiant, disrespectful act. His father, dealing with his own set of emotions, didn't see it.

Weis went looking for his son at the end of every game. He was always a family-first kind of man, and the value of family had been driven home even more strongly by a conversation he'd had earlier in the year with NBC executive Dick Ebersol. The previous November, Ebersol and two of his sons were in a plane crash. Ebersol and one son had survived; his 14-year-old son, Teddy, had not. "Dick's advice to me," Weis said, "was that I had a rare opportunity to be able to share these special moments with Charlie."

And share them he did. "I enjoy it when I walk over and see my kid," Weis said after the Michigan win. "I like Charlie's smile after a game. He's going to be pouting after a loss too, I can promise you."

And he was. Charlie Jr. made a point of telling his father how badly it made him feel when he observed the MSU players planting the flag. Charlie Weis, the Notre Dame head coach, made a mental note. In fact, he filed the image his son had painted for him in a special compartment all its own.

THE TY BOWL

IT WAS WEIS WHO coined the phrase to describe the September 24 matchup between Notre Dame and Washington: the Ty Bowl. He said it way back on Media Day, August 8, as the Irish opened preseason camp.

A game that otherwise would have been dismissed by most college football fans was now must-see TV. It had nothing to do with records. Washington had defeated just two teams—San Jose State and Idaho—in its last 14 games, while Notre Dame was coming off an overtime loss to Michigan State.

No, this had everything to do with the subplot that centered on the coaches. Shortly after Notre Dame fired him, Tyrone Willingham was hired at Washington, where athletic director Todd Turner was looking for someone to reverse the fortunes of a once-proud program. Of course, Notre Dame had asked Willingham to do the same for the Irish.

Under Don James' leadership from 1975 to 1992, the Huskies had a 150–60–2 (.712) record, six Rose Bowl appearances—four of them wins—and a 10–4 overall record in bowl games. But after James left, three coaches—Jim Lambright, Rick Neuheisel, and Keith Gilbertson—failed to keep the Huskies at the same level. Willingham replaced the Gilbertson, who won just one game in 2004.

Washington announced that it was hiring Willingham on December 13, 2004—the same day Weis was introduced at Notre Dame. Twelve days earlier, Willingham said he would take a step back and relax before deciding about his future. He also disputed a news report that said he had been in formal discussions with Washington officials about their coaching vacancy two weeks before he was fired from Notre Dame. Willingham called the contact with Washington "informal." But obviously, the Irish coaching staff suspected something. Ultimately, five former Notre Dame assistant coaches ended up following Willingham to Washington.

Weis might have coined the phrase Ty Bowl, but he quickly tried to defuse the hype. In the wake of the MSU loss, he wanted to turn the focus from Weis vs. Willingham to Notre Dame vs. Itself. "We can't worry about who we're playing when we play like we did against Michigan State," he told the press. "If we don't play better fundamentally, and with better techniques, we could lose to everybody. Right now, our point of emphasis this week, besides getting ready for an opponent, is fixing ourselves. You can't worry about your opponent if you can't handle your own problems."

It was a nice try, but Willingham's presence couldn't be ignored. Certainly the players would be distracted by all the Ty Bowl talk, if for no other reason than the media was inundating them with questions about their feelings regarding their ex-head coach. If they knew what was good for them, though, the answer would be "No comment."

"They won't be talking about it and neither will I," Weis said. "We all know what the distraction will be, but I can promise you they won't be talking about that. Every week I try to have a point of emphasis and this week the point of emphasis is going to be fundamentals and techniques. I'm not going to make a big deal out of it. We'll talk about how we're going to handle it and that will be it. It's not going to be a long conversation."

When he was asked if he would dictate what the players could say to the media, he replied, "They can say whatever they want. They're big boys, they can talk for themselves. But I know what they're going to say."

And, almost uncannily, he did. "We have the utmost respect for Coach Willingham and the staff he has at Washington," said Samardzija.

"We have the utmost respect for him and the staff, but we can't get caught up in that," said offensive tackle Ryan Harris.

"It's a big game for us and we have the utmost respect for Coach Willingham," said tight end Anthony Fasano, breaking into a grin when he realized he sounded a lot like the guys who had answered before him.

But no matter how hard everyone tried to downplay the Weis-Willingham meeting, the simple truth was, it was a great story.

Think about it. Head football coach gets fired. Players agonize over the injustice. Head coach resurfaces a couple of days later and a few thousand miles away. His old team travels across the country to play their old coach's new team just four games into the next season. Would the players cry and feel divided allegiance when they saw their beloved ex-coach standing across the field wearing different colors?

"The coaches don't play the game," said Zbikowski, one of the few players who did not repeat the "utmost respect" line. "We're playing

Washington. I'm playing against their receivers, not any coaches. We're three games into it. We're pretty settled down. That's the past."

There had been plenty of emotion that December day when Notre Dame fired Willingham three years into a six-year contract. If you were a player, Willingham was easy to like. He treated you with respect, like a man. He was a player's coach.

On the Notre Dame campus, though, Willingham's firing had created a firestorm, particularly among minorities, who were in a perpetual battle to have their voices heard. Now, with the Notre Dame-Washington game next on the schedule, some of those same issues and emotions were revived. "The Washington game is the one game I don't want Notre Dame to win this year," said Leah McGee, a Notre Dame senior finance major whose mother is of Irish descent and whose father is African-American.

Everyone knew Willingham was a good man. He coached for the right reasons. He truly wanted to make a positive impact on the lives of student-athletes. His heart was in the right place. But the Notre Dame football players also knew he wasn't getting the job done.

To no one's surprise, the person who had the least to say about all the Ty Bowl hoopla was Willingham himself. He kept his comments brief and to the point. "At the end of the day, the scoreboard will say Washington and Notre Dame, not Ty and Charlie," said Willingham. "This week is a unique circumstance, but it has always been my belief that life is in front of you, and that's where I put my focus."

Yet even Turner believed Willingham badly wanted to win this one. "He won't talk publicly about it," said the Washington athletic director. "He doesn't want his team to play the game for him. But you've got to know deep down in his heart, he'd like to make a statement."

Willingham also had bigger issues to worry about. He was trying to stabilize an unsteady program, but losses to Air Force (20–17) and Cal (56–17) made for a rocky start. Kent Baer's defense was allowing a 48 percent conversion rate on third downs, including a whopping 56 percent in those two losses.

With Baer running the Huskies defense, Weis believed he had a bit of an edge. First of all, he had players who had been in Baer's system when Baer was in South Bend. Players such as Hoyte and Zbikowski would be able to provide much insight. "It also helps when you have the playbook," Weis said. "You know, the playbook that Kent Baer has, we have too. When coaches walk out the door, they can take everything else with them. But when you have a copy of it, you have a copy of it. It kind of helps a little bit when you know the foundation of the playbook."

All week, Weis placed the emphasis on his team. "Our team has the utmost respect for Coach Willingham, his staff, his team, and their university," said Weis, with a line that was beginning to sound strangely familiar. "What this week is really going to be about is us fixing our own problems fundamentally and technically. That's going to be our point of emphasis."

He knew that, man-for-man, the Huskies weren't good enough to beat the Irish. Focusing on his own team's shortcomings would get the job done and, in the long run, help teach his team how to come through with outside factors infiltrating their preparation. Because when it came right down to it, Willingham and the Huskies were a team to beat or, more accurately, a team the Irish had to beat. A 2–2 start would make those road wins in Pittsburgh and Michigan a distant memory.

By Wednesday of Washington week, Weis looked refreshed, even upbeat. He greeted the media enthusiastically after practice, knowing the distractions presented by the Ty Bowl would be gone by the next day. There were no more media interviews scheduled, and Weis had all of Thursday, Friday, and Saturday morning to re-focus his team.

As the media would learn the day after the Washington game, the preceding Wednesday Weis had visited the Mishawaka, Ind., home of Cathy Mazurkiewicz and her son, 10-year-old Montana Mazurkiewicz. Montana—named, of course, after legendary Notre Dame quarterback Joe Montana—had an inoperable brain tumor and was dying. After showering Montana with the usual assortment of Notre Dame gifts, Weis agreed to let the boy call Notre Dame's first offensive play—a run or a pass. Montana asked for a pass right.

The visit hit home for Weis, whose 13-year-old daughter, Hannah, was battling her own health problems. "I'll remember that visit the rest of my life," Weis said the day after the game. "Here's this 10-year-old kid with inoperable brain cancer. I was told he had a couple weeks to live. If you looked at him, you would know that a couple weeks was more realistically a couple of days. He knew he was going. He had lost feeling in his lower body. While I was sitting there, he had pain in his shoulders and he asked his mother to rub him down. He was trying not to be a wimp."

Sitting there with Montana and his brother, Rockne, Weis talked Notre Dame football. "I gave him an opportunity to hammer me on the Michigan State loss, which he did very well," Weis laughed. "It reminded me of my son. Then I was able to get a couple of smiles out of him. His mom got to take a couple of pictures. She said it was the first time he really smiled in about three months. He talked to me about his love for Notre Dame football, how he just wanted to make it through this game. He just wanted to be able to live through this game because he knew he wasn't going to last very much longer."

Earlier on Wednesday, Weis had talked to the team about Montana. "I told them how important Notre Dame football is to a lot of people," he said. "I'm not big on 'Win One for the Gipper' type of deals, but I wanted the players to realize how important they are as football players at Notre Dame, that they represent a lot of people who they don't even realize they're representing. Sometimes you think of the media, sometimes you think of the alumni. You don't think of the 10-year-old kid who is dying of cancer."

On Friday, Weis received word in Seattle that Montana had died that day, just a few hours after the Notre Dame team reached its weekend destination. "I talked to his brother," Weis said, "and Rockne said, 'The only thing I really wish on behalf of Montana is that you guys would be thinking of Montana and playing in his memory.'"

As expected, it was an emotional day on the field for both teams. The Irish were playing to reestablish themselves as the same team that had beaten Pittsburgh and Michigan. They were playing to please their new coach, and, in a way, to show off for their old coach. And they were playing for a little boy who had worshipped Notre Dame football.

They also faced an emotional Huskies team in the echo chamber known as Husky Stadium. A 1–3 record was an unwelcome possibility for a squad that was already shaky. And they wanted to do their new coach proud.

Weis and Willingham met at midfield before the game and shared a laugh. "In a very friendly, cordial way, we both acknowledged that it's been a little bit of a circus," Weis said. "I think we were both glad to get to the kickoff and get it over with, because no matter how hard you try, you know what it's going to be about."

Washington started the game on offense and marched downfield. The Irish forced a turnover at the goal line and Notre Dame took over at their own 1-yard line. Quinn turned to Weis on the sidelines and said, "What are we going to do?" Weis didn't hesitate. After all, he had told Cathy Mazurkiewicz on Friday, "This game is for Montana and the play still stands."

He told Quinn, "I've got no choice. We're throwing it to the right. Let's call bootleg. Fasano is going to be open. Just try to get it out of there." So Quinn ran the play-action fake, rolled to his right, and launched a pass to Fasano. Fasano leaped over a Washington defensive back after making the catch for a gain of 13 yards.

Somewhere in Mishawaka, a family cheered.

Although the Irish moved the ball with ease, controlling the clock for 10 of the first 15 minutes and racking up yardage on the ground and through the air, they only led 12–3 at halftime. In the end though, Notre Dame beat Washington, 36–17. With 560 yards total offense, the Irish had now surpassed the 500-yard mark for the third time in four games. They had done that just once in 2004, and that came in a 41–16 defeat.

Quinn was sharp, as was his go-to receiver, Samardzija, who caught eight passes for 164 yards, including a 52-yard touchdown reception that extended his scoring streak to four games and raised his touchdown total to six. Walker etched his name in the Notre Dame record book by rushing for 128 yards to become the first player in school history to open a season with four straight 100-yard rushing games. Quinn completed 25 of 37 passes for 327 yards. He now had 10 touchdown passes and just two interceptions for the season.

Washington's offense had hurt the Irish downfield, and that was the one remaining concern that hung over Notre Dame's workmanlike victory. Notre Dame's secondary continued to show its shortcomings, giving up 408 yards passing. But the Irish forced three turnovers and didn't commit any of their own. Touchdown-saving tackles, forcing fumbles at the goal line, and intercepting passes in the red zone had become a trait of the Irish defense.

"We almost feel invincible," Quinn said. "I don't want to say invincible, because there are times we're not doing what we should be doing. But we've gotten to the point where we are able to be powerful and do the things we want to do."

As promised, when the Irish returned from Seattle, Weis had the football signed by the team and delivered it to Cathy Mazurkiewicz. "For Montana's sake, I hope he's smiling in heaven right now, and I'm glad he's out of pain," he said. "I'm glad we won, by the way, so I could bring his mother the ball."

Weis had begun to feel a bit guilty about the publicity he was receiving for reaching out to the dying boy. Someone from the university had originally asked him to go see Montana, and Weis had just tried to do the right thing.

Cathy Mazurkiewicz cherished the ball, but cherished the memory of her son and the meeting he had with Weis even more. "He told Montana, 'You can't worry about tomorrow. Just live today for everything it has and everything you can appreciate,'" Mazurkiewicz recalled.

As for the pass-right play, Mazurkiewicz still couldn't believe Weis called it. "Montana would have been very pleased," she said. "I was very pleased. I was just so overwhelmed, I couldn't watch. I just closed my eyes. I thought, 'There's no way he's going to be able to make that pass. Not from where they're at. He's going to get sacked and Washington's going to get two points.'"

No way, said Weis.

Too many greater forces were at work.

······

Chapter 15

THE THREE R'S: RELAX, REFOCUS, REBOUND

THE LAST TIME NOTRE Dame had played Purdue, you needed a gas mask to survive the stink. The Boilermakers didn't simply beat the Irish; they placed them in bubble wrap and shipped the package to Blowout City. Weis wasn't at Notre Dame Stadium for the 2004 rout, of course, but he undoubtedly saw the 41–16 score. And if he didn't, he probably caught a whiff of the stench all the way back at Patriots headquarters in Foxboro, Massachusetts.

The Irish had rebounded from a loss to Brigham Young in the 2004 season opener and come back with three straight victories, including wins over Michigan and Michigan State. Maybe it was a late start for a banner year in South Bend. Maybe that 5–7 record in 2003 had just been a bad dream.

Hello, nightmare. The Boilermakers sauntered into Notre Dame Stadium, where they hadn't won in 30 years, jumped to a 20–3 halftime lead, and never looked back. That 432-yard passing effort from Brady Quinn? Nice looking on the résumé, but really just another measure of a team desperately playing catch-up ball from the opening whistle. The final score was 41–16. The countdown to the end of the Willingham Era at Notre Dame had begun.

With Lou Holtz at the helm, you could time your calendar to the annual September Irish win against Purdue. He was 11–0 against the Boilermakers, and his teams outscored them by a combined 433–123 margin. But in 1997, the same year Bob Davie replaced Holtz, Joe Tiller was named to coach Purdue football. Tiller was Purdue's version of Weis: bright, clever, confident. He brought his "basketball on grass" philosophy from Wyoming and turned the Boilermakers into an offensive powerhouse. They won games, filled seats, and earned bowl invitations, including the Rose Bowl in Tiller's fourth season. (They lost, 34–24, to the Washington Huskies.)

Davie led the Irish to a BCS bowl in his fourth season too—the Fiesta Bowl. A season later, he was fired. As it turned out, Davie's last game was December 1, 2001, when he beat Tiller and Purdue.

Willingham beat Tiller in his first season. Then came a 13–point loss in 2003 and the stinker in 2004, which ended Purdue's 30-year quest for a win at Notre Dame Stadium. You could hear the giggling all the way from West Lafayette, Indiana.

Since 1979, Purdue had become something of a barometer for the type of season the Irish would have. Beating Purdue didn't ensure Notre Dame of an outstanding season. But losing to the Boilermakers had been an accurate gauge for the better part of a quarter of a century. Purdue had defeated the Irish eight times since 1979, and in each of those seasons, Notre Dame failed to win more than seven games. In fact, in those eight seasons, the Irish finished below .500 four times and at .500 once.

Weis and the Fighting Irish would be bringing their 3–1 record to Ross-Ade Stadium in West Lafayette to play a Purdue team still recovering from a double-overtime loss at Minnesota. While Tiller had been praised for his passing schemes, defensive coordinator Brock Spack had done a brilliant job against the Irish offense. From 2000 to 2003,

Spack's unit did not surrender more than a single touchdown to Notre Dame in any one game. In 2004, the Irish scored two touchdowns—and lost by 25 points.

Weis' first Notre Dame-Purdue match-up was expected to be close, if for no other reason than that the Irish weren't the same team they had been a year before. Certainly, the offense wasn't the same; Weis had seen to that. Spack might not have spent sleepless nights leading up to the game, but he was guaranteed to have some long ones. Weis' playbook demanded that sort of attention from an opposing defensive coordinator.

Of course, Notre Dame would have to guard against a Purdue squad that was motivated following its loss to the Golden Gophers. And Tiller had added an option attack to his offensive arsenal, taking advantage of quarterback Brandon Kirsch's running skills. The idea was to use the option to gash defenses that were spread out to defend the passing attack.

Irish defensive coordinator Rick Minter's old boss, Holtz, called the option game the great equalizer. "Urban Meyer got a good trend started," said Minter of the spread option elements made famous by the former Irish assistant. "West Virginia's Rich Rodriguez, Clemson's Tommy Bowden, and all those guys have fed off each other. It's about matchups and playing in space and making a one-on-one play. It's also caused them to become a little more physical in the sense that they are committing themselves to running the football more."

Weis, with his background in the pros, was a novice when it came to defending against the option attack. That's one of the reasons he hired a veteran defensive coordinator like Minter, who had faced Navy and its option attack during his two years under Holtz and Army's option during his tenure as Cincinnati's head coach.

"This is a unique running game," said Weis. "Like the run-and-shoot and a lot of offenses of the past, any team that runs an option requires some serious studying to make sure you can get ready to go in a week."

Weis said he also studied up on option football over the summer. What he learned was that Tiller's offense wasn't easy to defend against. In fact, the more calls he made to coaches who had faced the option, the more he realized what a wonderful job Tiller had done at Purdue.

In some ways, the two men were very similar. "He's very creative on offense; he always has been," Weis said of Tiller. "He's another one of those guys who evolves. He sees who he has and then figures out what to do. He's been good since the day he got there. Purdue's program has been steadily on the rise, and you have to respect anyone who has that type of imagination."

Throughout Purdue week, Notre Dame's players were bombarded with questions about their "rivalry" with the school just a less than a three-hour drive from South Bend. (There had to be an angle every week.)

"It's bragging rights for Indiana," said Darius Walker. "Whoever wins that game is basically the ruler of the state and can talk all the trash in that state for that particular year. I've heard a little bit of it," he admitted. "I'll just say we're anxious to get out there."

"The people from Indiana realize what this game is," said Irish center John Sullivan, who was preparing for his first start of the season in the absence of the injured Bob Morton. "I didn't really have that concept when I got here, but after playing in the game last year, it's a pretty heated rivalry. It's a big game for us. When you go out on the field at West Lafayette, that crowd is intense. You can tell there's a hatred for you."

The hatred intensified when Davie hired former Boilermakers coach Jim Colletto to coordinate his offense. Once Tiller arrived and turned Purdue's fortunes around, the disdain for Colletto among Purdue fans became obvious, particularly when the Boilermakers knocked off the Irish in Ross-Ade Stadium upon Colletto's return in 1997. Lining the tunnel as Colletto left the field, the fans peppered him with verbal taunts.

"It's in-state," said tight end Anthony Fasano. "For me, the first time we played them was at home. I think they had more fans than I've ever seen any other team have in our house. I knew then that they had a good following. As for their stadium, it was one of the rowdier places that we've played in. It was Brady's first start, and they were giving him hell. We threw the ball 60 times, and we didn't play as well as we wanted to."

The memory was particularly bitter for Quinn, who was beaten like Purdue's World's Largest Bass Drum in his first collegiate start at Ross-Ade in 2003, then was sacked seven times in the 2004 loss.

Right guard Dan Stevenson felt personally responsible for the beating Quinn took, since he was penalized several times and beaten a few others while trying to contain former Purdue pass-rush specialist Shaun Phillips. "Three offside penalties in a row, not a fun experience," he said. "I've definitely thought about that. Thankfully, I'm not playing tackle anymore. I'm not 320 pounds, and I'm not going against a quick defensive end like Phillips. That makes things a little bit easier."

The Irish and the Boilermakers play each year for the Shillelagh Trophy, a victory symbol donated in 1957 by Joe McLaughlin, a merchant seaman and Notre Dame fan. Following each Notre Dame-Purdue contest, a small football with the winner's initials and the final score is attached to the trophy stand.

The Shillelagh, of course, is also the prize for the winner of the Notre Dame-USC game—a point not lost on Notre Dame alum Weis. So naturally, before the Purdue game, the media asked Weis whether Notre Dame-Purdue was actually a rivalry at all or just another game. If he said no, there would be controversy. If he said yes, he'd have to come up with a good explanation.

"The obvious thing to do when you're at Notre Dame is to just say the rival is USC," Weis began. "Let me tell you something, the way our schedule is set up with so many teams in close proximity, you're competing on a lot of levels. You're competing for bragging rights in-state, for instance. You're competing for recruits. You're competing for so many things that you can never take a game and not view it as a rival. First of all, you'd be slighting the other people, and second, that's the way they're looking at it. So if they're bringing a lot more emotion into the game than you are, you're just missing the boat."

And he was just warming up: "That's what you go through every week in the NFL. The really good teams are the ones that treat each week as the only game that matters. When I say that, a lot of people think I'm just blowing hot air. But really, that's the only way I know how to do it. Everything we're putting into this is just for Purdue. We've got a bye next week. What are we supposed to save stuff for?"

Beyond winning this "rivalry" game, several Irish offensive players talked about keeping Quinn "pretty" after the pounding he had taken in 2003 and 2004. That's pretty as in no bruises, no blood, no grass or dirt stains on his uniform. Weis concurred with that goal: it would be nice to see Quinn spend this game upright for a change.

Weis' concern for Tiller's two-pronged offense was evident during Notre Dame's final practice on Thursday at the Loftus Center. The usual 20 minutes the media was allowed to observe practice was reduced to 12—just enough to see the warm-ups. When the players had begun to stretch, Weis sensed a level of relaxation that wasn't suitable when prepping for an opponent that had manhandled the Irish in each of the past two seasons. Weis had a few things he wanted to say to his team. In private.

They were too laid-back, in Weis' view. And some players on the offense were verbally ripping players on the defense. It was good-natured fun—the sort of humor you'll hear on every team—but too many players were becoming involved. So Weis stepped in.

"Okay, let me just rattle off some facts and figures for you," he said. It got so quiet you could hear a sweat bead drop. The Irish had reached a very critical point in Weis' first season. Defeat Purdue and head into a bye week with a 4–1 record and two weeks to prepare for USC ... or fall to the Boilermakers for a third straight year, drop to 3–2, and lose momentum going into the USC game. In the grand scheme of things, it wasn't a must-win. But 4–1 with a two-week buildup for the Trojans would make for a buzz on the Notre Dame campus that hadn't been heard since the No. 1 vs. No. 2 battle against Florida State 12 years earlier. How the team performed during this crucial period would go a long way toward determining where the Irish ended up at bowl time.

With Purdue coming off a tough loss to Minnesota, Weis expected the best and most consistent effort from the Boilermakers. "A good football team is usually more focused than they normally would be when they're coming off a loss," he said. "I've been affiliated with a good football team for the last bunch of years, and every time we'd lose a game, we'd have even more focus. There's always been an extra sense of urgency, and it didn't just come from the coaches."

A victory would underscore the notion that the Irish could go into enemy territory and take charge. "The irony of all ironies? If we win this game, we'll be 4–0 on the road and 0–1 at home," Weis said. "This team is starting to learn some valuable lessons. They're getting a little hardened on the road. I think they kind of like being on the road—not that they don't like being at home."

Weis had taken the potential negative of a season front-loaded with road games—which the national experts said Notre Dame could not overcome—and turned it into a positive. "One of the things I was trying to do on the road was build camaraderie," he said. "Kind of an 'us against the world' mentality. It's easier to do that on the road because there are no distractions."

For Weis, this was his third trip to West Lafayette. As a sophomore in 1975, he watched Notre Dame defeat Purdue, 17–0, and then two years later, cheered as old classmate Joe Montana lead the Irish to a come-from-behind, 31–24 victory.

Trip No. 3 to West Lafayette turned out to be Weis' most memorable. Notre Dame overwhelmed Purdue, 49–28, and it really wasn't that close. The Irish traded in their gas masks for a shillelagh.

None of Purdue's offensive weapons did serious damage. If anything, it appeared that Purdue had tried to stuff too much into their attack, and none of it worked very well. The Boilermakers were never in the game. They didn't score their first points until the third quarter, and by then Weis was thinking about how many starters he could rest in the fourth quarter. Rick Minter's defense gave up 514 yards but no meaningful points. Basketball on grass had been mowed.

Quinn finished very "pretty" in this one. You could have placed his white jersey back on a hanger, it was so clean. Notre Dame's pass protection was superb: zero sacks.

In his 26th start as Notre Dame's quarterback, Quinn turned in what most considered the best performance of his collegiate career: he completed 29 of 36 passes for 440 yards (283 in the first half), three touchdowns, and one interception.

"I would be remiss if I didn't talk about the performance of the quarterback, because he was outstanding—and I don't say that very often," Weis said. "If we didn't drop a couple of balls, he would have had another 100 yards."

Not that there was anything wrong with the receivers. In fact, it became obvious early that the Boilermakers secondary couldn't contend with Notre Dame's wideouts. Jeff Samardzija extended his scoring streak to five games with a pair of touchdowns, including a 55-yarder in which Samardzija turned a perfectly thrown out pattern into a long score by bouncing off Purdue's poor tackle attempts. Samardzija finished with 153 yards on seven receptions, while Maurice Stovall caught eight passes—seven in the first quarter—for another 134 yards. Samardzija's diving, one-handed grab deep in Purdue territory early in the game would become a trademark highlight of the 2005 college football season.

"Samardzija seems to find the end zone," Weis said afterward. "I guess I should throw it to him more often."

The man calling the game for ESPN that day was ex-Irish coach Bob Davie, who shared the broadcast booth with Ron Franklin. Davie obviously had forgiven a few people in South Bend and moved on since his firing. And he had nothing but gushing praise for the job Weis was doing at Notre Dame. From the first snap of the game, Davie called Quinn a future "first-round draft choice," and later lavished the same praise on Fasano.

Later in the broadcast, Davie added, "This has been a clinic, and if Charlie Weis gives a clinic, I'll attend, because I'm on the bandwagon." Davie also pointed out that when it came time to sell his house in South Bend, Weis was the buyer. He quipped, "If I'd known they were going to pay him so much, I would have charged him more."

The road had indeed been good to the Irish. Not only had Notre Dame knocked off four opponents away from home, but they had pretty much dominated all four. They defeated Pittsburgh by 21, Washington by 19, and now Purdue by 21. The Michigan game, a 17–10 victory, looked close on the scoreboard, but the Irish never lost control of the tempo after establishing superiority at the line of scrimmage in the opening drive.

The Irish had come a million miles since the 2004 season, particularly offensively. No longer did third and 13 seem like third and no way. Three-and-out series had become rare. A much higher percentage of third-and-short situations gave Weis a vast array of plays and formations to call upon. The level of confidence of the offensive players had gone from doubt to near-certainty.

The defense had surrendered too much yardage. But when a sportswriter suggested to Weis that Notre Dame's No. 94 national ranking in total defense was a sign of weakness, the coach snapped back: "First of all, what's our record? I think that's more important. You're playing the wrong angle here. You're worrying about stats. If we're up in a game, and we've been up in a few of them now, what are the other guys going to do? They're going to throw the ball and try to get some yards, and yards don't mean anything. It's how many points you score."

The defense was 54th in the country in points allowed. But excluding the Michigan State game, in which the Spartans scored 44, the Irish had allowed their opponents fewer than 20 points per game.

In reality, Weis wasn't happy with the yardage allowed. But the coaches were beginning to get a better grasp of just what they had defensively, and it was paying dividends in the most crucial statistical categories. The Irish were tied for 10th in the country in turnover margin—always a telling stat—with a plus-six. Five times, Notre Dame had forced turnovers in the red zone. Another time, the opponent turned the ball over on downs.

"Schematically, things are starting to fall into place," Weis insisted. "We're at the point now where we're *expecting* to see progress each week. This is no longer an evolving defense. The coaches have done a good job of putting the players in position, and now, because they're not thinking as much, they're just playing.

"I'll give you one example: Derek Landri is a guy you don't even notice out there because he's an interior lineman. But he's spent at the end of the game because he's all over the field. You'll see Zbikowski or Hoyte because they're involved in all the sideline-to-sideline type of plays. But you won't see those sluggers in there who prevent an inside run. It's not by coincidence. Somebody is making those plays, and somebody is creating some serious havoc in there, or else they would be able to run the ball inside. It all fits together."

That said, the Irish were far from a finished product, and Weis knew it. But they had followed his plan almost precisely. They clearly had gotten better. And they had forged a 4–1 record when virtually no one expected better than 3–2. Many had anticipated much worse.

Even better, they were a team who believed in themselves and the program. "My whole party line walking in the door was a mentality that I wanted the team to take, and I'd say the team has taken that mentality," Weis said. "That pleases me more than anything, as much as wins."

The following week, the first of two bye weeks, was a time to recover, relax a little, and then begin preparing for the Trojans. So pleased was Weis with the rout of Purdue that he allowed himself, his staff, and the players to relish the victory for an extra day. Rather than the usual Sunday gathering, the postgame meeting was pushed back to Monday. It may not have seemed like a big deal to anyone on the outside. What's one day? But for a demanding coach like Weis, little gestures like this were huge.

Naturally enough, the coaching staff focused heavily on USC during the bye week. The plan was to go a bit easy on the players who had played regularly through the first five games and turn up the volume for the backups who hadn't seen nearly as much action.

The difficult work for the regulars would be the mental preparation. Notre Dame's one-sided victories against Washington and Purdue had given Weis the luxury of removing many of his starters in the fourth quarter. That, coupled with Weis' cautious approach with starters during a bye week, would keep the Irish fresh for USC.

Weis even allowed himself a break, taking the bye week Saturday off and not meeting with his staff until early Sunday morning. (The players had until 8 p.m. on Sunday before they had to report for study hall.)

Weis had big plans for his Saturday off. Charlie Jr. was scheduled for a haircut from his dad, and the Irish head coach planned to videotape his wife riding one of her two horses after that. At 2:30 p.m., Weis was going to plop on the couch and watch the USC-Arizona game. Always looking for an angle, he planned to turn up the sound, too, because he might be able to pick up a tidbit from the broadcasters: "Sometimes coaches give the commentators a lot of information going into the game."

He encouraged his players to go home over the weekend, if possible. Just be safe, be smart, and be back at the prescribed time. "I hope they get away from here, to tell you the truth," Weis said. "Getting away from football is a good thing—as long as they're at study hall Sunday night at 8 o'clock."

None of the players was made available to the media during the off week. But Weis, increasingly cognizant of the needs of the media and in an attempt to keep things fresh, made all of his assistants available for interviews before seven of them hit the recruiting trail following Wednesday's practice. The assistants were quick to credit Weis with the early transformation of the program, but it was clear that this was a special staff in its own right. Everyone understood his role, and it appeared, at least from the outside looking in, that there was no battle of the egos.

Players can tell when they're being coached by skilled teachers, and there was no mistaking the skill of Weis' staff. The Irish had become one of the most dangerous college football teams in the country. Although they weren't blessed man-for-man with the nation's most gifted athletes, this was a veteran team with more than enough capable football players to challenge just about any opponent. Perhaps the bigger change was that the Irish weren't losing to teams they should beat.

One of the most telling statistics of the first five games was Notre Dame's 75–19 scoring advantage in the second quarter. It was a sign of Weis' ability to adapt quickly to the style and tempo of the game. Although he grew noticeably restless when the "offensive guru" tag was thrown his way, he also knew he had a certain advantage over a lot of other coaches: "Where I've come from, I've seen a lot of things," Weis said. "You build up a reservoir of how to handle the things you're going to go against."

Weis also was learning off the field about the differences between coaching pros and coaching college kids. In the NFL, it was agents and players' wives who tried to get his ear. At Notre Dame, it was parents.

And he had learned to tune out certain complaints. "I don't mind when parents call me up to talk to me about a health issue or a school issue, because I'm on the same page with them on that," Weis said. "I want them to be healthy, and I want them to do well in school. Just don't call me up and say, 'Why is my kid second team?' Because he *deserves* to be second team, that's why. I get very testy when that happens."

He had also learned how to juggle the emotions of a bunch of teenagers and twentysomethings. "You reward the kids on show teams by taking them to the game," Weis said. "I do that every week. Last week, we took extra guys, eight players who I felt deserved to go on the trip for how they'd been working. They all want to play in the game, but they also want to *be* at the game. It's one way of rewarding players for working extra hard."

It worked the other way, too. When sophomore Justin Hoskins, a promising running back who arrived with Darius Walker in the fall of 2004, had a bad practice the week before the Washington game, Weis left him off the travel squad for the trip to Seattle.

"Justin didn't deserve to make the trip," Weis said bluntly. "He wasn't banged up. He just didn't deserve to make the trip last week. The way we do it, it's a week-by-week deal here. We don't put anyone on the shelf. We go by what we see each week. When the players realize you're going to treat them fairly week in and week out, there are very few gripes."

Weis was just as hard on himself when it came to grading his performance so far. "Right now," he said, "I'd give myself an incomplete."

After an intense training camp and five straight weeks of games, Weis was finally able to immerse himself in his job and still spend quality time with his family. Charlie Jr. was just a couple of steps from dad on game day—always close enough to offer some advice, which his father seemed to enjoy sharing with the media. When the Purdue game had already been decided and the fourth quarter began to drag, Charlie Jr. told his old man, "Let's run the ball and get out of here, Daddy."

The reply: "Charlie, I'm trying, I'm trying."

Winning was easy, especially for a 12-year-old boy. Losing was a little more difficult. "It's easy when you're the coach's son and you win," Weis said. "You go to school, and you don't have to worry about it. But when you lose, it's a lot harder on them than it is on us. You don't even realize it. Everyone asks, 'Hey, what happened?' Like he had something to do with us winning or losing. So when we win, he enjoys it more than I do. When we lose, he probably hates it more than I do."

So far, it had been pretty easy for father and son. The bitter loss to Michigan State was now a distant memory to Charlie Jr., especially with the anticipation of the undefeated and No. 1-ranked USC Trojans coming to town.

Undefeated. Ranked No. 1.

Just like Weis had hoped they would be.

......

Chapter 16

THE BEST DAMNED GAME OF THE YEAR — PERIOD

THE SOUTH BEND REGIONAL Airport was beginning to take on the hustle and bustle of Chicago's O'Hare as the October 15 game between top-ranked USC and ninth-ranked Notre Dame grew near. The number of private flights into South Bend increased from the typical 30 a day to more than 200 by the morning of the game.

Weis was concerned when he heard that 6,000 people had been turned away from the pep rally in the Joyce Center the night before the Michigan State game. Knowing that perhaps three times as many people would be denied entrance for the pep rally the night before the clash with the Trojans, the university decided to move the Friday night cheer-fest to Notre Dame Stadium, which could accommodate more than 80,000.

Weis, who had been emcee at the pep rally the night before the Michigan State game, wouldn't be doing the honors at this event. He was 0–1 as pep rally emcee, and he wasn't taking any chances.

Many Irish fans arrive in town for a home game on Friday, giving them plenty of time to take in the sights of the historic campus. But with Pete Carroll's Trojans coming to town—the two-time defending national champs with the 27–game winning streak—fans began trickling in even earlier than usual. Thursday was like a typical Friday in terms of the number of visitors on campus.

Rumors spread as to which celebrities would be on hand for the game. The most rampant speculation centered on rock stars Bruce Springsteen and Jon Bon Jovi, personal favorites of New Jersey native Weis'. Supreme Court justice Clarence Thomas and actor Martin Short had been spotted in South Bend. So had actor Jim Caviezel.

Caviezel had played Jesus in the film *The Passion of the Christ*, and had become friends with Notre Dame safety Tom Zbikowski and his family. In front of hundreds at the university's famous Grotto, Caviezel led the recitation of the rosary early Thursday evening. Later that night, in a much less solemn event, former Irish walk-on Daniel Ruettiger (the subject of the 1993 cult film *Rudy*) was roasted at South Bend's Palais Royale, with proceeds going to a local charity.

Photos of USC quarterback Matt Leinart and running back Reggie Bush were taped to sidewalks all over the Notre Dame campus for students to walk on during the week. "Wanted" posters featuring former Trojan great O.J. Simpson also were abundant. Scarlet and gold T-shirts emblazoned with the words "Trojans Break" were a favorite of many Notre Dame students—a good condom joke and a dig at USC all in one.

By Friday, the campus was overrun with Notre Dame and USC fans. The huge crowd may have been partly Weis' doing. He concluded his Thursday evening press conference by mentioning the exact time the USC team buses would be arriving at Notre Dame Stadium for their walk-through. Hundreds of people, mostly Notre Dame students, formed a tunnel at the north entrance outside the stadium tunnel in anticipation of the Trojans' arrival. Students held up signs to commemorate the event, and not all of them were friendly. A bed sheet with the inscription "27–1" was held off to the side of the tunnel of students.

When the Trojans arrived a few minutes before the 2:30 walk-through, a group of students rushed to the bus and began rocking it back and forth—not with any intent to injure anybody, but as a clear sign to the Trojans that they had truly entered enemy territory. For Notre Dame, however, one of the nation's more conservative educational institutions, it was tantamount to a riot.

Well before the scheduled 6 p.m. start of the pep rally, the entire west side of Notre Dame Stadium in front of the press box was filled. Students from each dorm sat together, making for rowdy individual cheering sections. Before it was over, an estimated 45,000 to 50,000 people had filed into Notre Dame Stadium.

At 5:35, a wooden Trojan horse was rolled into the stadium. As smoke billowed from its nostrils, the Notre Dame leprechaun popped out of its underbelly. A corps of drummers and bagpipers slowly emerged from the tunnel. A couple of the Notre Dame dorms put on skits for the pre-pep rally entertainment. (Morrissey Manor, for instance, parodied the fact that Leinart was taking a ballroom dancing course in this, his fifth year at USC.) Then the Irish Guard and band marched into Notre Dame Stadium, followed by Weis, his staff, and the Irish players in suit and tie, who lined up at midfield.

Weis introduced the emcee, the inimitable Rudy himself, who had made an appearance early Friday morning on ESPN's *Cold Pizza*, broadcast in the shadow of Touchdown Jesus. Irish seniors Corey Mays and Maurice Stovall spoke. Mays, normally one of the most reserved players with the media, fired up the crowd when he alluded to the previous year's 31-point loss to USC and what was going to happen the following day: "Last year, we were down. Tomorrow, the only thing that should be down are these two damn goalposts right here!"

One by one, Rudy introduced the special dignitaries who had come to cheer for the Fighting Irish. No—*sigh!*—Springsteen or Bon Jovi. But Weis' old undergraduate suitemate, Joe Montana, was on hand after having made an appearance at Notre Dame's Thursday practice. "Tomorrow, it's not about USC," Montana said. "It's about Notre

Dame and respect. With your help, we'll bring Troy to their knees one more time!"

Heisman Trophy winner Tim Brown, who had retired from the NFL several months earlier, was followed by a deadly serious Chris Zorich, who symbolized the intensity and hard-nosed approach during Notre Dame's national championship run in 1988. Zorich delivered an impassioned plea for the fans' efforts to match that of the players'.

And finally, it was the man of the hour, Weis. Speaking in a calm, measured tone, he talked about respect: respect for each other, respect for your opponent, respect for your elders, respect for humanity in general, and respect for the game of football. He also said that if all four facets of the game could come together—offense, defense, special teams, and the fans—it would "give us a chance at one of the greatest moments in Notre Dame history."

Weis concluded by reflecting on "that team from California," as if USC didn't deserve to have its name mentioned at a Notre Dame rally. Ten months earlier, during halftime of an Irish basketball game, Weis had made a very public wish. Now he reminded everyone that the wish had come true. "I said at that time that I hoped they were undefeated," Weis told the Notre Dame Stadium audience. "Well, they are." With that, the Irish left the field. A few fireworks were shot off on the east side of the stadium. The crowd didn't seem to want to leave, but when they finally did, the party continued outside Notre Dame Stadium right through Saturday.

WEIS WAS A SENIOR at Notre Dame on October 22, 1977, when Dan Devine's Irish surprised the nation by coming out in green jerseys. Since that day, when the No. 11-ranked Irish crushed No. 5 USC by 30 points, the Irish had come out in green jerseys as a surprise on six other occasions. (Not counting the balance of the 1977 season, when the Irish stayed in green jerseys at home and wore white jerseys with green trim on the road.)

Eight years later, in 1985, with the Irish leading USC, 27–0, at halftime, Gerry Faust switched his squad into green jerseys at the intermission.

Notre Dame won that game, 37–3, but the halftime change left a bad taste. It was contrived, particularly because no extra motivation was needed with such a large halftime lead. The green jersey had become a crowd groaner, not a crowd pleaser.

Lou Holtz waited until the January 1, 1992, Sugar Bowl to bring out the green. The Irish wore white jerseys with green numbers and beat Florida, 39–28. Under Bob Davie, Notre Dame lost to Georgia Tech in the Gator Bowl in green jerseys. The one time Ty Willingham tried it, in 2002, the unbeaten Irish lost to Boston College, 14–7. Willingham never did put the Irish in green jerseys again. It was time to let that tradition die.

Weis did not disagree. He was a pragmatic, by-the-book kind of guy and did not believe in gimmicks. In fact, he said so four days before the game when a reporter asked about the green jerseys: "That emotional stuff doesn't last too long. We're going to have to play our best game to have a chance to win. That's what I am hoping we do."

Each day of USC week, Weis offered a laundry list of reasons why the Trojans were the best team in the country. For all the success USC had enjoyed en route to back-to-back national championships in 2003 and 2004, this was an even better team, at least on the offensive side of the ball. At 5–0, the Trojans were averaging a remarkable 51 points and 640 total yards, including a nation-leading 291.2 yards rushing per game. Leinart was on pace to repeat as the Heisman Trophy winner—that is, if Reggie Bush didn't walk off with it. This was a nearly unstoppable unit, and keeping them off the field didn't help. Against Arkansas in the second game of the season, the Razorbacks ran 28 plays to USC's eight, yet the Trojans led, 28–0, en route to a 70–17 victory.

Asked midweek whether the Trojans had any weakness offensively, Irish defensive coordinator Rick Minter turned on his Texarkana sense of humor. "It's still just Wednesday, right?" he drawled. "We haven't figured this one out yet. The weakness probably comes when they bench all their starters in the last two minutes of the game."

Minter, quarterbacks coach Peter Vaas, and offensive coordinator/ running backs coach Mike Haywood were the only Notre Dame coaches with a firsthand taste of the USC rivalry. "The media, the rivalry ... this is legendary, it's tradition," Minter said. "It's a big, big game. We make no small talk about it. We want to be a part of the rivalry. We want to live up to the hype of the rivalry and play great on defense. The game has parallels to the Florida State game when I was here, when we were No. 2 and they were No. 1. As your season goes on, the more games you play and win, the higher the stakes become. If we win, the stakes get higher. If we're sitting here 1–4, you guys might not even be here, because we'd just be another notch on their belt."

Weis referred to Bush and his 245-pound running mate, LenDale White, as a "pick your poison" proposition. Each was averaging eight yards per carry. If the Irish found themselves facing second and 2 all afternoon, it could quickly turn into another 31-point loss—the margin of defeat the Trojans had pinned on the Irish in each of the previous three seasons. "We're going to have to play at the top of our game just to have a chance of winning," Weis said.

And yet, when going over the list of top USC players, including an offensive line that had been underrated amid all the talk of the great skill-position players, Weis quickly glossed over the Trojan cornerbacks. Carroll's squad was down to three scholarship cornerbacks, and seniors Justin Wyatt and John Walker had shown vulnerability throughout the early part of the schedule.

The Trojans scored 63 points against Hawaii, 70 against Arkansas, 45 against Oregon, 38 against Arizona State, and 42 against Arizona. That helped camouflage some but not all the glitches in the Trojans defense. Plus, USC had been flat at times in the first half, only to turn on the jets in the final 30 minutes to pull away. For instance, Oregon had a 13–0 halftime lead on the Trojans, and Arizona State had a 21–3 lead before USC surged ahead. The Trojans had made a habit of turning on the afterburners against the Irish, too, outscoring Notre Dame a combined 68–0 in the second halves of their three previous games.

During the bye week, Weis started the buildup by first breaking the players down. He wanted to make them feel the shame of losing to Notre Dame's greatest rival by 31 points in each of the previous three

years. "I basically told them, 'You're already down 31, let's see where
we can go from there. Let's see if we can close the gap a little bit,' " he
recounted. "Then you take the rest of the time, and all you do is try
to build up their confidence. You play to their psyche and get them to
believe ... The No. 1 job I had was to get them believing that they had
a chance to win the game."

As motivation, he showed the players the first half of the USC-
Arizona State game—but not the second, when the Trojans devastated
the Sun Devils.

The fact that USC was a 12-point favorite was not an issue. Weis
had been the underdog before. The Patriots were certainly the underdogs in Super Bowl XXXVI against the St. Louis Rams, Weis pointed
out: "We had no chance to win, right? We were supposed to get killed
in the greatest show on turf ... How did it turn out? *Ka-ching*! That
was a ring and a bunch of money. That's all I know."

And, contrary to his philosophy during Michigan State week, he
embraced the campus hoopla, as well. "I screwed up the last home
game," Weis admitted. "I made too much of avoiding all the distractions that come with a home game. I'm not going to make that
mistake again. I want them to enjoy the experience. We know it's a
big game. You can't pretend like it isn't. At the same time, I want
them to have fun doing it. There's no sense being miserable and
worrying about every little thing. Coming out flat against Michigan
State could be attributed to me talking about how many distractions
there were."

Embracing the distractions on campus included getting involved
in the insane demand for tickets. Weis estimated he received about
300 ticket requests, some of which came from "long-lost best
friends." Andy Reid, the Philadelphia Eagles head coach, got one of
the coveted tickets, since his team had a Sunday bye. Weis also had
tickets for Patriots owner Robert Kraft and Atlanta Falcons owner
Arthur Blank.

Juggling the activities and emotions of the week while preparing for
the game was not going to be easy for the players. On top of everything
else, they were in the midst of midterm exams. Holtz' teams regularly

played some of their most lethargic games at the tail end of midterms week. Several players missed practices during USC week to study.

As they had been carefully groomed to do, Notre Dame players had nothing but respectful things to say about USC during the week. After all, you'd have to be a fool to add motivation to a team with a 27-game winning streak. Or an emotionally cranked-up SoCal native who found himself caught up in talk that quickly got away from him.

The latter description fit Irish defensive end Chris Frome, who was born in Van Nuys and now lives in Saugus, 22 miles away. "I really wasn't interested in USC," the senior told the press. "I didn't like what they stood for. Notre Dame isn't very comparable to USC as far as campus life. I wanted to come to a place that's more focused on academics and more focused on a well-rounded individual. USC is just powerhouse football. That's what they do."

Meanwhile, Weis was trying to keep Quinn, and talk of the Heisman Trophy, in check. It had suddenly become obvious that a victory by Notre Dame, with Quinn spearheading the win, would make him a serious Heisman contender. It was the first true Heisman hype at Notre Dame since Raghib "Rocket" Ismail finished second in the 1990 balloting to BYU quarterback Ty Detmer. But Weis knew how to handle Quinn, especially since the Irish quarterback had a less than stellar practice earlier in the week.

"I went a whole day without talking to him, just to make sure he understood that he has to play at a high level all the time," Weis said. "I wouldn't call it mind games, but I think you have to make sure a player knows he can always play better. You can read the papers all you want, but if you spend too much time believing what you read and you start thinking you're better than you are, then you're setting yourself up for a fall."

Weis acknowledged that midterms might have had something to do with Quinn's loss of concentration, which is why the two of them were going to spend a little extra time together Friday night. "We already have a date where he and I can just sit down and chat," Weis said. "I'll treat him very similar to how I used to work with Tom Brady the night before a game. We might not talk just about the game. I'll make sure he's loose and focused. But more important, I want him to anticipate what I'm going to do.

There was a South Bend precedent for Weis' little heart-to-heart with his quarterback: "At the Michigan State game when we were down 21," said Weis, "I walked over to him and said, 'Okay, it's you and me, buddy. We can't make an error the rest of the way. Let's get it to a two-score game.' You have to talk very matter-of-factly in those situations. If you panic, it's over. If he panics, it's over. The most important thing is for him to be ready for Saturday so he can go out there and have some fun."

Quinn had been hardened by the beatings he had taken, particularly during his first year as a starter, in 2003, and Weis quickly determined that the quarterback he inherited was "all-day tough."

Quinn also benefited greatly from a system that had been formed around his skills. "This offense is a quarterback-friendly offense," Weis said. "Everything is built around the quarterback. We don't put anything in the offense that the quarterback can't handle. We don't put anything in the offense that the quarterback doesn't like. If we put something in the game plan and he doesn't like it, I throw it out."

For Weis, matching wits with Carroll was also nothing new. During the late 1990s, when Weis was the offensive coordinator of the Jets, Carroll was the head coach of the Patriots. Weis' team had come out on top three of the four times the two had faced each other.

Weis didn't want to talk about those past successes against Carroll. He wanted to keep the focus on the Trojans' success. "All I know is, Pete has been a head coach for a lot of years, and I've been head coach for five games," Weis said. "I have a long way to go. Pete has set the bar in college football over the last several years. Since he's come over from the NFL, he's gotten the USC program to the top of the game."

While Carroll and Weis exchanged compliments throughout the week, they did disagree on one thing: the use of instant replay. As the visiting team in a nonconference game, it was Carroll's call. The Trojans head coach declined the use of instant replay. "I just have never liked it," Carroll said. "I like the traditional way games go, the rhythm of it … I've never not trusted the officials. I've always thought the officials are busting their tails and doing the best they can do. I'm willing to live with the way the game is."

During the week, Weis had a couple of conversations with his former coaching cronies, including Bill Belichick. And for an impeccable resource on the Notre Dame-USC rivalry, "I had lunch with Ara Parseghian on Friday," Weis said. "You have these guys available as resources. They've done it; I haven't. So instead of kidding yourself and acting like you're the man, go to the guys who have done it and try to get some information on how to handle a situation like this one."

Carroll had his own confidants, including legendary UCLA basketball coach John Wooden. Clearly, Carroll and Wooden had something in common. Like Wooden, Carroll was coaching a genuine dynasty. So when the Trojans won their second straight national title and had a legitimate shot to claim a third in 2005, he called on Wooden—winner of 10 national titles in his last 12 seasons with the Bruins—for a little advice. "I asked him how much he thought it was necessary to change from year to year to keep things fresh," Carroll said. "He made me feel uncomfortable because he looked at me like I was crazy. He said, '*You* don't change from year to year; your *players* change. Their personalities direct the adjustments that you make.' And he's right. We have our philosophy, we do what we do, and we deal with the subtle changes that come by the nature of a new season."

What about home field advantage? Wouldn't playing in South Bend give Notre Dame an edge? Sure, but don't forget Michigan State. "We lost to Michigan State here, and I'd like to have that game back," Weis said. "But you just have to take that as a learning experience. I have to believe that I'm worth three points; that's what we lost by. I have to look back and say, 'What could I have done differently, both leading up to the game and during the game, that could have made a difference?' But you can't dwell on that sort of thing. In the grand scheme of things, if you're playing at home for the next five weeks, you better be trying to use that as an advantage and not be talking about how it's a disadvantage."

As was his custom, Weis gave the players a 10-point printout of what they would have to do to defeat the Trojans. He revealed two of those of those points to the media: No. 5 on the list was containing No. 5, Bush; No. 2 was to play for 60 minutes. He wasn't prepared to reveal the rest of the points yet. It left everybody wondering what was No. 1.

The list was like a map: follow it and it will lead you to victory. "The players are confident; they know they have a chance," Weis said. "A lot of times players say, 'We're going to win,' but they don't really believe it. I think our players believe they have a shot at winning the game, and that's half the battle."

When told that tight end Anthony Fasano had said "when we win" instead of "if we win," Weis smiled and responded, "That's a good Jersey boy there."

Irish nose guard Derek Landri knew a little something about playing for a dynasty and how to play against one. His De La Salle High School team in Concord, California, had strung together 151 straight victories, and Landri was a part of that streak. "A lot of times, USC will beat a team before they even play," Landri said. "The other team just psyches themselves out mentally. You have to know that they have a lot of talent, but we're just as good athletically. They're physical, but we've got to know that we're just as physical as they are. We know what we're capable of, and that's more convincing than anything."

Leinart watched the Irish game films and knew this wasn't the same Notre Dame team he had beaten before. "Some teams try to get pumped up and try to convince themselves, but down deep inside, they know they can't beat us," he said. "Notre Dame is a great team. I know their attitude. I know they believe they can beat us, and I know they won't be afraid."

With the extra week to prepare, most of the important work had been done by the time the Irish reached Thursday of USC week. Weis held the practice in Notre Dame Stadium, just to get a feel for the home field where the Irish hadn't played in a month. Down in the north end zone, well away from the team as it stretched and then broke into special teams work, Joe Montana tossed around a football with his kids. He was in town to see his two daughters, both students at Notre Dame.

Weis met with the media in the Notre Dame Stadium interview room after the Thursday practice. The last time Weis had stood at that same podium, it was after the overtime loss to Michigan State. But his team was ready for the Trojans, Weis declared, and no bad karma was going to sway his mood. "They're perky, they're not nervous, which is always a good sign," Weis said of his players. "You're always worried about them getting a little too intense with the magnitude of the game, but they're not."

Over the years, the Irish were 0–4 against USC when the Trojans were ranked No. 1. "I understand we're an underdog in this game," said Weis, "but it would be pretty cool to win, don't you think?"

Everyone was in countdown mode, including Charlie Jr. "He's geeked," Weis said. "He told me this morning, 'Dad, I'm starting to get a little nervous.' "

He wasn't the only one.

BY 7:30 A.M. ON Saturday, fans were already arriving outside of Notre Dame Stadium—*seven hours* before kickoff. ESPN's *College GameDay* was set up on the grass between the north stadium tunnel and Touchdown Jesus. Students with signs began to congregate in hope of snagging their moment of fame—a fleeting appearance on national television. One Irish fan wore a T-shirt that read "Notre Dame: 7 Heismans, 0 Murderers," with, naturally, a picture of O.J.

USC fans were out early as well. At one local McDonald's, half a dozen Trojan fans piled in to fuel up on McMuffins and caffeine. One fan showed off a tattoo on his right calf with the words "Southern Cal" wrapped around a Trojan head. Another had indelibly etched the rivalry on his body: a tattoo on his upper right arm depicted a Trojan sitting on a horse, holding the decapitated head of a leprechaun. Some fans obviously took the 77th meeting of the intersectional rivalry that had begun in 1926 a little more seriously than others.

And just in case the boisterous home crowd needed something else to scream about, Weis was sending his Irish out in green jerseys.

"Last summer, I said to our equipment manager, 'Let's order a batch of these green jerseys. Maybe we'll get in a bowl game,' " Weis later explained. "Everyone thought I was on drugs for saying that. But I felt this was like a bowl game."

It certainly felt like one.

THE NOTRE DAME STRATEGY was simple: hold on to the football as long as possible. And it almost worked, Notre Dame's time of possession—38:40 to USC's 21:20—kept the Irish, who never trailed by more than seven points, in the game.

Notre Dame took a 21–14 lead in the second quarter when Jeff Samardzija caught a 32-yard touchdown pass and Tom Zbikowski returned a punt 60 yards for a score, breaking three would-be Trojan tackles at the end of the run. USC tied the score, 21–21, in the third quarter. Two plays into the fourth, the Irish moved ahead, 24–21, on D.J. Fitzpatrick's 32-yard field goal.

Two missed opportunities would come back to haunt the Irish: a reception by Fasano that he fumbled after crossing the USC 20-yard line in the third quarter, and a missed field goal by Fitzpatrick from 35 yards out with the Irish clinging to a three-point lead in the fourth quarter. On the play before Fitzpatrick's miss, Quinn badly overthrew a wide open Asaph Schwapp on a third-down pass that likely would have kept the drive alive or, at the very least, given Fitzpatrick a shorter field goal attempt.

Bush, who finished with 160 yards rushing, scored his third touchdown of the day to give USC a 28–24 lead with 5:09 left in the game. But the Irish bounced back with an eight-play, 87-yard drive engineered by Quinn.

"I said to him right before the drive, 'Hey, buddy, this is the type of drive where legends are made,' " Weis told reporters after the game. "He looked at me, and he knew exactly what I was saying to him. I said, 'Here's what we're going to do: I'm going to call a bunch of three-step drops. We're going to throw a bunch of slants. We're going to get them reeling. We're going to get some yards with the run after the catch. I'm going to mix in a couple draws, and we're going to go down there and score. Be patient, we've got plenty of time.' And Brady executed it as well as could possibly be imagined."

The Irish led, 31–28, with 2:04 remaining. Had Notre Dame Stadium rocked and swayed any more, civil engineers would have been called in to check for structural damage. The Fighting Irish were only minutes away from beating the defending national champions, breaking USC's 27-game winning streak, and triggering the kind of celebration that hadn't been seen in South Bend for years. The sound was deafening.

All that separated Notre Dame from the victory was a USC fourth and 9 from the Irish 26-yard line. Hold USC here, and the game was likely done. There was just one flaw in that plan: Matt Leinart.

The unflappable USC quarterback looked at Notre Dame's coverage and called a fade route at the line of scrimmage. Moments after the ball was snapped, wide receiver Dwayne Jarrett slipped slightly past Irish cornerback Ambrose Wooden, and Leinart delivered the kind of Heisman-quality pass that even Weis had to admire. Jarrett, who was bothered by blurred vision in his right eye for part of the game, caught the ball almost in perfect stride, broke free of Wooden, and raced 61 yards to the Irish 13-yard line, where Wooden finally pulled him down.

Carroll could have chosen to kick a field goal, tie the game, and take his chances in overtime. But the man wore a wristband with the inscription "Compete." He was going for the win.

After a Leinart incomplete pass, Bush gained six yards, then five for a first down at the Notre Dame 2. Less then 20 seconds remained as Leinart rolled to his left and made a dash for the end zone. Just as Leinart reached the Irish 1, Mays drilled the USC quarterback, sending him into a propeller-like motion—and knocking the ball out of his grasp and out of bounds.

Where the ball left the field of play remains in doubt. But the stadium scoreboard operator didn't stop the clock. As the clock raced to zero, Notre Dame fans began to storm the field and Irish players started to celebrate. Without instant replay—remember Carroll's decision to ban reviews?—there was no way for the officials to determine where the ball went out of bounds, or even when.

Weis walked to the middle of the field for an explanation. A USC assistant coach came sprinting down the sidelines, out of the coaching box, to call a time-out—a time-out the Trojans didn't have. After a lengthy discussion, the ball was spotted inside the 1-yard line, and seven seconds were put on the clock.

As the referee prepared to restart the clock, Leinart, who had taken a physical beating from the Irish, looked to the USC sideline, where Carroll was signaling for him to spike the ball to stop the clock. It was, as Carroll later revealed, a decoy. Carroll wanted Leinart to sneak the ball in the end zone. Leinart, shaken by the pounding he had taken over the course of the game, wasn't sure he could make it. But when he turned to Bush, the star tailback encouraged him to run the play.

Leinart took the snap and was stopped on his initial surge up the middle. But then he spun to his left. (Spun? Maybe those ballroom dancing classes really had paid off.) He cleared the pile of bodies and lurched into the end zone—aided by an illegal shove in the back, later dubbed the Bush Push—with just three seconds remaining.

The Trojans missed the extra point, but the Irish only had time for a kickoff return that USC swarmed. The Trojans had survived, 34–31.

"I was in shock," said Leinart in the postgame press conference. "I didn't want to celebrate until the clock hit zero because who knows what can happen in three seconds. I'm still really speechless. I imagine this will go down as one of the greatest games ever played."

An exhausted Bush, who fought leg cramps near game's end, wept afterward. So did Leinart. "Just tears of joy," said Leinart. "I was more like, Oh my God, what just happened?"

Here's what happened:

- USC and Notre Dame played the Game of the Year … the Game of the Century (at least so far) … maybe the Game of All Time. It was that good. It was so good that the College Football Hall of Fame, right there in South Bend, should have immediately requested the game tape and started running it in a continuous loop, in perpetuity.

- Leinart (17 of 32 for 301 yards) and Bush (160 yards on 15 carries and three touchdowns) performed like, well, like Heisman Trophy candidates.
- Yes, the Bush Push was against the rules, but no way were the refs going to call it a penalty. It just wasn't one of those rules that officials routinely enforce.
- Brady Quinn completed 19 of 35 passes for 264 yards and a touchdown. For significant stretches of the game, it could be argued—and was, vociferously, and not just by Irish fans—that Quinn outplayed Leinart.
- Plain and simple, Notre Dame football was back: the Fighting Irish had returned to the Gold Standard.

No one who watched the game could dispute that a star had been born in Brady Quinn. Not that he cared about a Leinart–Quinn comparison. "Obviously, everyone is pretty disappointed, especially when you have a change of events like that toward the end," said Quinn. "Seeing how you want it to come out, and then seeing the exact opposite, all in a matter of minutes … People were pretty shocked and devastated."

"It's the highest I've ever been and the lowest I've ever been," said Fasano. "They don't give trophies for second place," said Darius Walker.

No one was in the mood for moral victories, including Weis. His postgame comments were calm and measured—until someone suggested that perhaps the Irish could take something positive out of the difficult defeat. "If you're looking for me to say this is a great loss, you'll be waiting a long time!" Weis snapped. "Losing is losing. That's the way it is. There are no moral victories. But I did tell them not to hang their heads. It was a gutsy performance out there. That was a street fight. It was two good football teams going at it, and for that, they should keep their heads held high."

After the Michigan State loss, Weis said that he had to account for three points. Now the Irish had dropped another three-pointer. But it would be difficult to point a finger at Weis. He had done everything humanly possible to make sure his team, his school, his fans were ready for everything the Trojans threw at them. By allowing USC just 21:20 possession time, Weis had provided his team with a near-perfect game.

Weis wasn't about to blame the officials for the loss, and he respect-ed Carroll's right to bypass instant replay—which likely could have helped in spotting the ball a yard or two farther back. Faced with the ball at the 2-, 2½-, or 3-yard line, Carroll might have settled for a field goal and overtime. But without replay, the officials spotted the ball where Leinart had been tackled.

Weis also agreed that Bush's "helping hands" for his quarterback on the goal line was against the rules. "Yes, it's illegal. Would I do the same thing? Absolutely," Weis said. "I don't want to be a hypocrite and say, 'Well, they were cheating.' Hopefully, any running back I had would be pushing right along with him."

Weis declined to second-guess the defensive coverage the Irish had been in when Leinart completed the fourth-and-9 pass to Jarrett. "We had a great call on, the perfect defense, and they just made a play," he said. "It was a fade route with a low success rate, but this time it hap-pened to succeed."

The bottom line? "You don't make excuses for losing the game," said Weis. "It comes down to the end. Do I wish the clock had run out? Sure, then I'd be happy right now, but it didn't, and I don't make excuses."

After addressing the media, Weis went to the USC locker room to offer his congratulations—and he took his son with him. "I said, 'Come on, Charlie, we're walking over to their locker room,' and he thought I was hallucinating," Weis said. "It's easy to be gracious when you've won a game. It's tough to be gracious when you've lost a game, especially a game as heartbreaking as that. I thought it was a good les-son for my son."

Weis walked the short distance from the interview room to the cramped visitors locker room. As he began speaking, USC players shushed each other. "That was a hard-fought battle," said Weis, stand-ing a few feet inside the door. "I just want to wish you luck the rest of the way. I hope you win out."

A few USC players clapped. Others nodded their heads. They knew Weis was right: it had been a hard-fought battle. And the dif-ference between the two teams, at least on this day, was as thin as a chin strap.

As Weis returned to the Notre Dame locker room, he explained to Charlie Jr. exactly why he had congratulated the USC players in person. It was as simple and as corny as good sportsmanship.

The gesture wasn't lost on Carroll, who was equally gracious and sincere in his praise of Notre Dame. As he prepared to board the team bus for the short ride to the airport, Carroll said, "We'll be happy to leave South Bend."

And then someone asked about those 31-point USC victories over Notre Dame in 2004, 2003, and 2002.

"That," said Carroll, smiling, "may be a thing of the past."

Chapter 17

······

THE SECOND
SEASON

COACH WEIS WASN'T BUDGING. At his Tuesday press conference, three days after the Best Damned Game of the Year—Period, Weis locked the door and threw away the key to the Trojans game.

A day earlier, in recapping the USC game, he answered all questions pertaining to the loss. He covered every agonizing detail. He calmly reflected on the impact of his squad's second three-point setback in his first six games on the job. And a casual aside from a reporter about what a "great game" it had been nearly got the questioner's head bitten off.

"It *might* be great if you won," Weis said through clenched teeth. "It's *not* a great game if you lost. You can say whatever you want; it's not going to be one of my greatest games, because we lost."

Now it was Tuesday, and not only was the USC game off-limits, so were the five games prior to that.

The "first season" was over.

Time to move on to the "second season."

"As you talk to our players and coaches this week, they're only going to be talking about the second half of the season," Weis bluntly told the press. "So don't bother asking questions about the first half because they won't be talking about it. We're looking ahead, not backwards."

With that, he opened the floor and was immediately flooded with questions about ... well, you know what.

It was understandable. The USC game had been one for the ages, and no one—well, almost no one—was ready to let it go just yet. And so, at their own risk, the reporters inevitably returned to what had taken place three days earlier. When a reporter began a question with, "Last week the defensive line ... " Weis cut him off. "I'm not talking about last week," he said. "I'm only talking about BYU."

Everybody got that?

Are you sure?

Okay, next question ...

DÉJÀ VU ALL OVER AGAIN

ACCORDING TO WEIS, THE October 22 game against Brigham Young would be Notre Dame's "home opener" of the second season. You either followed his calendar, or you followed none at all. "The media always wants to know what my message is," Weis said. "That's my message. We're getting ready for the first game of the second half of the season. BYU is our opponent."

Got that?

And it wasn't just the media that was getting stiff-armed on all discussion about the first six games. Notre Dame players had been alerted too. Weis had already spoken to senior linebacker Brandon Hoyte, one of the team captains, about the second season. "If I told you we were opening up this week against BYU at home," he asked Hoyte, "how fired up would you be?"

"Pretty fired up," said Hoyte.

"That's the way we're approaching the week," said the coach.

To get his message across to his players, he had to walk the walk, not just talk the talk. He had to sell the notion on all levels. His players were not going to hear him say one thing in practice and another thing at a press conference. Instead, what they heard was, "The players just finished midterms in the classroom, and they just finished midterms on the field. This is a midsemester break. We're fired up about the second half."

Indeed, Weis was grateful that it was mid-semester break at Notre Dame. While a typical work week gave him 20 hours with the team, he likely had more of the players' attention, since they weren't in class. He wouldn't overdo it. Not the two-a-day mentality again. After all, the season was already half over. But he had to grab their full attention.

The Cougars presented a bunch of new challenges for the coaching staff and players. Behind closed doors, Weis referred to BYU as a gimmick football team. They ran an offensive set similar to the one used by head coach Mike Leach at Texas Tech: a wide-open attack predicated on the pass, but punctuated effectively with the run. It had made Texas Tech into a bowl-caliber program and turned Leach into something of an offensive guru. BYU, using major elements of that offense, had surprised Colorado State—as well as the Irish coaching staff—by rushing for 274 yards in beating the Rams the same day the Irish fell to the Trojans.

First-year head coach Bronco Mendenhall, who had been the coordinator of the defense that held the Irish to 11 yards rushing in BYU's 20–17 season-opening victory in 2004, had brought in offensive line coach Robert Anae from Texas Tech to coordinate the Cougars attack.

Weis and his staff figured BYU quarterback John Beck would throw the ball all over the field, but the running back combo of Curtis Brown and Naufahu Tahi, a bruising 240–pounder, would keep the defense honest. The BYU offensive line averaged 310 pounds per man and aligned in unusually large splits, so the Irish defensive front would be faced with a distinct challenge.

On the other side of the ball, Mendenhall used an unorthodox 3-3-5 defense, which often confused offensive blocking schemes and added a high degree of uncertainty on blitzes. The scheme had totally flummoxed Notre Dame the year before.

Even BYU's special teams played "left-handed." Near the top of Weis' Top-10 list for the week was the need to protect Irish punter D.J. Fitzpatrick. Weis expected the Cougars to try to block every punt. BYU's punting scheme also was different in that it used three personal protectors for the punter, which allowed the seven men up front to focus on containing Tom Zbikowski, Notre Dame's talented returner.

Of minor concern at the moment, but laden with implications for the postseason, was the release of the season's first BCS rankings on October 17. Notre Dame hadn't budged from ninth in the AP poll—a generous ranking considering the Irish had lost twice. But they fell three spots to No. 12 in the coaches' poll, and now, in the first BCS rankings, a system in which six computer programs are put into play, the Irish were No. 16. Notre Dame would have to finish among the top 12 in the final BCS to qualify for one of the four BCS bowls: Rose, Fiesta, Orange, and Sugar.

Notre Dame's strength of schedule (or lack thereof) caused the drop. Purdue had just lost its fourth game in a row. Michigan State had just lost for the second straight week. Michigan had an unexpected three losses. Washington still had just one victory. Pittsburgh had lost four times. In other words, Notre Dame's opponents during the "first season" had not done so well, and that made the Irish victories seem much easier than the preseason prognosticators had anticipated. You couldn't explain to a computer how good the Irish had become. So Notre Dame's 4–2 record, despite its valiant effort against the mighty Trojans, left the Irish lucky to be behind "only" 15 other teams in the one poll that ultimately mattered.

"We're going to have to beat BYU this week to see if we can't get in the mix," said Weis with a tone of dismissal. "That's what I think.

We'd better beat them, because if we don't respect BYU, they're definitely a good enough team to come in here and beat us."

Notre Dame was still solidly in the BCS mix, especially if the Irish could run the table. And if the Irish beat 3–3 BYU, the remainder of the schedule wasn't exactly imposing. Tennessee was a solid team with an excellent defensive line, but certainly not up to the standards of recent squads. Navy was scrappy and ran a funky option attack, but Notre Dame would undoubtedly be favored against the Midshipmen. Syracuse was in the midst of one of its worst seasons in school history. And Stanford, against whom the Irish would end the regular season, was struggling to become bowl-eligible. No wonder Weis insisted on treating BYU as a major power.

He knew the post-USC week would be difficult emotionally and that there would be some sort of letdown. But the loss ultimately could put everything in perspective. "It would have been a bigger trap if we had beaten USC, because when you win a game like that, you're on such an emotional high that it's tough to bring people down," Weis said. "Now, obviously, we have to build everyone back up, but I think that we have a good plan, as far as the psychological approach to get that done."

The recovery wasn't limited to the players, either. "I've got to get the coaches on board too, because they're also human," Weis said. "They were as disappointed as the players were."

And then there were the Irish fans. Weis worked the campus into a frenzy for the USC game, beginning with the wild and crazy pep rally on Friday night. Now the disappointed students were just trickling back to South Bend after midterm break. Still, Weis had faith in them. "Any time a program plays hard for 60 minutes with a lot of guts and a lot of effort, they become favorite sons. People recognize the players giving it their all," he said. "The number one thing we need to do is come into our place this week and win at our own stadium on our own field in front of our own fans and get this program headed in the right direction."

Weis thought he could exploit BYU's 3-3-5 defensive scheme—and its tendency to blitz (that's what the Cougars had done so successfully a season earlier against the Irish at Provo)—not by running the ball, but by passing it early and often. It was a good plan.

On game day, the Irish opened with a five-wideout, empty-backfield, no-huddle offense, with Quinn throwing passes on 8 of the first 9 snaps of the first series. Notre Dame marched down the field to take a 7–3 lead on a 10-yard scoring pass from Quinn to Maurice Stovall. It was the first of a record 6 TD passes for Quinn as he completed 32 of 41 attempts for 467 yards.

The Irish ran the football just eight times for minus one yard in the first half, while Quinn completed 25 of 30 passes for 287 yards. Weis was amused when an NBC sideline reporter asked him at halftime whether the Irish would try to run the football more in the second half. "Not if they're going to bring seven or eight on every play," he said. "If they're going to do that every play, we're going to throw every play."

It was a day of records. Stovall broke a 39-year-old school record set by Jim Seymour by snagging 14 passes from Quinn. Stovall also broke the Irish mark for touchdown catches in a game with four. "People overlook how much time Maurice has put into working on his technique and watching film," explained Quinn, who was in a playful mood after the 49–23 victory. "He's such a good kid. A lot of people don't see how hard he's worked to have that success. Plus, he's a good singer and he dances pretty decent, too."

Jeff Samardzija scored twice, tying Derrick Mayes' 1994 mark of 11 touchdowns in one season. Quinn, who seemed determined to shred the pages of the Notre Dame record book one by one, also set a single-season mark by upping his touchdown pass total to 20.

Weis had counted on the BYU blitz and got it. He also got a near flawless performance by Quinn. Weis' game plan and Quinn's execution were in marked contrast to the 2004 season opener, when the Irish looked helpless and clueless against the Cougars. "This team plays with more confidence," said Mendenhall. "This team is more efficient. This team is more determined. And this team executes at a higher level."

Still, this team was far from flawless. BYU took the lead twice in the first quarter. The Irish committed 11 penalties. Weis bemoaned Notre Dame's shoddy tackling and poor ball security. Leading 28–10, the Irish allowed BYU to creep to within five at 28–23 with 5:38 left in the third quarter. But the Irish scored the final 21 points of the game to win by 26.

"It really wasn't that easy," said Weis of the wide-margin victory. "There were times when BYU moved the ball almost at will, but in the first half there must have been close to half a dozen third-down stops. When it's all said and done, they scored 23 points, and as wide-open as their offense is, that's not a bad number."

It had been a difficult week. No matter how much Weis emphasized putting the disappointment of USC behind them, he knew his players were suffering a severe letdown. So he was proud of the way they had responded once the whistle blew: "The game wasn't perfect, but that's usually true of a season opener." Even the opener of a second season.

As Weis spoke in the stadium interview room after the game, a television high on the wall was showing the Tennessee-Alabama game. The score was tied, 3–3, but the Crimson Tide eventually claimed a 6–3 victory. For Tennessee, which would visit Notre Dame in two weeks, the loss was the Volunteers' second of three straight losses. If Tennessee wanted to begin to salvage its season, a victory against the Irish would be a nice start, as well as sweet revenge—the Irish defeated the Volunteers the previous season, 17–13, in Neyland Stadium.

Notre Dame, meanwhile, had a BCS bowl bid to play for. The Irish could not afford to lose a single game.

BUSY BYE WEEK

THE PHYSICAL NATURE OF Notre Dame's victory over BYU—on the heels of the epic battle against Southern California—made the second bye week of the season a welcome rest. As he had done during the first off week, Weis allowed plenty of recovery time for his frontline players, who worked out in helmets, jerseys, and shorts during the three-day practice week: "They've now got an opportunity to get rested up, work on all the things we messed up, and get ready for Tennessee."

Certainly Weis had done everything in his power to prevent a letdown following the emotional loss to USC. But the Irish just weren't sharp against BYU. They simply couldn't get their bodies to perform at the highest level for 60 minutes.

Evidence of their wavering focus included what Weis called line-of-scrimmage penalties, such as false starts, that are more the result of a lack of concentration than anything else. The Irish fumbled the ball three times and generally protected the football poorly, including the defense. Cornerback Mike Richardson fumbled after an interception without any contact. And Zbikowski, near the end of a scintillating 83-yard interception return that put the last touchdown on the board, held the ball haphazardly over the final stretch of ground. "As good of a play as Zibby's was, I'm not the biggest fan of a guy getting 30 yards from the end zone and suddenly holding the ball like a loaf of bread," Weis said. "That doesn't fire me up."

As Tuesday's practice began, the backup offensive linemen formed a tunnel of bodies and beat the skill position players with blocking pads as they raced through the gauntlet holding footballs. Running back Justin Hoskins, who had missed the previous week for unspecified reasons, was told to hop to the front of the pack since, as Weis put it, he had been "on vacation for the past week." Immediately, Hoskins had the ball jarred loose.

Another backup who saw a little extra practice time was sophomore quarterback David Wolke. Quinn had established himself as a bona fide star. As his numbers increased, so did his chances of being invited to New York for the December Heisman Trophy presentation. The flip side of Quinn's success, however, was the lack of work afforded his backup. Should something happen to Quinn, the Irish would have to depend on Wolke, who had seen precious little time on the field.

Wolke played in garbage time against BYU, but was asked to do little more than run out the clock. He was on the field for a grand total of four minutes and 48 seconds—six snaps. He attempted zero passes, which made sense, since the Irish were up by 26 points.

Weis tried to keep Wolke sharp in practice situations by surprising him with reps when he least expected. "After the fundamental and technique period, right in the middle of team reps, I'll put him in there for a couple of plays," Weis said. "The role of the backup quarterback is to be ready at any time. I don't tell him when the reps are coming because that's the way it is in a game. The role of the backup quarterback, when you have a clear No. 1, is more mental than physical."

The Irish practiced on Tuesday and Wednesday of the bye week, and then seven Irish coaches, including Weis, hit the recruiting trail. Asked to comment earlier in the week about Notre Dame's recruiting effort, which included 19 verbal commitments at that point, Weis took aim at the so-called recruiting experts.

"First of all, what do they know?" Weis said. "All these gurus of recruiting ... I mean, give me a break. Do they sit there breaking down film, or are they just watching some kids playing a high school game? There's a lot that goes on in the evaluation process. But if you're asking me if I'm happy with everyone who has said they're coming? Absolutely."

The Irish had reached a point of caution in the recruiting class of 2006. Only about six spots remained open, and there were many more scholarship offers out there than there were openings. One potentially useful NCAA loophole: if a couple of Notre Dame's recruits started a semester early (January, not August 2006), they could be counted in the 2005 recruiting list—which had eight unfilled slots.

The signing date was February 1, 2006, but Weis had more patience for some than for others. When California kicker Kai Forbath slow-played the Irish, Weis dropped him and accepted a commitment from a local placekicker, Ryan Burkhart, of tiny Wakarusa, Ind. "If he's the right guy, we'll be waiting on him," said Weis. "That wouldn't hold true for everybody."

When a reporter suggested that the Irish would be a national title contender in 2006, Weis said, "To be honest with you, I'm disappointed we lost the two games we did and we're not in it right now. You're talking to the wrong guy if you think I'm ever going to think otherwise."

With the exception of the planned recruiting trips, it was shaping up to be a rather quiet second bye week. But then came the news that New York Giants owner Wellington Mara died. Mara, along with Bill

Parcells, had given Weis his first job in the NFL. Weis attended Mara's funeral after tending to recruiting on Thursday.

And then came an item on NFL.com that caused Notre Dame fans to reach for their heart medicine. "At least one NFL team has found out that it won't need the luck of the Irish to lure away Charlie Weis from Notre Dame," wrote the website's Adam Schefter. "Weis' six-year contract at Notre Dame includes a modest $1.5 million buyout, a number that caused one NFL head coach to remark this week, 'That's it?'"

What?

"That's it," Schefter continued. "The buyout means that, despite the fact that he has one of the country's most heralded recruiting classes coming in next season, Weis has positioned himself to leave Notre Dame after this season for the NFL if he so chooses. And he might. Should Weis cap Notre Dame's impressive season with a win over Tennessee and then another win in a major bowl game, he could vault himself into the No. 1 coaching prospect on the radar of NFL owners. As it is now, he already is way up there. One team, and quite possibly more, has been quietly investigating Weis behind the scenes and finding out what kind of head coach he would be, and they love him. NFL opportunities will be there for him. This doesn't mean he is going; it just means it is under consideration. But this is a developing situation sure to get lots of attention in the weeks to come."

Schefter's comments were sheer speculation. Every coach, college and pro, has a buyout clause in his contract. The fact that it was "only" $1.5 million did not mean that Weis was any closer to leaving Notre Dame than the day he signed the contract with the Irish. Were certain NFL teams interested in him? Undoubtedly, considering his track record.

Was there a shred of hard evidence to suggest he was thinking of leaving Notre Dame?

No.

The facts? At least one NFL team asked about Weis through his agent, Bob LaMonte—who at the time also represented eight NFL head coaches (Jon Gruden, Mike Holmgren, Andy Reid, John Fox, Mike Sherman, Mike Martz, Jim Mora Jr., and Mike Nolan). In just seven games, two of which the Irish lost, Weis had begun to establish himself as a coaching heavyweight. Few college football experts had expected Notre Dame to have more than three wins after its first seven games. Instead, the Irish were 5–2 and ranked No. 15 in the most recent BCS release. Anything beyond that was pure—or impure—speculation.

Weis was aware of the speculation. And, as usual, he had anticipated it and made a plan. "The week of the first bye, Kevin White and I sat down and I said there would be a possibility that people would start talking about things like the NFL," said Weis. "I wanted to confirm to him that he never had to worry about there being any interest on my part."

When the NFL.com story hit, Notre Dame's plans to announce the extension of Weis' contract were already well in the works. By Saturday, October 29 (the second bye weekend), Notre Dame made it official: Weis was now signed through 2015.

"In a very short period of time, Charlie has clearly and impressively demonstrated the ability to take the Notre Dame program where we all want it to go," said White in a statement released by the university. "Whether you talk about on-field results, off-the-field understanding of the Notre Dame athletics and academic culture, recruiting, public relations, or any other area, Charlie already has indicated that he possesses the abilities to position our program to compete at the elite level of college football."

Not a half-bad midterm report card.

"We're excited that Charlie wanted to extend his commitment to Notre Dame, combined with the university's interest in furthering its relationship with him." White continued. "All of us are enthusiastic about what the future holds for Notre Dame football with Charlie Weis as our head coach. We're confident that we've got the best coach in America ensconced at his alma mater for the remainder of his career."

Weis was equally enthusiastic.

"Since the first day I arrived at Notre Dame as head football coach, one of my primary goals was to be able to see this job through to the time my son, Charlie, would graduate from the University of Notre Dame and to stay in this position until I retire," he said. "By restructuring this contract, adding an additional five years, this allows me to accomplish that goal."

Irish fans might think the Schefter article helped seal the deal. But that was not the case. "When I first came here, I made it pretty evident from the day I walked in the door that we were doing it on a permanent basis, not on a quick fix or to buy some time to go somewhere else. My intent was the same from the day I got here. This puts an end to any of those questions and rumors."

Clearly, the most pressing issue regarding the timing of the announcement was securing the recruits who had already committed and those Weis and his staff were still pursuing. Weis said none had asked him about the possibility of him leaving for the NFL. But he knew it would only be a matter of time before they did, particularly with the story quickly spreading nationally.

"Any time people put out stories that are unsubstantiated, they have to be addressed sooner or later," Weis said. "The best thing to do was to make it sooner and get it out of the way. I'm not big on distractions, and yesterday I eliminated myself from being a distraction."

The next day, ESPN's Chris Mortensen reported that Weis' new contract was in the $30–40 million range for the 10-year period. But Weis was not wrong when he said, "If it was about money, I'd be coaching in the NFL." There were also other ways to make the big bucks. By Weis' count, he had turned down 17 book offers. He also told his agent that he wasn't interested in the seven-figure offer for his cooperation and involvement in a movie about his rise to the Notre Dame football throne. Some day? Perhaps, but only after he had actually accomplished something.

Some observers and more than a few Irish fans wondered why Notre Dame offered a contract extension to Weis after just seven games. Jason Whitlock, a columnist for the *Kansas City Star*, pointed out that Willingham had gone 8–0 to start his first year with the Irish, and no contract extension was offered to him. Whitlock then dropped the R-word—racism—and called the new Notre Dame coach, "the Great Weis Hope."

The truth was, Weis' extension probably had more to do with the reported interest of NFL teams and the groundwork he had put in place since December. Weis hadn't earned his extension based on seven games, but on all the things he had accomplished in the 11 months since he was hired—including putting together an outstanding recruiting class.

Asked on Sunday about his views regarding the racism accusations against Notre Dame, Weis steered way clear of the debate. "I learned a long time ago, long before I got into the business world, to be color blind," he said. "Anyone who is a success in life better practice that philosophy."

As for the university's detractors, someone was always trying to declare Notre Dame to be the evil empire. Only at Notre Dame could an athletic department that ranked among the top three in graduating African-American athletes be accused of racial injustice.

BEWARE THE WOUNDED ANIMAL

THE ARRIVAL OF THE Tennessee Volunteers, with their 78.3 winning percentage under head coach Phillip Fulmer and a record of 75–5 in November over the past 20 years, brought plenty for Weis and his Fighting Irish to worry about. The Volunteers would enter Notre Dame Stadium with a 3–4 record, including three straight losses for the first time since 1992. Notre Dame had defeated 9th ranked Tennessee, 17–13, the previous year, but it took an interception return for a touchdown by since-departed linebacker Mike Goolsby to pull it off. The Irish had managed just 216 yards total offense.

Notre Dame had a much more dangerous offense in 2005, ranking fifth in the nation in passing, ninth in total offense, and 11th in scoring. But the Volunteers were led by a massive, talented defensive line and a cat-quick linebacker corps. Tennessee was struggling, but it was still a formidable opponent.

Now No. 8 in the AP poll and No. 14 in the BCS rankings, the Irish could take a huge step toward solidifying a BCS bowl bid with a victory over Tennessee. Only Navy, Syracuse, and Stanford remained on the regular-season slate. If Notre Dame could just put its two weeks of preparation time to good use and create enough offense against

Tennessee's vaunted defense, the path to a postseason bowl was relatively clear.

Weis knew his players respected Tennessee, but he was a bit concerned about the psyche of his squad if they dwelled on Tennessee's 3–4 record. The Volunteers had played four teams that were ranked in the top 10 in one poll or another when the game was played. They defeated LSU on the road, but lost to Georgia, Florida, and Alabama, struggling mightily on offense in the process. Tennessee was averaging just 16 points per game, which was 108th in the country. The Volunteers ranked 99th in total offense, 101st in passing efficiency, and 98th in rushing offense.

Following Tennessee's 16–15 loss to South Carolina, Fulmer assessed the damage. "What you saw out there was unacceptable," he said. "In my 13 years here, we haven't had a season like this one. It's been tough."

It was all so un-Tennessee-like. And yet, with victories against the Irish, and then Memphis, Vanderbilt, and Kentucky, the Volunteers could salvage their season and finish 7–4.

On the Monday of Notre Dame week, Tennessee offensive coordinator Randy Sanders announced, with Fulmer's blessings, that he was stepping down as playcaller for the remainder the season. Sanders, 40, a former Tennessee quarterback who never left the Volunteers program after his eligibility expired, was staying on as quarterbacks coach, with Fulmer calling the plays while consulting with the rest of the offensive coaching staff.

"This isn't a response to criticism," Sanders said. "This is a response to what I see on the field. Somewhere along the line, things have gotten out of kilter a little bit offensively this year. I don't necessarily think it's all my fault. But the fact is, it is my ship."

Actually, it was Fulmer's ship with Sanders directing a good portion of the voyage, and Fulmer wouldn't let Sanders take all the blame. "This has been an extremely difficult season for everyone, especially Coach Sanders," Fulmer said. "I want it to be understood that by no means are the results of the season any one person's fault."

Weis mulled over the turn of events in Knoxville with an abundance of caution. The coaching change could energize Tennessee, or further demoralize it. As for the record, Notre Dame assistant Mike Haywood called the Volunteers, "the best 3–4 team in the country." Haywood meant it as a compliment, but some fans in Knoxville compared it to being called the world's tallest midget.

"They very easily could have won every game they've played," Weis said. "So don't talk to me about Tennessee being 3–4 because this team could easily be 6–1 or 7–0, and we're definitely concerned. All you have to do is watch the tape. This is the scariest 3–4 team that you're ever going to go against because they're capable of beating everybody every week. They know it, and our guys know it too."

Weis would be facing a challenge as a playcaller. Tennessee defensive ends Parys Haralson and Jason Hall had so far combined for 20 tackles for lost yardage and 10.5 sacks. After leading the SEC with 18.5 tackles for loss, interior defensive lineman Jesse Mahelona was named an All-America by *The Sporting News* as a junior, and was named one of 12 semifinalists for the 2005 Lombardi Award. With speed and talent at linebacker, led by Kevin Simon and Omar Gaither, and a secondary with an abundance of athleticism (although lacking size and proven play-making ability), the Volunteers ranked fifth in the country in rushing defense, allowing just 2.7 yards per carry. No Tennessee individual opponent had rushed for 100 yards; Georgia's Thomas Brown came the closest with 94 yards. The Volunteers allowed just three runs of 20 yards or more in seven games, and a mere three touchdown passes—about the same number Quinn was averaging per game.

Looking at it all, Weis downplayed the problems Tennessee faced with Fulmer calling the plays for the first time since his coordinating days: "There'll be no difference. It's just like if I turned the playcalling over to someone else. It would be the same list of plays; only the order in which you call them would be different. It's just a matter of how you call the plays on game day, and we won't know that until after we play the game."

With temperatures expected to be mild the Friday before the Tennessee game, another huge pep rally crowd was anticipated. The university announced that pep rallies for the final three home games would require a ticket; they were free, but fans would have to stand in line to get them.

Recruits were beginning to stand in line too. Notre Dame was becoming a cool choice again for the top prep stars. With 19 verbal commitments and dozens of big-name players still strongly considering the Irish, Weis vowed that Notre Dame's recruiting fortunes would be far richer—and more consistent—than they had been under the most recent coaching regimes. "I don't intend to be a one-year wonder in recruiting," Weis said. "I intend this to be an every-year, passionate thing."

Weis had taken a different approach to recruiting than had his predecessors. He hit the recruiting trail hard after arriving from the Patriots, and then spent the bulk of May on the road, laying the groundwork for the class he would sign on February 1, 2006.

He chose carefully, evaluating not only a player's talents but also his personality and his ability to accept tough love. That particularly came into play with the quarterback, who received the largest and toughest doses of that love.

Weis readily admitted that some top-rated prep quarterbacks fell off Notre Dame's recruiting list because he didn't believe they had what it took to withstand his exacting demands. "I'm a tough coach, and the quarterback is not absolved from being given up in front of the team," Weis said. "At a lot of places, the quarterback is off-limits when it comes to constructive criticism. Heaven forbid you might hurt his feelings. Well, that's not me."

Quinn fit Weis' mold for a quarterback. Not only could he handle constructive criticism, but he also had the intelligence to decipher the plan on the field, on the run. "Sometimes football players can't transfer intelligence to football intelligence," Weis said. "Where a guy might be a great interview, he might be a dumb football player. Brady is a very bright football player, and he's really fun to be around because you usually only have to tell him something once. Sometimes when a player makes a mistake and you correct him, he gets defensive. When Brady makes a mistake, he understands why you saw it differently than the way he saw it."

In an interview on NBC the Thursday before the Tennessee game, Quinn explained things from the players' point of view. "You can call it tough love, but I really think our team has started to appreciate it," Quinn said.

And respond to it. The Irish scored on their first two drives against Tennessee, which was a season first for Notre Dame. They led 21–10 at halftime, survived a Volunteers comeback to tie the score in the third quarter, and scored 20 unanswered points in the final quarter to pull away to a 41–21 victory.

Quinn, Samardzija, and Zbikowski were the stars. Quinn completed 20 of 33 attempts for 295 yards and three touchdowns. Samardzija caught seven passes for 127 yards and one touchdown. And Zbikowski scored twice, once on a 78-yard punt return and later on a 33-yard interception return.

"He lifted my spirits," Weis said of Zbikowski. "Any time you're not an offensive player and you're responsible for two touchdowns, that's a major factor in the game."

Once again, the Irish defense came up big, holding Tennessee scoreless over the final 16:49. The offense came through with big plays when the Irish were threatened. Fitzpatrick kicked two fourth-quarter field goals and Zbikowski had that electrifying punt return.

"Today we got production on all three levels," Weis said. "There was a lot of hidden yardage today—interception and punt return yardage. I have a lot of confidence the defense can make big plays. The offense is not going to lay 50 on 'em every time. It's going to have to be a group effort. You don't pull away from an opponent because one side of the ball does well. It's because all three phases start clicking."

Weis was showered with a bucket of water after the game for the first time as Notre Dame head coach. "I'm going to get the videotape and find out who did that," Weis smiled. "Anyone want to give him up now?" By the morning after the Tennessee game, Weis had his video evidence: defensive linemen Trevor Laws and Justin Brown had been caught on tape wet-handed. "I've done my research," Weis said. "We'll address that later this afternoon."

While the Irish certainly didn't play their best football game of the season, they had shown degrees of resiliency and toughness that made Weis proud. "The fact that we didn't give up any points in the fourth quarter and that we scored showed how the mentality of the team is changing," said Weis of Notre Dame's 20–0 fourth-quarter run. "Even when the game was tied in the third quarter, the defense stiffened, and they played very good ball in the fourth quarter. There was no panicking on the sideline. We kept our composure and then we pulled away. That's what good teams are capable of doing."

Weis no longer questioned his team's willingness to go the distance. "We're far from perfect," Weis said. "Our coaching staff isn't error-free. But the one thing you can say about this team is that they're playing hard and they're playing hard for 60 minutes."

The same could be said of Notre Dame's next opponent, Navy. In fact, the Midshipmen were willing to go the extra mile, by land or by sea.

THE STREAK

NOTRE DAME'S RELATIONSHIP WITH the military academies is deeply rooted, both on the football field and on the Notre Dame campus, with ties dating back to the days of Knute Rockne.

The Irish first played Army in 1913, when Rockne teamed with his roommate, quarterback Gus Dorais, to stun the Cadets, 35–13. They were helped by a revolutionary invention: the forward pass.

In 1927, Notre Dame played its first game against Navy. Since then, the rivalry, if you can call it that, has been ruled by the Irish. Going into the upcoming game, Notre Dame had a 68–9–1 series advantage and a mind-boggling 41–game winning streak against the Midshipmen.

As the 79th game between Notre Dame and Navy approached, the two programs announced an extension of the series through 2016. Every other year, the game was played in Notre Dame Stadium. Navy's "home" game against Notre Dame was played at various neutral sites across the country, so as to accommodate the larger crowds that wouldn't fit into the 36,000-seat Navy-Marine Corps Memorial

Stadium in Annapolis, Md. In recent years, venues included Giants Stadium in East Rutherford, N.J.; Veterans Stadium in Philadelphia; Jack Kent Cooke Stadium in Maryland; the Citrus Bowl in Orlando; and Croke Park in Dublin, Ireland, where the series would be returning in 2012.

Weis had an appreciation for the military academies, particularly the Naval Academy, because of his connection with Bill Belichick, whose father, Steve, had coached at Navy for 34 years (1956–1989) under seven head coaches. In addition, Weis' old boss, Bill Parcells, had coached at Army and Air Force.

Much like BYU, the Naval Academy had a gimmick: triple-option football, which negated the physical advantage of an opponent by forcing the defense to play strict, assignment football. That in itself was reason enough for the Irish players to keep focused on the game. That, and the consequences of losing to Navy. Nobody wanted to be on the team that ended the streak.

"They *better* be thinking that way," said Weis.

Navy was different from most football teams, both in terms of their commitment to excellence and the absence of a breaking point. If the game turned out to be close, Navy wouldn't quit. If it was one-sided, Navy wouldn't quit.

"They have a different mentality than we have about everyday life," said offensive lineman Bob Morton. "When they go out and compete, it's fun for them and they're going 110 mph. It doesn't matter how many times they hit the dirt; they're going to get right back up. That's the kind of personality they bring to the football field. As a football player, you always think you can get that one last hit where you go, 'Okay, the game is over.' With these guys, it never happens."

"My only experience against an academy is that they're top-of-the-line guys, they play hard every snap, and they do their assignments," said Samardzija. "They're not freelancers. You've got to understand going into the game that they're going to give it their best shot, no matter what."

Facing Navy head coach Paul Johnson's well-structured game plan, Weis knew his offense would have a limited number of possessions, probably single digits. So the offensive goal was ambitious: score on every possession. No matter what happened against the triple option, Navy wouldn't be able to outscore the Irish if Quinn & Co. took care of business.

The defense would have to do its part as well. "When you play Navy, it's an assignment game because if anyone breaks down with their triple-option threat, you can get exposed by the quarterback. You can get exposed by the single back. You can be exposed by either slot," Weis said. "If you say that one guy is more important than the other when you're playing against an option team, you're sorely mistaken. Everyone has to execute his assignment. If not, you'll lose."

But Notre Dame also had some advantages. One of them was Weis' ability to put himself in the position of the players and see the game through their eyes. He had mentioned after the Tennessee game that he agreed with Quinn's calls at the line of scrimmage most of the time, because he was inclined to view the game the same way Quinn viewed it. "Even some of the times I've disagreed with him, I never make a snap judgment," Weis said. "I try to see the game from the quarterback's eyes. For any good coach, it's really important to try to look at the game that way."

Weis developed his technique by watching the end zone and the sideline angle of a play. When he reviewed a Notre Dame game tape, he saw each play from both angles, back to back. By watching both angles, he could get closer to seeing what the player saw.

Quinn laughed at the notion that Weis patiently waited to hear the quarterback's explanation before jumping to a conclusion. "If I do something that is completely unorthodox or something that has no rhyme or reason in our game plan," Quinn said, "he doesn't necessarily look for my input."

But Quinn did buy into the notion that Weis saw things in a way most coaches didn't. "He was talking about a particular route that Jeff Samardzija was running," Quinn said. "I said something to Coach along the lines of, 'Why didn't Jeff do this?' And he said, 'The way the cornerback was playing him, it's not like he could get inside, so he couldn't run the route that way.' I asked Jeff about it, and Jeff said the exact same thing. Coach was looking at that play through Jeff's vision."

Going into the Navy game, the Irish were ranked No. 7 in the AP and coaches' polls, and had moved up to No. 11 in the BCS rankings, thanks to losses by Florida State, Wisconsin, UCLA, and Virginia Tech.

Making good use of their tremendous size advantage up front, the Irish quickly took a 7–0 lead against Navy on a leaping touchdown reception by Stovall. But Navy responded with its own lengthy scoring drive—16 plays, 68 yards—and the tempo suddenly favored the Midshipmen.

With the Irish leading, 14–7, late in the first half, Navy entered Irish territory and was primed to either tie the game or pull to within four points heading into halftime. At the worst, the Midshipmen would get the ball to open the second half trailing by just a touchdown. But when Navy quarterback Lamar Owens' pitch was fumbled, linebacker Corey Mays recovered with 2:29 left in the half. Three plays later, running back Darius Walker scored. Following a Navy punt, the Irish added another touchdown on a pass to Fasano with 40 seconds remaining. A close game had become a three-touchdown advantage for the Irish.

Navy went on another long touchdown drive to start the second half. But Quinn soon hooked up with Stovall for his second and third touchdown receptions of the game. Quinn finished the game with four touchdown passes—and his first interception in 131 passes—en route to a 42–21 victory.

After the Irish had won their 42nd straight game against the Navy, the Notre Dame players began drifting to the southeast corner of the stadium, where several thousand Midshipmen stood in the stands. Before the Irish saluted the home crowd by raising their gold helmets in front of the student body, the Notre Dame players stood shoulder-to-shoulder with the Navy players as the band played "Navy Blue & Gold."

The show of solidarity had been orchestrated by Weis.

Quinn's 284 yards passing moved him past Jarious Jackson for the single-season yardage mark at Notre Dame. Quinn also passed current director of personnel development, Ron Powlus, on the school's all-time touchdown total list with 53.

The Irish had only nine offensive possessions against Navy, but they scored six times while holding Navy's offense to more than 40 yards under its rushing average. The defense was stingy when it had to be.

Weis, for his part, admitted that he had been cranky all week, just to keep his players on edge. He hadn't cared what his team thought about his midweek mood, and he hadn't cared what they thought about being in full pads at the end of the week. "It's irrelevant," Weis said. "You never let them think that you're happy, because then they start to loosen up a little. You just stay on them and keep your foot on their throat the whole time. It was not a good week for them."

"He was making his paycheck this week, let's say that," Mays said diplomatically.

I PLEDGE ALLEGIANCE

WITH SYRACUSE COMING TO town burdened by seven straight losses under first-year head coach Greg Robinson, Notre Dame's last home game didn't appear to be much of a threat to its bowl chances. The Irish, winners of three straight, were on a direct path to the Fiesta Bowl. It would be their first appearance in the Tempe, Ariz., bowl since a 41–9 thrashing at the hands of Oregon State following the 2000 regular season, Davie's most successful at Notre Dame.

Installed as five-touchdown favorites for the Syracuse game, the Irish figured to send their 34 seniors (not all of whom had used up their eligibility) out on a positive note. Weis was publicly cautious, of course, reminding everyone about Robinson's two Super Bowl rings as defensive coordinator with the Denver Broncos in 1997 and 1998, and about an Orange defense that ranked sixth in the nation against the pass.

During the week, Weis received verbal commitments from three acclaimed prep prospects. Pledging their allegiance to Notre Dame were linebacker Morrice Richardson from Atlanta, offensive tackle Chris Stewart from Klein, Texas, and wide receiver Richard Jackson from Clermont, Fla. The commitments meant Notre Dame had 22 pledges—a staggering total compared to where the Irish had recently been at this stage of the recruiting process. Never had the Irish been this far ahead of the game in terms of verbal commitments, with the national signing date still some two and a half months away.

NCAA regulations prevented Weis from talking about the specifics of the commitments. But he could speak in general terms, and clearly the Irish were in position to sign one of the top five classes in the country. One list had the Irish at No. 2.

Why the dramatic turnaround? "We're winning, and kids look at that," said Weis. "And there's now a familiarity with our program. It's the same school, but it's a different program."

Weis' plan for the final home game was to get each of the 34 seniors into the lineup against the Orange. This was important to Weis. The seniors, in particular, had made the greatest sacrifices during the transition from Willingham to Weis. They had put in four, and in some cases, five years with Davie, O'Leary, Willingham, and now Weis, the most recent "new guy." Weis was well aware of their important role in converting the Irish into a legitimate BCS contender, and he hoped to salute them all.

"It's been a pretty wild ride when you consider we had, what, three and a half coaches?" said fifth-year senior guard Dan Stevenson. "It's definitely not what I expected when I came here, but there's no better way to end it." With just Syracuse, Stanford, and a bowl game remaining, Notre Dame's seniors had a chance to win 10 games this season and finish their careers on a high note.

For Stovall, who was playing his final game at Notre Dame Stadium, the 2005 season had been a dream fulfilled. "I'm a little sad, and I'm also excited," he said. "I'll try not to fall into that trap. If I'm thinking this is my last game, I won't be focused on executing what I have to do for us to win."

Stovall had a special place in Weis' heart. Before the 2005 season, Stovall appeared to be on the verge of letting a promising career disappear. After catching 18 passes as a freshman, including a critical touchdown at Michigan State that earned him a spot on the cover of *Sports Illustrated*, Stovall's career fizzled out. He caught 22 passes as a sophomore and 21 as a junior. But most of his damage in 2003 came in one game — a loss to Purdue. In 2004, he missed three games with injuries. His toughness was questioned. His commitment was questioned. His future in football after Notre Dame looked pretty bleak.

All that changed under Weis. Stovall, along with Samardzija, had established himself as a legitimate NFL prospect. "Maurice Stovall is one of my favorites," Weis said. "First of all, I love him as a kid. He can play for me any day on any level. If I was coaching on the next level, he could play for me there too. For me to say that, I shouldn't have to say any more."

One senior who would miss out on the experience of running into Notre Dame Stadium for the last time was fifth-year senior fullback Rashon Powers-Neal, who had been suspended from the team before the USC game for unspecified reasons. Asked if Powers-Neal might rejoin the squad for the final home game, Weis acknowledged that it had been discussed. But Notre Dame's goal-line back early in the season would not dress for the final home game.

Another issue arose at the tail end of Navy week when *Chicago Sun-Times* columnist Greg Couch broached the subject of Weis' weight and health. "He seems to be gaining weight. A lot of weight. And fast," Couch wrote. "Maybe it's none of our business, really, but while Weis seems right for Notre Dame, is Notre Dame right for Weis? Is coaching?

"He is the most prominent, most visible coach in college football, with a fresh, new 10-year contract worth up to $40 million. Yet he seems to be backsliding into a condition he once thought of as life-threatening."

Couch quoted rotund former Utah Utes basketball coach Rick Majerus, who said he couldn't speak for Weis, but that his own nocturnal urge to study tape lent itself to some late-night eating binges. Couch said he wasn't "pointing fingers at Weis for his weight." But he added, "It's a health issue. And he's the ultimate reflection of a very real problem in sports coaching."

The story mentioned the two heart attacks that Weis' father had suffered and that he died at age 56. Weis was now 49. Couch also noted the gastric bypass surgery Weis had after being "shocked at how huge he had become, more than 340 pounds," when he saw pictures of himself at the Super Bowl. The surgery and its effects on the body were described in great detail.

The story struck a nerve with Weis, who relayed to the *Chicago Sun-Times*, through Notre Dame's sports information department, that since he wouldn't be talking to anyone from their newspaper in the near future, there was no need for their beat reporter, Jim O'Donnell, to bother asking any questions for the rest of the season.

Weis was more concerned about game-planning for Robinson. The two had matched wits four times since Weis had become an offensive coordinator for the New York Jets in 1998. Weis' team won three of the four times and averaged 25 points per game against Robinson's Denver Broncos and Kansas City Chiefs defenses. "He's a very good coach, and he's very close with Pete Carroll," said Weis of Robinson. "Their philosophies are very similar. He coached in the NFL for 14 years. He's got multiple Super Bowl rings. This guy has been running defenses at a high level for a long time."

Still, Syracuse was riding in on a seven-loss streak. Yet Weis' theme of the week was Notre Dame's 26-point loss to the Orange that ended the 2003 season. Weis focused on the poor effort of the Notre Dame players that day in Syracuse. And he didn't mind hinting at the concept of getting revenge against the Orange, without actually using the word.

At that 2003 game in the Carrier Dome—played one week after Notre Dame beat Stanford by 50 points—it was obvious several of the Irish players gave up in the second half. Syracuse running back Walter Reyes scored five touchdowns for the Orange, and the Irish limped home with a 5–7 record for the season. "I have a seven-minute tape I'm going to show them from the 2003 season, and I think that will be a very humbling experience for them and a quick reminder that this game is about playing Syracuse as well as being respectful to the seniors," Weis said. There would be zero tolerance for undisciplined football.

"It was surreal," said Morton of the Syracuse tape. "At first it felt like I was just watching a really bad football team. At the end, Coach asked us, 'How many people were actually there?' All of a sudden my hand went up and I realized, 'That missed blocked there, that miscommunication there, was something that was on my shoulders.' It was really humbling.

"We're in a different spot right now, but the same thing can happen. Syracuse has a lot of the same personnel. The tape definitely motivated us for practice today and motivated us for this week."

Weis had learned to cover all the angles as a head coach, including the Midwestern weather. So far, it had been warm and fair in South Bend. But the forecast for Syracuse week was for temperatures to plunge from the unseasonably warm 50 degrees to the 20s, with wind chills reaching single digits.

On Tuesday, Weis practiced inside the Loftus Center because the weather remained mild. But by Wednesday, as the temperature turned frigid and the wind whipped through the Cartier Field practice facility, Weis wanted his team outside so they could get used to it.

Weis trimmed about 20 minutes of outside practice as the wind pierced the bodies of the players. "I was actually pleasantly surprised at the execution, to be honest with you," he said. "The weather got their attention more than I got their attention. They were pretty spunky."

Despite Weis' best efforts to prepare his players for the seniors' final home game, the Irish came out a bit flat against Syracuse. Syracuse, with one of the nation's most unproductive offenses, had some success against the Irish early on, taking a 3–0 lead. After a scoreless first quarter—Notre Dame's first of the year—Weis left his perch along the sideline to talk to the offensive players sitting on the bench. The players thought he was about to blister them for their lackluster performance. But Weis sensed that perhaps his players were trying a bit too hard in the senior finale. "Relax, relax," he told them. "Gain your composure. You're acting like you're down 50 points!"

Even Quinn was a little anxious. "We talked on Friday, and I told Coach that I felt tight that night," said Quinn. "There is always that feeling that you want to play your very best game for the seniors, for everything they've done for you."

With a 25-yard completion to Stovall on the next-to-last play of the first quarter, Quinn became the first quarterback in Notre Dame history to throw for more than 3,000 yards in a season. He also became

Notre Dame's all-time leading passer with 7,618 yards — 16 more than Powlus — on a fourth-quarter completion to Samardzija.

Quinn managed to find Stovall and Samardzija for touchdowns in the first half. It took pressure from Chase Anastasio on a couple of Syracuse punts to provide the offense with good field position. Both Irish touchdowns in the first half came on short drives — just 36 and 40 yards.

Notre Dame held a modest 14–3 lead at halftime, despite failing on all seven third-down conversions in the first half. But the Irish defense played its role well. Syracuse failed to enter Notre Dame territory in the second quarter and went 11 possessions between scores. The Irish then methodically pulled away, with a Leo Ferrine interception for a touchdown, a couple of Fitzpatrick field goals, and a Walker touchdown run to cap the second straight 100-yard performance (123 yards total) by the Irish sophomore and his sixth of the season.

Once the Irish took a 34–3 lead midway through the fourth quarter, Weis emptied his bench. Even senior walk-on quarterback Marty Mooney, who had never attempted a pass during his four years with the team, completed a slant pattern to Mike O'Hara, another senior walk-on. Weis later called that "my favorite play of the game." The backups gave up a touchdown, and the final score was 34–10.

After the game, Notre Dame's seniors ran around the outside of the field in their final home appearance, as oranges were thrown onto the turf — indicating the students' hope for an Orange Bowl berth. Tostitos chips — the sponsors of the Fiesta Bowl — were also tossed about. Oranges or chips? They would find out in two weeks.

As the players filed into the Guglielmino Athletics Complex the next morning, Weis noticed that they looked as if they had lost to Syracuse: "You walk in and everyone looks like doom, and I said, 'The score was 34–10, right? Do I have the right score on this game?' "

In fact, the Irish had come to expect much more of themselves, and they knew they really hadn't put together 60 consecutive minutes of consistent football since the USC game. Yes, they beat BYU by 26 points, Tennessee by 20, Navy by 21, and Syracuse by 24. But they had also learned the Weis credo, a philosophy Weis learned from Bill Parcells: "Find whatever your level is, and then go past that."

Weis elaborated: "That's my role now, to try to find those buttons to push and then push them higher. That's not just players, but coaches as well. You push everyone to have higher expectations."

Now 8–2, ranked sixth in the AP poll and eighth in the BCS, the Irish had just won a football game by 24 points and they were disappointed in their performance. They expected more of themselves.

Only one more obstacle stood in the way of a BCS bid: a trip to Stanford in Palo Alto. Focus, insisted Weis, would not be an issue.

THE $14.5 MILLION DRIVE

STANFORD WOULD BE NO gimme. The game was on their home turf, and they were playing for their own bowl bid. At 5–5, Stanford needed one more win to earn a postseason invitation.

Stanford was an unpredictable team. Under Walt Harris—the highly respected head coach who left Pittsburgh after winning the Big East—the Cardinal defeated Navy by three points to open the season, but then suffered one of the great upsets of recent years, a 20–17 loss to Division I-AA UC Davis, followed by a blowout loss at home to Oregon. Stanford rebounded with consecutive victories against Washington State, Arizona, and Arizona State. But they couldn't put an undefeated (at the time) UCLA team away, squandering a three-touchdown lead and losing by three in overtime. Then USC crushed Stanford, 51–21. A three-point win over Oregon State and a 24-point loss against California left Stanford equal in the win-loss columns—and desperate.

On paper, Stanford looked more like a 2–8 team than a 5–5 team: 2.8 yards per rush, a Pac-10-worst 35 sacks allowed, outscored 98–33 in the fourth quarter, outgained by 105 yards per game. Quarterback Trent Edwards left the two most recent games with injuries to his left shoulder and left hand. T.C. Ostrander, a promising backup to Edwards, played pretty well in relief, but Ostrander couldn't rally his team in the second half of the 27–3 loss to Cal.

They could be so dangerous offensively and so porous defensively, and yet the defense was dotted with notable performers, including nose tackle Babatunde Oshinowo, defensive end Julian Jenkins, outside linebacker Jon Alston, and linebacker Kevin Schimmelmann. Cornerback T.J. Rushing was one of the nation's most dangerous kick returners.

The Irish had learned through the years to respect the Cardinal. A No. 1-rated Irish squad in 1990 fell to Stanford, 36–31, at Notre Dame Stadium, with Cardinal head coach Dennis Green orchestrating the upset. Legendary San Francisco 49ers head coach Bill Walsh returned to the Farm and knocked off the No. 6-ranked Irish, 33–16, in Notre Dame Stadium in 1992. The teams started meeting annually in 1997, and Stanford defeated Notre Dame three out of the next five games; Notre Dame won the last three times the teams met (2002–04).

The Irish needed two fourth-quarter touchdowns in 2004 to pull out a 23–15 victory against Stanford. Otherwise they would have missed qualifying for the Insight Bowl. (In retrospect, maybe that wouldn't have been such a bad thing.)

There was also no love lost between the two teams, partly because of the way Notre Dame had behaved in 2003 when they whipped Stanford 57–7. It was Senior Day in Palo Alto, and the Irish took the field while the Stanford seniors were still being introduced for their last hurrah. And then Willingham called for a fake punt in the fourth quarter with a 50-point lead.

"We're not going to be disrespectful to Stanford," Weis said. "I can promise you that."

With the BCS bid on the line, Weis didn't have to perform magic tricks during Stanford week to motivate his team. Win and you go, most likely, to the Fiesta Bowl; lose and you hate yourself for eight months for finishing 8–3 and having to go to the Gator Bowl. Weis was careful to speak fondly of the Gator Bowl, but he wanted his squad to be included among the eight best teams in the country.

"I hope for our whole university and everyone affiliated that we go out and play our best against Stanford," Weis said. "I hope we win and have an opportunity to go play in one of those big games on January 2 or 3 and see how we can make out."

Weis submitted his usual 10-point chart of priorities for the game against the Cardinal, but number one on the list was the only one that really mattered: win and go to a BCS game. It was as simple as that.

At the regular Tuesday press conference, Weis was asked to grade himself after 10 games. "I'm doing all right," he said. "Trust me, when you get to the level I'm at now, you're definitely your own biggest critic. You never look at yourself and say, 'I really did well.' The best you'll say is, 'I did okay.' You could call 50 good plays and two bad ones, and you'll harp on the two bad ones. That's part of being a perfectionist."

As the season had progressed, the questions in these press conferences had gradually become much broader in scope. Weis proved to be a fascinating interview — quick to elaborate on offensive and coaching philosophies, and introspective even on the most mundane of topics. So now he was asked what he thought about the interview with Tom Brady that had aired recently on *60 Minutes.*

Weis said he was blurting out Brady's responses before his former quarterback even spoke. He knew, for example, that Brady would say that his favorite Super Bowl ring was "the next one."

"You don't look back; you always look forward," Weis said. "You're always looking toward the next ring. There's one I'd like to get at Notre Dame in the near future. I'd like to be able to put those pro rings away."

His goal, he explained, was simple enough: win every time you play. "That's the goal for any competitive player or coach," he said. "You don't have to wait for somebody else to expect it for you. Any time you lose, it's a disappointment. So should the fans be disappointed when you lose? Yes, because you should be disappointed when you lose. You should expect everyone else to be disappointed when you lose. It comes with the territory."

Now that he had raised the bar, anything less than a national title run in 2006 would be a disappointment. And he wasn't the only one who thought so. Quinn, in particular, had become a Weis Mini-Me — a perfectionist. Weis had seen it start back in the spring and increase with the competition of the 2005 season.

"Leadership can't be faked," Weis said. "You can't ask people to be leaders if they aren't leaders. Leadership has to be something that you really have; it has to be something inherent. Quinn obviously has it."

Weis also remained steadfast in his commitment to Darius Walker, who entered the Stanford game just 80 yards short of becoming the ninth player in Irish history to rush for more than 1,000 yards in a season. Walker gained more than 100 yards in each of the first four games of the season, and then leveled off over the second four-game stretch. Junior Travis Thomas had played well in a backup role. But in recent games against Navy and Syracuse, Walker had come of age. Weis preferred having a bell cow running back—someone who could carry the ball 25 times in a game. And Walker was showing improved running technique and increased productivity in the home stretch of the season.

Walker didn't have breakaway speed, but he was starting to snap off longer runs because he was correcting his technical mistakes. Instead of turning his back to the line of scrimmage and spinning when a tackler approached, he was staying square to the line of scrimmage and making moves with his feet underneath him. Instead of stopping to make a cut, he was making cuts on the move. These were signs that the nimble sophomore was really starting to get it.

"Everyone wants to hand the ball to Reggie Bush, but there's only one Reggie Bush," Weis said. "I'll take Darius and Travis any day. That's who I have and I like who I have."

All and all, Weis liked the way his team was progressing. They had missed out on a couple of golden opportunities at home, but they rebounded from the USC loss and were undefeated since the "second season" began. "I like the players," he said. "I like the coaches. I like the team. I wouldn't say I'm satisfied because we've lost two games that we had an opportunity to win, and I'd like to be talking about the Rose Bowl and not talking about getting to 9–2 and playing in a BCS game."

Thanksgiving fell during Stanford week, so the players didn't get a chance to celebrate it at home unless they lived nearby. The plan was to practice at 8 a.m. on Thanksgiving, then fly out to Palo Alto later that evening. Weis offered a single piece of advice to his players who were stuck in town for the holiday: call someone they hadn't spoken with in a long time. Just pick up the phone and reach out to someone.

Weis and his wife, Maura, were thinking about Keith Penrod as the holidays approached. Penrod, a Mishawaka, Ind., native, had been a fixture around the Notre Dame program for nearly three decades. Doctors told Penrod's parents when he was born that he wouldn't live more than 48 hours. He was baptized less than 12 hours after his birth, and this year was about to turn 53. He had spent the bulk of his life cheering for Notre Dame.

Penrod suffered from cerebral palsy, a debilitating impairment of muscular power and coordination. He had surgery when he was 19, which enabled him to walk. But for much of his life, Penrod was confined to a wheelchair and his makeshift "Irish mobile" golf cart, which he used to drive around the campus. The golf cart, adorned in Notre Dame colors, even had a horn that played the "Victory March."

As a youngster, Penrod got around either in a wheelchair or by crawling around on his hands and knees. He played sports with his siblings in the backyard. He was a goalie in soccer or hockey, a catcher in baseball, or a center in football—all positions that required the least amount of mobility. He earned 10 letters in high school as the manager of various athletic teams. He attended his first Notre Dame football game in 1969 (a 13–6 victory over Air Force) when a priest gave his father a couple of tickets. Penrod had been coming back to Notre Dame ever since, always making sure he lived close to the campus.

Penrod began attending Notre Dame football practices during the Parseghian era. The late George Kelly, then an Irish football coach and eventually an athletic administrator, looked after him. When Willingham left Notre Dame, Penrod wasn't sure if the next head coach would accept him. A guy zipping around in a wheelchair at practice makes some head coaches a bit uncomfortable. What Penrod didn't count on was a new head coach with a daughter who also had special needs.

Not only was Penrod welcomed at practices, but Weis gave him almost unlimited access. As the team stretched for the start of practice, Penrod could be seen driving his wheelchair between the rows of players as they began another day's work. An astute football observer, Penrod was completely in his element on the practice field. In recent years, he had been asked to leave practice the same time the media was expected to depart—about 20 minutes after the start. Not anymore.

Penrod attended almost every Notre Dame home game through the years—football and basketball—but had never accompanied the Irish football team on a flight. This year, he was going to Palo Alto as Charlie Weis' guest.

So there he was, sitting in his wheelchair along the Notre Dame sideline in Stanford Stadium. Well after the Stanford seniors were introduced, the Irish took the field. Fifteen seconds after the opening kickoff, Notre Dame led, 7–0, thanks to a short Quinn pass that Samardzija turned into an 80-yard touchdown. The rest of the evening wouldn't be quite so easy.

Stanford matched Notre Dame's opening score after a rare Quinn interception (only his sixth of the season). The Irish jumped back out on top with an eight-play, 72-yard drive, this one capped by a Samardzija touchdown. But the Cardinal answered with a three-play, 51-yard scoring drive to tie the score at halftime. Some of Stanford's all-time greats, including John Elway, were on hand for the halftime celebration.

If Notre Dame was looking for the perfect game, this wasn't it. The Irish scored on their opening drive to start the second half, this time on a Quinn-to-Stovall connection. But Fitzpatrick, who had set the Notre Dame record in the first half for extra points in a season—a perfect 50 for 50—hit the left upright. Twice the Irish took a nine-point lead in the second half. Both times Stanford, now working behind Ostrander in the absence of an injured Edwards, cut it to within a touchdown.

Weis was trying to win a football game while juggling kickers. Carl Gioia, who kicked the last extra point of the Syracuse game when Fitzpatrick went down with a knee injury to his kicking leg, had been handling kickoffs against Stanford. Fitzpatrick missed a 42-yard field goal in the third quarter, and Weis went to Gioia, who kicked a 29-yard field goal. Then Gioia kicked a line drive on the ensuing kickoff and T.J. Rushing returned it 87 yards for a score. So Weis went back to Fitzpatrick, who promptly missed a 29-yard field goal with

2:15 remaining in the game and the Irish leading, 30–24. The field goal would have given Notre Dame a two-score lead. Instead, the Irish would have to sweat it out.

On the second play of Stanford's ensuing series, Ostrander hit wide receiver Mark Bradford over Irish cornerback Leo Ferrine. Seventy-six yards later, Stanford was at the Notre Dame 4-yard line. On second down, Ostrander connected with tight end Matt Traverso for a touchdown, and Michael Sgroi's extra point gave the Cardinal a 31–30 lead with 1:46 remaining.

Fiesta Bowl CEO John Junker probably wanted to weep. So did Notre Dame fans.

With a BCS bid and their $14.5 million payday on the line, the Irish started at their own 20-yard line with two timeouts remaining. To begin the drive, Weis called a play the Irish hadn't used since early October. They hadn't even practiced it in recent weeks. But in anticipation of Stanford's soft coverage, Weis quickly gathered the offensive players together, discussed individual assignments, and then sent Samardzija running a crossing route underneath the deep coverage. When he caught the football, there was no one close to him, and he sprinted to the 50-yard line for a 29-yard gain.

"A draw-the-play-in-the-dirt-with-a-stick play," is how Samardzija later described it.

With excellent field position, the momentum shifted back to the Irish. Quinn hit Samardzija again for 17 yards, and after a short Quinn scramble, Stovall won a jump ball with Rushing inside the 10. On second-and-goal from the 6, Walker burst up the middle and stretched the ball over the goal line for a 36–31 lead with just 55 seconds left to play.

The situation dictated a two-point conversion attempt. And Weis, who didn't want to send a kicker out there again, jumped on it. So from the three, Quinn lined up in a shotgun formation and acted as if the snap had gone over his head. Walker took the direct snap from center and easily scored on the conversion for a 38–31 lead.

("A copycat play," Weis said later. "It's Kevin Faulk and the Patriots in the Super Bowl from a couple of years ago—the exact same play.")

Moments later, defensive end Victor Abiamiri sacked Ostrander to end the game. Sighs of relief among the Irish and their supporters far outnumbered smiles. Notre Dame had survived—just barely.

But as Charlie Weis would be the first to tell you, a win is a win, and what had been all but unthinkable at the beginning of the season—a trip to a BCS bowl—was now all but guaranteed. A huge chunk of credit went to Walker, who played the best game of his two-year collegiate career. He rushed for 186 yards on 35 carries and added 55 receiving yards. And when Walker needed a break early in the fourth quarter, Thomas scored untouched on an eight-yard run.

Meanwhile, the Irish defense held Stanford to one-of-11 on third down, one week after limiting Syracuse to three-of-15 on third down.

For the regular season, Walker had finished with 1,106 yards rushing; Samardzija had 191 receiving yards against Stanford to finish with 1,190 and break the Notre Dame single-season mark set over three decades earlier by Tom Gatewood (1,123 yards in 1970); and Stovall had 136 yards to join Samardzija in the 1,000-yards Club with 1,023. "I'm really proud of this football team," Weis said. "You don't win every game by a hundred points. It just doesn't work that way. Most teams would have thrown in the towel once the score went to 31–30. But we kept our composure, went right down the field, scored, got the two-point conversion, and then finished the game on defense."

"We were completely calm," Samardzija said. "Everyone understood what he had to do. It was laid out there for us. We had 1:50 on the clock. We couldn't settle for anything less. We haven't been in a situation like that for a while. But I think we have guys on this team who know how to handle situations like that. We just kind of took it with a leadership attitude. No one was panicking. Everyone just went out and did his thing."

Samardzija declared the Irish BCS worthy because there was "no other team that should represent their own school and college football than this one right here." Added Walker, "We've had one of those seasons. It seems like Notre Dame gets better every week. We've played well enough to get the BCS bid. We've worked hard all season. It would be nice to have it."

Weis, as always, went straight to the point: "We're 9–2. We're one of the best teams in the country. Only two teams can play for the national championship, and we're not going to be one of them. But the next best thing is to be one of those six teams playing in the big games. Sign me up. I don't care who we're playing. Let's go."

Chapter 18

······

BREAK OUT THE CHAMPAGNE

THE 2005 NOTRE DAME schedule, once considered too formidable and almost impossible to overcome, was now being declared too easy. As the December 4 Bowl Championship Series selection show drew near, critics were suddenly questioning the quality of Notre Dame's regular-season opponents. More than pride was at stake in this revisionist view of history: one of those precious eight BCS bowl bids was on the line, along with the $14.5 million payday that comes with it, a payday that independent Notre Dame wouldn't have to share with any conference.

Underdogs in four of its first six games (conveniently forgotten by these same critics), Notre Dame had gone 4–2 with a pair of three-point losses. The Irish then won their final five games, four in convincing fashion. They ended the regular season with a 9–2 record, were ranked seventh in the Associated Press poll, and finished eighth in the

BCS rankings. Yet as the Big Four bowls—Rose, Fiesta, Orange, and Sugar—whittled their respective shortlists, Notre Dame's worthiness had come into question.

There were eight BCS spots, but only two places available for an at-large team such as Notre Dame, Oregon, Ohio State, or Auburn. Oregon, with its 10–1 record (a loss to USC), had a legitimate claim to a BCS bid. So did Ohio State, which was fresh off its come-from-behind victory against archrival Michigan. The Buckeyes were 9–2, with losses to Texas and Penn State. And then there was Auburn, which had survived the always tough play of the Southeastern Conference and finished with a 9–2 record. What it all meant was this: two worthy teams were going to get stiffed.

Fiesta Bowl officials were diplomatic about it, but there was little doubt they coveted Notre Dame. After suffering through a one-sided Utah victory against Pittsburgh a year earlier, the Fiesta Bowl was going to do whatever was necessary to put fannies in the seats and viewers in front of their televisions. If that meant choosing Notre Dame over 10–1 (and Pac-10 member) Oregon, they would do so without hesitation.

On November 22, four days before the Irish squeezed past Stanford, Oregon head coach Mike Bellotti, athletics director Bill Moos, and three other Oregon athletic department officials visited Fiesta Bowl president John Junker in Tempe, Arizona, to make a case for the Ducks. It wasn't a very subtle presentation, but it was direct and honest. The gist of it was this: choose Oregon and we'll bring lots of fans, spend lots of money, and put on a good show. We did it for the 2002 Fiesta Bowl; we'll do it for the 2006 Fiesta Bowl.

South Carolina head coach Steve Spurrier, whom Weis had called a predictable playcaller following Spurrier's short-lived NFL coaching career, voted Notre Dame No. 14 in his final poll. Did Spurrier really think the Irish were only the 14th-best team in the country? "They haven't really beaten anybody," Spurrier said. "They didn't hardly beat anybody with a winning record. Personally, I think it's a crying shame why they allow them to go 9–2 and still play for the big money. I just don't think it's fair. Why do we have to treat those guys differently?"

Junker wasn't about to be swayed by Steve Spurrier. After all, Spurrier didn't have to sell Fiesta Bowl tickets, impress corporate sponsors, or make sure the TV ratings were high enough. Junker was a college football junkie, but he was also a businessman and a pragmatist. Inviting Notre Dame and Ohio State was too enticing to ignore. The two programs were national heavyweights and magnets for television viewers. They had played each other only four times—1935–36 and 1995–96—and split the series. What was there not to love about a 2005 postseason match-up?

In less than a year, Weis had transformed Notre Dame's program from near chaos to nearly undefeated. He was speaking to the press that day, but he could have just as easily been talking to Fiesta Bowl officials. The message was the same: Notre Dame had returned to national prominence.

"Something critical happened in that game Saturday night," said Weis of his team's six-play, 80-yard, game-winning drive against Stanford. "We were in a close game and won. There's definitely a lesson that can be learned in every game, and each week, there's a separate lesson to be learned. The fact that something bad happened at the end of the game and the team came back and won, that's just as important as any other lesson, because a team doesn't start winning those close games until they experience it. Now that they know they can do it, it'll make it a little easier the next time."

Weis said he wouldn't publicly lobby for a BCS bowl bid, but it was obvious he thought Notre Dame would receive an invitation—and deserved one. And there was no real need for him to politick. He knew that the Irish were an attractive commodity.

"People look at records at the end of the year," he said. "I look at records when you play them. For example, Michigan State deserved to beat us. We didn't play well that day. We didn't coach well that day. But at the time, Michigan State was one of the best teams in the country. So they end up 5–6, and everyone says, 'Well, Notre Dame lost to a 5–6 Michigan State team!' The Michigan State team we played at that time ended up 5–6, but they were not a 5–6 team when we played them."

(Lobbying? No, just stating a few facts.)

"So we lost to Michigan State and we lost to USC," Weis went on. "I mean, take a look. It doesn't take too much to figure out. Take a look at the teams we beat that people say weren't any good this year. Last time I checked, I think Michigan turned out okay. Purdue was highly regarded when we played them. You can't look at how they turned out. Look at where they were when you were playing them. We went into Pitt the first game of the year and we were supposed to lose by a hundred."

It was more like three, but Weis' point was clear.

The bowl bid wasn't the only issue on the table for Weis. Even if playing in a bowl this season was a given, winning one wasn't. Notre Dame hadn't won a postseason game since the 1994 Cotton Bowl. Wherever the Irish played, Weis wanted to leave the field with a W.

"People aren't going to remember the Stanford game after the bowl game," he said. "They're going to remember the bowl game. You're either going to be 9–3 having lost a bowl game or 10–2 having won the bowl game. It's either going to leave a good taste or a bad taste. I'm hoping for the former."

He was also hoping that his star quarterback would get some much-deserved national props. Now that the regular season was complete, the speculation about Quinn's chances to win the Heisman, as well as his future plans—stay in school or turn pro—was placed on the front burner. Quinn's name had been included in the season-long Heisman talk, though he was usually listed behind frontrunners Bush and Leinart of USC and Texas quarterback Vince Young. But if nothing else, Quinn was expected to be invited to New York for the awards ceremony.

Even Weis, obviously a big Quinn fan, would have had difficulty voting for someone other than Bush. But Quinn, said Weis, deserved to be in the front row during the Heisman presentation. His 2005 performance had earned him that much.

"I've said all along it would be tough for me to pick against that No. 5 from USC," said Weis, referring to Bush. "I've seen all three of these quarterbacks play, and Leinart is real good and Young is real good, but I wouldn't trade my guy for either one of them."

Yet Quinn wouldn't be invited to New York. Just the top three — Bush, Leinart, and Young — were asked to attend the ceremony.

"I just don't get it," said Weis. "Their rationale was that there was a clear drop-off between No. 3 and 4. In the past, they've invited as many as six, but they thought that three was the magic number. I disagreed … But my biggest gripe was the subjectivity. I felt he was deserving of making that trip, and I think it leaves a bad taste in his mouth."

Asked if he was surprised to be at Notre Dame on December 10, the day of the Heisman presentation in New York, Quinn couldn't completely conceal his emotions. "I'm definitely disappointed that I'm not in New York," Quinn said. "But at the same time, I have the opportunity to practice and prepare for an upcoming bowl game, which for me is more important than being somewhere where you're probably not going to be receiving the award. I think we all know who's going to win that."

If Quinn was bitter, he didn't show it. "No, not at all," Quinn said. "It's not up to me to decide who goes to those sorts of things. Really, when you look at the players who are there, they deserve to be there. They've had tremendous seasons. Everyone there is 11–0 and playing for a national championship. How can you argue that you should be there when you're 9–2 and playing in the Fiesta Bowl instead of undefeated and playing in the Rose Bowl? It's not up to me to say, 'Oh, I should be there.' "

Earlier in the season, Quinn had declared his intention to return to Notre Dame for his senior year, even though it was apparent he was developing into a legitimate NFL quarterback candidate. But now that the question of his future was a frequent topic, Quinn made sure to leave himself an opening if he chose to turn pro. If the word from the NFL general managers was that he would be a top-five pick, Quinn would have to at least consider the option. A "99% chance," said Quinn, of the probability of his return to Notre Dame.

Weis was 100% sure what Quinn *should* do.

"I would definitely tell him that he needs one more year in school," said Weis on ESPN's *Rome Is Burning*. "He would be a first-round draft choice this year, but the difference between being a Top-10 pick and a first or second pick is millions and millions of dollars. The people in the NFL would like to see him seasoned for another year. They know he'll be coached by a guy who understands the professional game, and we're only going to enhance his value by him staying here another year."

Weis said Quinn, who was a year away from earning degrees in finance and political science, had already declared his intention to return, and his word was good enough for him. "Brady is not the type of person that's going to sit there and tell you he's coming back and then not come back," Weis said. "Obviously, you have to understand what happens at this time. NFL agents try to get to these kids and their families and encourage them to come out early so that they can make money. That's the bottom line. That's what this is all about. Somebody says, 'Hey, you're going to be a first-round draft choice, and you're going to make millions of dollars!' Well, my feeling is, you're going to make a lot more millions of dollars in one more season."

Weis made it clear that he didn't object in principle to a player leaving early, provided he fulfill one obligation. "If a guy wants to go out early, as long as he's graduated from Notre Dame, I'll support it," Weis said. "The only time that I have a problem with these guys wanting to leave here before their eligibility is done would be if they haven't graduated. Getting a Notre Dame degree is part of the package when you come here. If you leave here without one, you'll probably never go back and get one. The odds say you won't."

The Associated Press named Quinn a third-team All-America. Anthony Fasano was a finalist for the John Mackey Award as one of the nation's elite tight ends. Jeff Samardzija was a finalist for the Biletnikoff Award and a second-team AP All-America. He was eventually named Notre Dame's first consensus All-America since cornerback Shane Walton in 2002. Tom Zbikowski was named to the third team at safety.

For the first time in three years, the banquet to mark the season's end would be a true celebration. Two years earlier, the Irish had been coming off a 5–7 season in which Notre Dame lost games by 38, 37, 31, and 26 points. A year earlier, the public banquet was cancelled in the aftermath of the Willingham firing, and a private ceremony was held for the players and the coaches. This time, the Irish would bask in some glory for a night, with Lou Holtz returning to his beloved campus.

The banquet was scheduled for Friday, December 2—two days before the bowl bids were to be announced. Before the event, Holtz met with the media and waxed poetic about his days in South Bend. It was the old Holtz, face sparkling as he talked about his magnificent six-year run, from 1988 to 1993, when the Irish won 64 games. "Notre Dame has changed a lot," he said. "They now have tremendous facilities." Pause. "They pay coaches now too."

Then he turned serious. "But Notre Dame has not changed its values, its purpose, and its mission. Facilities just enhance Notre Dame, but Notre Dame will always be the same."

There was very little resemblance between Weis' 2005 squad and Holtz' teams, other than the positive results. Holtz preferred to run the ball. In fact, he preferred just about anything to a passing attack. But he and Weis did share one common trait. "There isn't any doubt about who's in charge," Holtz said. "People can name the head football coach; it's more difficult to name the leader. Titles come from above; people alone determine leaders. The person they'll choose as the leader is someone who has a vision and a plan. From talking to Charlie, he has a vision and a plan. How close his plan is to mine, I couldn't tell you. But we both had a vision where we wanted to go, and we both had a plan."

As a head coach, Holtz was an outspoken advocate of a team-first approach, which Weis demanded as well. "What impressed me the most about this Notre Dame team was the attitude they've had, the unselfishness, and how well they've represented Notre Dame," Holtz said. "It's important for Notre Dame football to be on top. This has been one of the great years in college football, and the interest in Notre Dame has been one of the biggest stories. Many people would like to emulate Notre Dame's program. This was a very special team. They very easily could be playing for the national championship. They are a very well-coached, fun team to watch play. The football team should reflect the university. This team did Notre Dame proud."

Holtz knew the expectations placed upon the Notre Dame football coach as well as anyone. He was one of the guys who had helped create and sustain those expectations. He won a national title in his third year. From that point on, anything less than a national title run was considered a disappointing season. At one point, the Irish won 23 straight games. A few years later, they strung together 17 straight victories and deserved to win a national championship over a great Florida State team that the Irish had defeated during the regular season.

"Once you're here," said Holtz, holding his right hand just above head level, "there's only one story, and that's down here. It seems like everything is negative, no matter what you do."

Holtz also couldn't resist taking a parting shot at his ESPN studio partner, Mark May, in front of the Notre Dame banquet crowd. May had dismissed the football team's chances even before the season started. "Mark May is a beautiful individual, and I love him dearly," Holtz said. "The fact that he did not get a good education at Pittsburgh is not his fault."

Nearly 2,000 people attended the 85th Notre Dame football banquet. They embraced Holtz as he spoke, and the feeling was mutual. And then it was time for local sportscaster Jeff Jeffers, who worked at WNDU, to introduce the current head coach.

"On the evening of September 3, I happened to walk by the Irish locker room underneath Heinz Field in Pittsburgh," Jeffers began. "Charlie Weis was walking out to check the field, and just as he left the room, he reached up and slapped the sign that said Play Like a Champion Today. That private moment spoke volumes. I knew that he understood 'it.' 'It' is the knowledge that Notre Dame football and its tradition cannot be understood unless it is embraced.

"Over the past few months, we've seen a total transformation of Notre Dame football. More importantly, we've been able to learn a lesson from a very good teacher, which is what Charlie Weis really is. We learned that 'pass right' was more than just a play to see how high Anthony Fasano could jump. We learned that after the most disappointing, heartbreaking loss to our archrival, the right thing to do was to visit the locker room of the winning team in order to teach his son that celebrating victory and understanding defeat are similar lessons. We learned that future military officers who will be entrusted with our safety deserve the ultimate act of respect, that standing with them after a game endorses and salutes their efforts on the field and their future way of life.

"But the best lesson is that the teaching, the winning, the excitement, the optimism, and the anticipation has only just begun. Ladies and gentlemen, the head coach of the Fighting Irish, Charlie Weis."

At recent banquets, at this precise moment, the air in the building suddenly seemed quite thin. Irish fans had stopped believing in Bob Davie's words, and they never truly connected with the emotionally distant Ty Willingham. But when Weis spoke on this night, the air was thick with excitement and admiration.

Weis' first topic was a familiar one: family. "About a year ago at this time, I received a phone call from associate athletic director John Heisler inquiring whether I'd be interested in the head coach's position at the University of Notre Dame. So I sat down with my family, and we talked about the possibility of leaving professional football to go to the life of college football. We were really intrigued by going to a college community and being involved in that community. It was really important to our family to go somewhere where we could really be a family."

After Weis was officially offered the job, he said, "I tried to find out why exactly Notre Dame wasn't at the top of the college football world. I heard all the reasons: the academic requirements, the schedule, everything known to mankind. But I didn't realize until I got here that all the resources Notre Dame needed to win were already in place. All it needed was to be tweaked a little bit. So they gave me enough money to hire the best coaching staff in America. They gave me the resources to hire a personnel department. They gave me an opportunity to come here and just be me, which is easier said than done for an obnoxious, sarcastic guy from New Jersey."

Shortly after arriving in South Bend, Weis went on, he knew he'd made the right call: "When I got here, about the middle of spring, I realized in a short period of time that there was a collection of young men here with a desire to be great. They didn't want to be 6–6; they didn't want to be 5–7. They wanted to be on top of the football world, and that's half the battle."

That half, Weis figured, was already won: "I looked around at this group of guys, and these are the same guys who walked off the field a year ago after a bowl loss with a 6–6 record and felt humiliated. Today, these same guys have their chests held out and their heads held high, and they feel good about where they've come."

But even on this night of celebration, Weis was a perfectionist. He was glad that Irish fans were happy about the season, he said, but "to be honest with you, we're not as happy as a lot of the alumni because we realize how close we were to actually playing for the national title."

The crowd loved it. And they loved it even more when Weis said, "We're going to go to whatever bowl they dial up. We don't care where it is; we're coming. Once we get this monkey off our back and get that bowl win out there, we're going to set our goals even higher next year and continue that for as long as I'm here."

Wrapping up, Weis turned to his team. "I promised only one thing when I came through this door: We would have a hardworking football team that was intelligent, tough, and nasty. Fellas, you achieved all those goals, and I appreciate it."

Two days after the banquet, Notre Dame accepted the Fiesta Bowl's bid to play Ohio State. With its No. 1-rated rush defense and an improving offensive unit, led by quarterback Troy Smith, the Buckeyes had lost just twice, and that was against No. 2 Texas and No. 16 Penn State. Ohio State had talent to burn. And Notre Dame had that little seven-game losing streak in bowls.

Motivation? That shouldn't be hard for Weis and his staff to generate.

"Oh, it will be mentioned," he said of the bowl losing streak, breaking into his signature Cheshire grin. "It will be mentioned … every day … multiple times. Yes, it will be emphasized."

Most of Notre Dame's seven bowl losses hadn't even been close.

The streak started with an undeserved trip to the Fiesta Bowl (the Irish were 6–4–1) to take on Colorado on January 2, 1995. Kordell Stewart, Rashaan Salaam, & Co. drubbed the Irish, 41–24. Three seasons later, after traveling to Baton Rouge and defeating LSU during the regular season, the Irish played the Tigers again, this time in the Independence Bowl: LSU 27, Notre Dame 9.

The only two close ones were the 31–26 loss to Florida State in the January 1, 1996, Orange Bowl and the 35–28 loss to Georgia Tech in the January 1, 1999, Gator Bowl.

The last three bowl trips had been decided by an average of 23.7 points per game: 41–9 versus Oregon State in the January 1, 2001, Fiesta Bowl; 28–6 against North Carolina State in the January 1, 2003, Gator Bowl; and 38–21 to Oregon State in the December 28, 2004, Insight Bowl.

But Notre Dame's motivation in the Fiesta Bowl against Ohio State didn't stop there. For the players, the historical perspective stung less than the recent criticism of their program. "You want the politically correct answer or the true answer?" responded linebacker Brandon Hoyte when a reporter asked whether shots taken at the Irish bothered him. And then he gave the true answer. What bugged him the most was what people had been saying and writing about the Irish the past few years: "It's definitely something that's a motivational factor."

Playing Ohio State made Brady Quinn feel a bit nostalgic. He'd grown up in Dublin, Ohio, and he'd attended Ohio State games. If he hadn't fallen in love with the Notre Dame campus and environment during his recruiting visit, he would have chosen the Buckeyes.

BEFORE QUINN AND THE Irish could turn their full attention to Ohio State, they had to deal with final exams. That meant Weis, who understood the rigors of academics at Notre Dame, had to give his players some space. This was definitely something new.

The run-up to the Super Bowl can be one week or two. Having four to five weeks to prepare for a bowl opponent is very different. The extra time might have been more welcome, though, if final exams weren't looming. Weis held just two practices in the first three weeks after the Stanford game, although coach Ruben Mendoza stayed on top of the team's conditioning regimen. While the coaching staff began gathering and studying information about Ohio State, his players didn't have to worry about the Buckeyes' X's and O's until after final exams.

In fact, from the outset of the bowl preparations, Weis was deter-mined to keep his players fresh, both mentally and physically. Expose them to too much information on the Buckeyes too soon, and by the time they reached Arizona, they'd be yawning at yet another explana-tion of Ohio State's game plan.

Weis consulted with a few football coaches who had prepared for bowl games, starting with his own staff—Bill Lewis, Rick Minter, and Peter Vaas—and culminating with a meeting with Miami Dolphins head coach Nick Saban, who had spent the majority of his head coach-ing career in the college ranks. "Fortunately, some of these guys have screwed it up first and have since fixed it," Weis smiled. "So I'm hoping to bypass the screw-it-up phase and get to the second phase right off the bat."

They warned Weis against making the early bowl practices too physi-cal. There is the temptation to try to do too much with the extra practice time. Some coaches had treated the early-December time as a kind of early spring practice. Others installed the game plan four weeks before the bowl game to give their players plenty of time to zero in on the opponent. "By the time the game came around, they were either too bored or too beat up to play the game, and they'd go out to the bowl game and not do too well," Weis said. "They've learned how to tone it down and be more time efficient."

Instead, he was taking a "training camp mentality. Don't worry about how quick you get them in, but when you get them in, give them a full dose of fundamentals and techniques, and don't overload them with the game plan all at one time."

With the one-year anniversary of his hiring less than two weeks away, Weis restated his willingness to take responsibility for everything that had not gone well. "I'm content with our season being 9–2 and being in a BCS game," he said. "But I think both Ohio State and Notre Dame, as happy as we are to be in a BCS game, sit back at night and say, 'What if?' When you're the head coach, you have to be personally account-able. I personally felt responsible for our two losses. I'm happy to be in the situation we're in for our team. We've made significant progress in a year, but I'm never going to be really happy until we win all of them."

On December 23, the last day of practice in South Bend, Weis concluded the week with a press conference. He was less interested in talking about football than about how well his players had done in class that term. He had recently been handed a copy of the players' grade-point averages; a 3.04 cumulative GPA for the fall 2005 semester. He was ecstatic.

"I'm not going to say it's never been done in the history of Notre Dame football, but their grades were just great," Weis said. "Normally, I'd talk about football and Ohio State, but I'm very proud of this team's performance in the classroom. Out of 98 players, 56 of them had over 3.0. That's phenomenal. I don't know how these guys do it. When I was in school, I thought my grades were pretty good, but I didn't have football to deal with. They have an aggregate grade-point average of well over 3.0. I don't know if that's ever been done before. But it shows me that these guys really consider academics important."

Tyrone Willingham had recruited a bunch of young men who took their responsibilities as student-athletes seriously. And Notre Dame's academic support system had created the kind of environment that encouraged academic and athletic success—simultaneously.

"As far as we can tell, and we keep pretty good records going back 20 years, that is the highest grade-point average on record," said Pat Holmes, in his ninth year at Notre Dame and his fourth as director of the school's academic services for student-athletes.

Notre Dame fans were also setting records. The Fiesta Bowl allotted 15,000 tickets for Notre Dame season ticket-holders; there were 45,589 requests. That was the most ticket requests ever received for any bowl game in Irish football history. All 2,500 tickets allotted to Notre Dame's students quickly sold out as well.

Weis was setting some records too. He had already negotiated a contract extension with the security of 10 more years after the 2005 season. Now he was in a position to cash in with endorsements, speeches, and other moneymaking opportunities. *Business Week* reported in December that Weis' fee for speaking engagements had risen from $20,000 to $50,000. "Charlie Weis—the innovative, weight-challenged rookie who rose to big-program savior by an unlikely route—and his agent, Bob LaMonte, will sit down to discuss whether Weis wants to spin his newfound celebrity into a pot of money and, if so, how large a pot," said *Business Week.*

LaMonte said Weis had already received 50 proposals for "endorsements, books, and speeches." Said Weis, "I want to be very sure I don't spread myself too thin. I think I can be good at some of these things, but I'm not going to whore myself out."

In less than a season, Weis felt secure enough, financially, to begin construction on an eight-bedroom house with an indoor horse-riding pavilion for Maura, a playground and pool for Hannah, and a regulation baseball diamond for Charlie Jr. Asked what was in the house for him, Weis said, "Contentment."

The weeks before Christmas had given Weis a dose of reality. First, Bill Belichick's father, Steve, the longtime Navy assistant coach whom Weis loved and respected, had died at the age of 86. Then came the shocking news that 18-year-old James Dungy—the son of Indianapolis Colts head coach Tony Dungy—had committed suicide in Florida. Weis, as he had done repeatedly during the 2005 season, used it as a lesson for his son.

"I went home last night and had a long conversation with Charlie about how a parent's worst nightmare is having to hear news like that about their kids," Weis said. "Our hearts and prayers are with Tony because that definitely affects me. I'm a football coach who is a family guy, and I definitely think that Tony epitomizes what that really is."

But now, with Christmas just two days away, Weis was feeling contented at his final press conference before leaving for Arizona. For the first time in 15 years—since before either of his children had been born—he would spend Christmas at home with his family. There would be no football practice or staff meeting to attend. "It's going to be kind of weird," he said. "I'm sure I'll be driving my wife nuts by about Christmas night."

Weis wanted his players to wrap themselves completely in the Christmas spirit and to put Irish football on the back burner for a couple of days. "Tomorrow they'll be with their families," Weis said. "I told them to make sure they spend some time letting those people know how important they are, especially over the holidays, when it's important to let people know what they mean to you. I told them to forget about football. I said football this weekend doesn't count. Throw it out. Not important. I'd rather they spent time with their family and friends. This is a time when Notre Dame football takes a backseat."

When the press conference was finally over, Weis flashed a mischievous smile. It was time to play Santa Claus. "Okay, now here's what I want you to do," Weis said. "Let's put these cameras and tape recorders away. I have lunch for you guys upstairs in the recruiting lounge. This is my Christmas present to you."

WEIS WASTED LITTLE TIME establishing what kind of week it would be for the Fighting Irish in Scottsdale, Arizona, where they would be based while preparing for their game against Ohio State. Shortly after the team arrived, on December 27, he stated flatly, "We didn't come here to drink margaritas."

A day earlier, the Ohio State contingent had landed at Phoenix's Sky Harbor Airport, with Jim Tressel summarizing the magnitude of the Buckeye-Irish battle. "We played twice in the '30s and twice in the '90s, and that's the end of it," said Tressel. "We're not that far apart, and with the great tradition of both football programs and both schools, what more could we ask for?"

The Fiesta Bowl had been good to Tressel and Ohio State. It was in Sun Devil Stadium that the Buckeyes had defeated Miami, 31–24, to complete a perfect 14–0 season and win the national championship in January 2003. A year later, following the 2003 regular season, the Buckeyes returned to Tempe and defeated Kansas State, 35–28, while holding off a fourth-quarter Wildcats charge. This was Tressel's third trip to the Fiesta Bowl in four years. This game wasn't for a national championship, but it was a chance for the Buckeyes to make a statement: that Ohio State football program was well ahead of Notre Dame's.

Weis arranged to take his squad to the Insight Bowl in Phoenix on December 27. A party of 150 people, including members of the Notre Dame squad, was treated to dinner in the Chase Field restaurant down the right field line. One year after losing to Oregon State in this very bowl, the Irish watched as Arizona State mounted a comeback to defeat a Rutgers team from Weis' home state of New Jersey.

Clearly, this year's Insight Bowl was a good diversion from the long week ahead. It also was a holiday treat for a successful season. But the Bank One Ballpark was also a reminder of how far the team had come since the previous year. "He didn't say that, but he's always trying to come up with psychological ploys," said Zbikowski. "I'm sure that had something to do with it."

Ohio State defensive coordinator Jim Heacock told the press he had studied all the tape of the Irish, and it was a mixed bag. Sometimes they came out in a no-huddle offense, as they did against Michigan. Sometimes they threw the ball on virtually every down, as they did against Brigham Young, to take advantage of the Cougars' poor secondary. Sometimes they fed the ball to Walker to help him balance the passing game, as they did against Syracuse and Stanford, when Walker carried a combined 61 times. "Weis does a great job of not letting you zero in on stopping one thing," Heacock said.

The Irish head coach loved the compliment: "When you're a game-plan-oriented play caller, you can usually throw tendencies out the window. At this point, it's Wednesday, and I can't tell you what I'm calling on second-and-10. I have a pretty good feel about how the game is going to start, but the game is going to change. They're going to dictate some things, we're going to dictate some things, but the game is going to change. Good playcallers have the flexibility to set up a plan and envision it, but they're willing to deviate when things don't go exactly the way they want."

As the Notre Dame players stretched for the start of their second practice in Scottsdale, someone flew a remote-controlled model airplane over the south end of Notre Dame's practice field (actually a nearby baseball field on the campus of Scottsdale Community College). Had the master of preparation finally allowed a breach of security? Was there a camera planted in the nose of the airplane to get a glimpse of Notre Dame's pregame plans?

Quinn had another theory. He glanced up at the plane and told Weis, "You wanted crowd noise."

Most of all, Weis wanted the Irish to approach the Fiesta Bowl as if they were pros. Offensive lineman Bob Morton, who had been to two previous bowls with the Irish, noticed a difference. "It's definitely more of a business atmosphere than we've ever experienced," he said. "I feel like we're more focused on the task at hand. I feel more ready than I have been before."

Tressel was taking a more relaxed approach to bowl competition. "For bowl games, Tressel is more laid-back," said Ohio State left guard Rob Sims. "This is still like our vacation. Even though it's real intense and we want to win this game real bad, this is a chance for us to enjoy ourselves and for Coach to say congratulations for having a great season. He's with his family and enjoying himself. We hit it hard for three hours and then relax."

Would the Irish have the advantage because of their hunger to finally win a bowl game, or would the edge go to the Buckeyes, who knew how to be successful in postseason play?

"Each game doesn't have a memory," said Ohio State center Nick Mangold. "This game isn't going to remember that our seniors have won three bowl games and they haven't won one. Coach Tressel has done a great job of preparing us. But from everything I've heard, Coach Weis is a great preparation guy. I think they're going to be more than ready to get after it."

"We're experienced, and we know how to approach these bowl games," Sims added. "We know how to have fun and still be serious at the same time. Notre Dame is dangerous because they have that thirst for it. They're hungry for it."

No one's hunger to end Notre Dame's seven-bowl-game losing streak was more intense than Zbikowski's. He'd answered enough questions about Notre Dame's streak, and he'd heard much too much from Notre Dame's critics: "The guys who said we were going to be 0–6 are the same ones who say we can't win a bowl game."

All season, Weis had backed away from questions about Notre Dame's performance under Willingham. Why would he start responding to them now? Willingham's bowl record was of no consequence, period. "I'm 0–0 in bowl games," Weis snapped. "I've never been involved with Notre Dame in a bowl game. I couldn't care less what they did before I got here. I'm only worrying about now. I'm just worrying about January 2. What happened last year with Ohio State playing in a bowl game and Notre Dame playing in a bowl game is irrelevant. The only thing that's relevant is what happens Monday."

More relevant was the scrambling ability of Ohio State's quarterback, Troy Smith. Smith had rushed for more than 500 yards in the regular season, in addition to passing for nearly 2,000 yards. Weis declared this his single greatest fear entering the game.

To Ohio State's credit, the Buckeyes seemed well prepared for the fact that Weis and Notre Dame would be the center of the pregame talk. The Ohio State players and coaches remained respectful of their upcoming opponent. Ohio State offensive coordinator Jim Bollman praised Notre Dame's defensive scheme, but he had spotted some obvious weaknesses in Minter's players—namely, the ability to get behind the Irish secondary.

The closest thing to a boast by Ohio State all week was a statement by wide receiver Santonio Holmes, who declared the Buckeyes to be the best pass-catching corps in the Fiesta Bowl: "You can't really compare them to us because they really only have two guys [Jeff Samardzija and Maurice Stovall] getting the job done for them, whereas we have three guys getting the job done for us." (Holmes was talking about himself, Ted Ginn Jr., and Anthony Gonzalez.)

That was about it for controversy. Otherwise, it was a week of mutual admiration.

THE NOTRE DAME–OHIO STATE matchup didn't rival the hype of the BCS championship game between Texas and USC in the Rose Bowl, but it did give Weis a national stage from which to sell the Irish program. There were plenty of reporters on hand (some were double-dipping, covering the Fiesta Bowl on January 2 and the Rose Bowl two days later) for Weis' often entertaining press conferences.

- ON NOTRE DAME'S 9–2 RECORD: "The players dwell on the nine; the coaches dwell on the two. Coaches are miserable by nature. It's part of the package."
- ON WHY NFL COACHES HAVE HAD SUCCESS IN COLLEGE: "First of all, the NFL schedule is unbearable, and when you come to college and you're used to working those hours, it puts you at a pretty good advantage because sometimes you can out-work people."
- ON RECRUITING: "The one disadvantage the NFL has over college is that there's a salary cap in the NFL, and everyone has the same size pie to work with. Here, unlike the NFL draft, you have a chance to go get 10 first-round draft choices every year. Just go out and out-work everybody. That's what the programs that win year in and year out do: they go out and get themselves the best players. You can talk about how good the coaches are, but the bottom line is, you have to go out and get the players. The players are the ones who make the difference."
- ON HIS SUPER BOWL RINGS: "I'll tell you one of my standard lines. When I go into a recruit's house, if I can get him to look at my hand instead of my face, I've got a good chance. A kid starts to tell me he wants to go to another school because he has a better chance to play in the NFL if he does. And I'll go, 'So you want to play in the NFL, huh?' Then I put my ring hand over my face. They usually get the point."
- ON HIS FOUR SUPER BOWL RINGS AND JIM TRESSEL'S FIVE COLLEGE CHAMPIONSHIP RINGS: "My one trumps all of his—size-wise."
- ON NOTRE DAME'S INDEPENDENCE: "Any time you're affiliated with a conference, you're considered regional. We're national. That's a great resource. We have Notre Dame clubs all over the country and all over the world. Trust me, I know, because they're all asking me to come and speak."
- ON WHOM HE'S MORE LIKE, BILL PARCELLS OR BILL BELICHICK: "When you've worked under two Hall of Fame coaches, you try to take the best of both worlds. Because I'm a Jersey guy, people automatically think I'm more like Parcells, which is not a bad

thing. But I'd like to think Coach Belichick influenced my career just as much, especially with the cerebral approach he takes to the game. If you don't know what you're doing after growing up with those two guys, then you've missed the boat."

- ON BRADY QUINN'S READINESS FOR THE NFL AFTER ANOTHER YEAR IN COLLEGE: "Coming in the door, he'll be more ready to go. He knows the philosophy we're putting in and the offense we're putting in. He could go play for the Patriots right now, and if they put him in the game, he could run the plays without one day of practice."

- ON WHETHER HE WAS HAVING FUN AT THE FIESTA BOWL: "My family is having fun. Everyone is content. We've had very few problems. I like the way the week is going. But the only way I'll have fun is if we win the game. I cannot have fun until after the game is over. If we win the game, I'm going to say I had a lot of fun. If we lose, I'm going to be miserable."

QUINN, EVER THE WEIS protégé, was also dealing well with the press. At his first meeting with them, at the Camelback Inn, where the media was housed, Quinn offered a definitive statement regarding his return to Notre Dame.

"When you look at the situation, I'm a big believer in my faith," Quinn said. "I believe God helped me make the decision to come to Notre Dame, and I feel the same way about Him giving me a feeling that it's in my best interests to come back for another year, finish out school, and be prepared for the real world whenever football ends. I see a lot of guys not finishing their degrees. It just takes them so long when they try to come back, and I have so many goals and ambitions outside of football."

(Across the land, a grateful Irish Nation breathed a sigh of relief.)

"It really is best for me to come back for an extra year and get the tutelage from Coach Weis that you can't receive in the NFL," Quinn went on. "He's not there anymore. He's here now. So why not use that as long as you can and go for every goal that you want? I want to win a national championship, and I think our team has the ability, without a doubt, to win it in 2006, especially with the people we have coming back on offense and defense."

Even with the NFL question all but settled, this would prove to be a rather distracting week for Quinn. His older sister, Laura, was dating Ohio State star linebacker A.J. Hawk. Hawk had even broken bread with the Quinn family over the holidays.

Compounding the distraction was the fact that Laura was preparing for a job in sports communications, so she was more than willing to play up the brother vs. boyfriend story. She conducted interviews with her brother and Hawk, playing one off the other and leaving both players squirming with discomfort. She was a guest on several television shows, including ESPN's *Cold Pizza*. On game day, she wore a specially made jersey—half Quinn's and half Hawk's.

She had deftly manufactured her 15 minutes of fame.

ON NEW YEAR'S EVE, Weis and his staff were required to attend a Fiesta Bowl black-tie dinner. "The best part about it is that John Latina hasn't been in a tux since he got married," Weis said of his offensive line coach. "We're going to be sure we get plenty of pictures of that."

Weis wanted his team to stay in. Some of his players wanted to go out. A handful of the younger players, particularly those who were not expected to play a significant role in the game, weren't really happy with the way the trip was going. "There was a big blow up the other day," said defensive lineman Trevor Laws on December 30. "We talked about it, and everybody decided we were doing it the right way. It's a business trip."

Weis gave his players a chance to make the decision. Well, sort of. He had gone to the "leadership committee"—the older players who represented each position—and asked if he felt they should alter his strict plan that included much earlier curfews than those imposed on Ohio State. "I wasn't going to listen to them anyway, but I gave them the opportunity to talk about it," Weis said. "I didn't look at this trip as a chance to paint the town red."

Weis set up a "multifunction thing" for the players on New Year's Eve. The Irish had come too far and worked too hard to let it all slip away for a few hours of merriment. So the curfew stood. But the grumbling continued.

"When I got here, I was jealous of Ohio State," said cornerback Leo Ferrine. "I was like, Man, it's messed up that Ohio State is out there until three in the morning. While they're drinking and having fun, we're studying our playbook."

One player who had tried to have too much fun in Arizona had already been sent home — injured defensive end Chris Frome. "Let's call it a violation of team rules that I didn't appreciate," Weis said. "So I encouraged him to pack up his stuff and go home."

Weis spoke to his players about his past experiences in the Super Bowl. Coaching on the highest level with some of the most talented and pampered athletes in the world, who had plenty of money to party with, Weis had seen the Patriots take a professional approach to Super Bowl preparation. His favorite story: receivers David Givens, a Notre Dame graduate, and Deion Branch stayed up much of the night studying their playbooks during Super Bowl week.

Notre Dame's fun was limited to the trip to the Insight Bowl, seeing the movie *King Kong* as a team, and experiencing New Year's Eve before the clock struck midnight. "We do get a couple hours off at night, but we've got so much football going on that most of us want to sit in the room or lie down," Laws said. "It's a lot different than how other teams are doing it and what we did last year. Hopefully, it pays off."

The Irish jerseys for this game would be home-team blue. After declaring himself "0–for" in green jerseys, Weis ordered that they be left in storage back in South Bend.

On the morning of January 1, 2006, a little more than 24 hours before kickoff, Weis received the Eddie Robinson Award as the nation's top coach, as voted by the Football Writers Association of America. When a reporter began to ask Weis about being the underdog in the game, the coach cut him short. "Labeled by who?" Weis asked. "We're no underdog. These are two great football teams. I don't worry about being an underdog or point spreads. Those things are irrelevant to me. You have two teams with an equal chance of winning."

By halftime the next day, that was no longer the case. Smith, who had worried Weis so much, was too fast, too quick, too elusive for the Irish defense. Notre Dame scored a touchdown on its first drive, then watched Smith lead Ohio State to three touchdowns in five possessions and a 21–7 halftime advantage. The Buckeyes were 5-for-5 on third-down attempts in the first half and had already gained 391 total yards by intermission. The score would have been more lopsided, but Notre Dame blocked two Ohio State field goals.

Notre Dame worked its way back in the game, inching within eight points late in the third quarter. And when Zbikowski scooped up what appeared to be a fumble by Ohio State wide receiver Anthony Gonzalez and returned it 89 yards for a score with about three minutes remaining in the quarter, the comeback seemed nearly complete. But replay officials ruled that Gonzalez never had possession of the pass. Ohio State's Josh Huston kicked a 40-yard field goal on the next play to give the Buckeyes a more comfortable 24–13 lead.

"Obviously, it was *the* play," Weis said. "The only thing I said to the official was, 'I hope that guy is right, because that changes the whole complexion of the game.' They have all the different TV replays. I'm going based upon what I saw on the big screen. I disagreed with it, but I'm prejudiced. I wanted it to be the other way."

With 5:27 left in the game, Walker scored his third touchdown of the night and pulled the Irish to within seven points, 27–20. Twice on the ensuing drive, the Buckeyes were faced with third-and-long situations. And both times Smith, found an open receiver. Antonio Pittman's 60-yard touchdown run sealed the 34–20 victory for the Buckeyes.

The dispirited Irish began to make their way out of Sun Devil Stadium, skipping their usual salute in front of the Notre Dame fans. Then Quinn yelled, "Hey!" and the players who were shuffling to the end zone tunnel stopped and followed their quarterback to the Notre Dame cheering section, where they sang the Notre Dame Victory March together for the last time of the season.

Weis later reported to the interview tent outside of the stadium. When the cardboard placard sitting in front of him with his name on it fell to the pavement, he muttered, "That's about right. That name tag should go down."

As usual, Weis made no excuses. He knew Ohio State dictated the flow of the game. The Buckeyes outrushed the Irish 275–62, outpassed them 342–286, and flat out outplayed them: "There's no reason to make any second guesses or complain, because they were definitely the better team."

Smith had made the difference. The Fiesta Bowl MVP completed 19 of 28 passes for 342 yards and also gained 66 yards rushing. He took advantage of Notre Dame's suspect secondary, most notably cornerback Ambrose Wooden, who had the difficult task of trying to cover Ginn (167 receiving yards, one touchdown; 73 rushing yards, one touchdown).

"I was disappointed with the number of big plays we allowed," Weis said. "That was the critical factor. A lot of times when you look at statistics, they're nickel-and-diming you, and you can live with that. But when you give up that many big plays, they're kicking your butt."

Weis liked how his team had stayed in the game, despite the statistical disparity. Plus, in recent years, the Irish would have been blown out of a game like this. Instead, they'd still had a chance until Pittman's long scoring run sealed it with 1:46 remaining in the game.

Now the Irish had to regroup and try to turn a 34–20 loss to Ohio State into a positive. Good luck.

"There are two ways you can go after a loss like this," Weis told his players. "You can feel sorry for yourselves or you can take that bitter taste in your mouth and say, 'I don't want to have that bitter taste next year.' It's one or the other. Which way do you want to go?"

Mostly, they wanted to go home. It had been a long week, made even longer by yet another bowl loss.

Ohio State was in no such hurry. They had beaten the Irish soundly. Now it was time to chirp a little.

Hawk, who led Ohio State with 12 tackles, including two sacks of his girlfriend's brother, finally stated the obvious after a week of Weis worship: Tressel and his coaching staff were pretty good too. "Everyone was talking about Coach Weis having four weeks to prepare," Hawk said. "What about giving Coach Tressel four weeks to prepare? He's won four out of five bowl games at Ohio State. That's where I think the focus should have been from you guys. Our coach did a great job finding the perfect balance."

Finding the perfect balance would also be Notre Dame's challenge in the offseason. They had lost another bowl, but they had also won nine games and received a BCS invitation and put some serious money in the Notre Dame coffers. Some fans claimed that Notre Dame was right back where it was following the one-sided loss to North Carolina State in the 2002 Gator Bowl in Willingham's first season. But that wasn't true. Never had Willingham's teams showed the explosiveness displayed by Weis' offense. Plus, Weis was in the midst of constructing one of the truly great collections of talent in his first full recruiting season.

As for the defense, well, that was a major concern heading into the offseason. But now that he had established his offense, Weis would certainly turn his attention to shoring up the other side of the ball.

He could also remind his returning Irish players of where the 2006 BCS Championship would be played: just up the road in Glendale, Ariz.

Wouldn't it be something if that's where Notre Dame broke its bowl losing streak?

Chapter 19

CHEER, CHEER FOR *NEW* NOTRE DAME

I N THE HURRIED POSTGAME atmosphere following Notre Dame's 34–20 loss to Ohio State, Weis, Brady Quinn, and Brandon Hoyte were ushered into an interview tent outside of Sun Devil Stadium and quickly addressed the highlights (or, in this case, the lowlights) of the game. The autopsy didn't take long. The assembled reporters were more interested in hearing Ohio State's version of the Fiesta Bowl anyway. After a mercifully brief stay in the tent, Weis and his players were replaced by Ohio State coach Jim Tressel and several Buckeyes stars.

Weis climbed into a waiting golf cart and was driven to the Notre Dame locker room on the other side of the stadium. He had conducted his last interview of the season. He wouldn't deal with another microphone or notepad until February 1, the day the Class of 2010 signed letters of intent. Still, one question in particular would linger during the next four weeks: Why had the Irish played one of their worst games of the season?

An easy answer was the fact that Ohio State owned the postseason. This was Tressel's fifth year at Columbus and his fourth consecutive bowl victory, three of them coming at the Fiesta Bowl. Winning a bowl game was almost a rite of winter for the Buckeyes.

Notre Dame didn't have that sort of postseason momentum. Actually, it had none. The loss to Ohio State was its eighth consecutive bowl game defeat. While the Buckeyes were an established program under Tressel, the Irish—and Weis—were still growing as a football team. It wasn't an excuse for the Notre Dame loss, just a fact. Tressel's program was simply better developed at this point, and his team was more talented and, at least on January 2, 2006, better coached.

Weis prided himself on being able to control the elements that contributed to the outcome of a game. He had carefully detailed his five-week plan of preparing his team for Ohio State. He had consulted with head coaches who had been in bowl games before. He had adapted his plan to fit that advice, but the format didn't work. The Irish weren't crisp: they were even a bit flat against the Buckeyes. One observer on the Notre Dame sideline sensed a lack of enthusiasm among the players throughout the game. That seemed hard to fathom, given the national stage and the quality of their opponent. But there were tiny cracks in pregame preparations; the curfew complaints were evidence of that.

Weis, the master manipulator of all things that pertained to the outcome of a game, had miscalculated and lost his vicelike grip on the Fighting Irish. Combine that with the talent of Ohio State, and you finish on the wrong end of the Fiesta Bowl.

"We did things that we didn't normally do," Weis said. "We dropped balls that we don't normally drop. What do you attribute that to? Rather than attribute it to the players just messing up, which is the easy way out, the more important thing is to try to figure out not only what happened, but also why it happened. I've got the what down; I don't have the why yet."

The Irish finished ninth in the country in the Associated Press poll, their highest postseason ranking since 1993. Considering that they had begun the season unranked, it was a big accomplishment. Weis would address the Fiesta Bowl more thoroughly as soon as the Irish completed their recruiting efforts.

Of course, there wasn't much to do in the last month of Weis' first complete recruiting season. Virtually everything had fallen into place for the Irish as they put the finishing touches on the Class of 2010. Notre Dame had 26 verbal commitments. Weis spent the month working on recruiting juniors for the following year and visiting each of the 26 committed players, just to make sure there wasn't any last-minute wavering.

On January 7, 11 players who had verbally committed to Notre Dame participated in the prestigious U.S. Army All-American Bowl in San Antonio. The U.S. Army All-American Bowl was being played for the sixth time and Notre Dame recruits had always been well represented at the event, due in large part to the involvement of recruiting analyst Tom Lemming, who was based in the Chicago area and had a history of favoring Notre Dame when it came to rankings and getting players placed in all-star games. This year, because the Irish were having a particularly strong recruiting campaign, the number bound for South Bend at the all-star game was even higher. The 11 commitments were running back James Aldridge, offensive linemen Matt Carufel, Chris Stewart, Bartley Webb, and Dan Wenger, wide receiver Barry Gallup, quarterbacks Zach Frazer and Demetrius Jones, tight end Konrad Reuland, and defensive backs Darrin Walls and Raeshon McNeil. Two other Irish recruits—offensive tackle Sam Young and defensive tackle Gerald McCoy—both of whom had yet to verbally commit to a school—also wound up in San Antonio for the all-star game. St. Louis running back Munir Prince, who had previously committed to the Irish, declined an invitation to the event. Also participating was Arkansas quarterback Mitch Mustain, who had previously committed to the Razorbacks, but had since backed out.

Mustain wanted to come to Notre Dame. There was no doubt about that. But when the offers were first extended earlier in 2005 to Frazer, Jones, and Mustain, it was with the understanding that the first two quarterbacks to accept would land spots in South Bend. Frazer was the first to say yes, and Jones was ready to make his commitment fairly early in the process. Mustain wasn't as certain.

As the 2005 season unfolded, Mustain had second thoughts about his home-state Razorbacks. He saw the evolution of the Notre Dame passing game under Weis. He saw the quantum leap in Quinn's development. Notre Dame's offense, Mustain decided, was a perfect fit.

The problem was, Weis had already accepted verbal commitments from Frazer and Jones. He probably could have accepted Mustain's commitment, too, and simply told everyone that it was in the best interests of the program to stockpile quarterbacks of that caliber. After all, Mustain was the highest-rated prospect of the three and Notre Dame's top choice. But when Weis made an agreement, he stuck to it.

Mustain remained hopeful that Notre Dame would "re-offer" him a scholarship. He even tucked a Play Like a Champion towel in his uniform pants for the all-star game. Rumors spread that the Irish would save a spot for the Springdale, Arkansas, standout, who also happened to be the high school teammate of offensive lineman Bartley Webb. In the end, however, Weis declined to add Mustain to the scholarship list. He couldn't. He had given his word to Frazer and Jones.

"He really wanted to come," said Weis, referring to Mustain, although not by name, on Signing Day. "It would have been nice if that would have worked out. But the way it worked out is the best for everyone involved. It's really important these kids trust what you're saying when you say, 'This is what we're going to do.' If you go back on your word, you're going to have a problem. Those guys sit there and say, 'Great, we get another great football player here, but what about us? This is what you told us you were going to do.' Kids don't want to be lied to, just like we don't want to be lied to."

Another player who really wanted to come to Notre Dame was Sam Young from Coral Springs, Florida, considered the top offensive tackle prospect in the country. But Young—unlike Minnesota offensive lineman Matt Carufel, who announced his decision to attend Notre Dame during the all-star game—was not yet ready to make an announcement. A week after the San Antonio game, Young canceled his visits to Michigan and Penn State. He had narrowed his choices down to Notre

Dame, which he had visited in June, and USC, where he had made a December visit.

When Young announced a press conference for Thursday, January 19—two days before his scheduled visit to Notre Dame—everyone wondered if he would choose Notre Dame before his official visit. Indeed he would. As it turned out, Young was Notre Dame's only official visitor in January—an unprecedented recruiting procedure. Most of the recruiting commotion at Notre Dame in January was with current high school juniors. Notre Dame now had a class of 27 for 2010. (McCoy, the highly rated defensive lineman, eventually signed with Oklahoma.)

"Sam Young is here today because of our recruits," Weis said. "When he was down at the All-American game, he observed how close our recruits were hanging out together. Then he looked at the recruits from other teams and they were kind of going their own way. He told me that he decided right then where he was going."

That connection was already being developed among some of the nation's top high school juniors, who visited South Bend the weekend of January 14 and attended a men's basketball game against Big East foe Providence. Among the junior visitors was Westlake Village, California, quarterback Jimmy Clausen, whom many believed would make the controversy over the Frazer-Jones-Mustain situation moot by the fall of 2007. Clausen, the hands-down top-rated player/quarterback in the Class of 2011, was at the very top of Notre Dame's list, and vice versa. Clausen's brothers—Casey and Rick—both played at Tennessee. The oldest one, Casey, was bitter when then-Irish offensive coordinator/quarterbacks coach Kevin Rogers wasn't sold on his skills coming out of high school. He took particular pleasure leading the Volunteers to a 28–18 victory against the Irish in Notre Dame Stadium in 2001.

But those wounds had healed within the Clausen family. And although schools such as Tennessee, USC, Florida State, Michigan, LSU, and Oklahoma were high on the list of the youngest of the Clausen clan, the Irish were expected to land Jimmy, who also had a teammate—running back Marc Tyler—on whom Weis had designs. In fact, when Sam Young became commitment number 27, the Irish had one more scholarship to give. Three of the members of the Class of

2010—receiver George West, running back James Aldridge, and offensive lineman Chris Stewart—were enrolled for the spring semester of 2006, which counted against the previous year's total. That meant that if the Irish stopped after Young's commitment, only 24 spots would be counted for 2006, leaving one early-entry prospect for 2007. That spot would be held, some speculated, for Jimmy Clausen.

On January 17, the start of the spring semester, West, Aldridge, and Stewart showed up for classes at Notre Dame. "It was a real tough decision for me to come early," West told the *South Bend Tribune*. "There was a part of me that wanted to go out and enjoy my senior year. But I understand this is an opportunity to do something special. The pluses outweigh the minuses."

Said Aldridge, "I guess that makes us pioneers in a way."

Their early arrival was yet another example of Weis' influence during his short tenure at Notre Dame. In previous years, this had not been an easy sell with the admissions department. In fact, it was forbidden. Then again, none of the previous head football coaches at Notre Dame had made a pitch quite like the one Weis made to Dan Saracino, the university's director of admissions. Notre Dame's stance had always been that the freshman year of studies was vital to incoming students. Saracino credited the 98 percent return rate of sophomore students at Notre Dame to the learning environment created during that first year of college.

Yet former Irish defensive coordinator and defensive line coach Greg Mattison, who was now on Urban Meyer's staff at Florida, once said that the Irish had to eliminate about five prospects a year because of Notre Dame's refusal to allow early entries. Coupled with a narrow recruiting base due to academic restrictions, losing five or more prospects per year simply made a difficult process that much tougher. Weis changed the policy by earning the trust of Saracino. Plus, the academic credentials of the three individuals were impeccable, which inspired confidence from the admissions department in Weis' judgment.

Meanwhile, five Notre Dame seniors—Hoyte, receiver Maurice Stovall, linebacker Corey Mays, offensive lineman Dan Stevenson, and kicker D.J. Fitzpatrick—were selected to play in postseason all-star games.

Stevenson and Hoyte were headed to San Antonio for the January 21 East-West Shrine Game. Mays and Fitzpatrick took a trip to Honolulu for the Hula Bowl, where they would be playing against a West squad coached by Tyrone Willingham. Stovall was headed for the January 28 Senior Bowl in Mobile, Alabama, considered the top destination for NFL coaches, scouts, and pro prospects.

Anthony Fasano—who still had another year of eligibility but was a few credit hours away from earning his undergraduate degree—officially announced his decision to enter the NFL draft. It was one of the worst-kept secrets of the 2005 season among the media. Fasano had decided early on that he would be leaving Notre Dame, and his solid 2005 performance only reaffirmed his decision.

"I knew going into the season that there was going to be a decision if I played up to expectations," said Fasano, who finished with 47 receptions in 2005 and 92 in his college career. "Going through the season and having a productive year, I got the sense from the NFL that I would be taken and be able to help a program early on."

Weis was not in a position to dispute Fasano's decision. All season he had sung the praises of his tight end, calling him a complete player, both as a blocker and a receiver. Plus, he was on the verge of earning his undergraduate degree.

Fasano eventually went in the second round to Dallas, followed by Stovall in the third to Tampa Bay and Stevenson in the sixth to New England.

When February 1—Signing Day—arrived, the contrast from one year earlier was striking. In 2005, Weis had been in Florida and announced his first recruiting class via satellite while preparing for the Super Bowl. This time he addressed the media from the auditorium in the Guglielmino Athletics Complex. All was calm in Weis' world, which hadn't always been the case at Notre Dame on Signing Day. Like most schools, Notre Dame often waited in nervous anticipation for each signed letter of intent to come across the fax machine. Not this year. By noon, the scheduled time of Weis' press conference, all 27 signed letters of intent were in the Notre Dame football office. The 2010 recruiting class had come together in textbook fashion.

"We had a couple bumps at the end," Weis said. "But the fact is everyone of our guys told me, 'I'm committed.' If you're going to expect them to trust you, then you're going to have to trust them."

The 27 players came from 17 states. The Irish added six offensive linemen, five defensive backs, four wide receivers, three running backs, three defensive linemen, two quarterbacks, two linebackers, a tight end, and a kicker. Lemming listed nine of the 27 among the nation's top 100 players. Nine were selected Gatorade Players of the Year in their home states. Lemming rated the Notre Dame class the third best in the country. Longtime analyst Max Emfinger and Scout.com rated the Irish number five. Rivals.com placed Notre Dame at number eight, while California-based SuperPrep ranked the Irish class at number nine.

Weis had offered scholarships to 58 players, 47 percent of whom accepted. Only 37 took official trips to Notre Dame, which meant that an incredible 73 percent of those who visited had decided to sign with the Irish.

One by one, Weis went through the list and sung the praises of his new class. He anticipated signing another full complement of 25 (with room for 26) in 2007. The trend toward early commitments and the desire by recruits to make earlier decisions had forced all coaches to get a jump on the process—the reason for Weis' emphasis on junior recruiting. In fact, Weis declared himself a proponent of an early signing date—in August—before the start of preseason camp. That would eliminate some of the recruiting work during the season and also give the verbally-pledged player the security of knowing that a commitment to Notre Dame was reciprocated, even if he should suffer a debilitating injury during his senior year in high school.

Although Weis wasn't about to project any of the freshmen as starters in 2006, he did acknowledge that the small classes in 2004 and 2005 (32 originally for both years, and that had been reduced to 24) certainly created more opportunities for young players to contribute. Weis said any position that had a senior starter departing was open for the taking, even by a freshman. "I'm not in love with anybody," Weis said. "I'm in love with the guys who give me the best chance to win. If a freshman can come in and beat out a senior, so be it."

Weis' priority from a numbers standpoint had been the offensive line. He wanted at least five linemen, hoped to get six, and would have taken a seventh. He showed patience early in the process when several marginal prospects were inclined to commit early. "We did not want to reach at this position," Weis said. "We needed guys we felt could earn their way into the two-deep, walking in the door." Among the significant offensive line contributors in 2005, all but center John Sullivan would be gone after the 2006 season, and that meant Weis had plenty to sell.

Although he praised the recruiting efforts along the defensive line, Weis failed to land a knockout performer. That obviously would be at the forefront of Notre Dame's priorities in the next recruiting class.

Young had been commitment number 27, and the Irish saved the best for last. Young was a prototype offensive lineman with the frame and agility of a basketball player and a football player's temperament. "I see what I've been used to seeing for a lot of years, only he's a high school kid," said Weis in his assessment of Young. "I see a man playing among boys at the high school level. Obviously, college is going to be a different deal, because you're going to have a higher level of competition, but Young is pretty impressive."

Even Weis' wife, Maura, who had been around her fair share of pro offensive tackles, was impressed. "I never remember anyone looking as big as this guy," she told her husband.

Young picked Notre Dame over USC. The Irish also won a head-to-head victory with the Trojans in their pursuit of tight end Konrad Reuland. The recruiting victories didn't offset the four straight losses to the Trojans on the field, but this was significant progress.

"I didn't know anything about Notre Dame other than the Knute Rockne movie and *Rudy*," said Young, who admitted he was lukewarm about the Irish before he visited in June 2005. "But the Notre Dame experience was different from what I thought it would be. I was really impressed by the academics, and the overall campus was absolutely beautiful. You never really get a chance to know all that just watching them on TV."

Young would soon get a closer look at Weis, who vowed to get even with his new lineman for making his decision to come to Notre Dame two weeks before telling the coach. "He played me until the end," Weis laughed. "I talked to him about payback this morning. Of course, that was after his letter-of-intent fax had come across."

Weis had not just found plenty of football talent; he had a 27-man class that seemed to fit Notre Dame. That's why there was very little concern over "decommitments" in a year when more than 100 Division IA players verbally committed to one school and eventually signed with another. That's why Signing Day was calm and peaceful inside the Gug.

Hard work would be the backbone of Notre Dame recruiting under Weis. It had become a 12-month endeavor. It had to be, because Top 25 programs everywhere were doing the same thing.

"Just because a kid is from a Catholic school five miles away doesn't mean you're getting him," said Weis. "You can't say, 'We're Notre Dame, so everyone is going to want to come here.' You need to go out and represent your school and be aggressive in recruiting. The game has changed in recruiting, and it's a much earlier game. You better be on them early and you better get them on board."

Weis' work with the Class of 2010 was just beginning. He had already told the 27 recruits that theirs was going to be the class that started Notre Dame back to the top. "That doesn't mean we don't have a chance to compete this year and next year. I'm talking about perennially being at the top. This class sets that foundation."

Two-and-a-half months later, on the morning of the annual Blue-Gold spring game, that foundation became stronger. Clausen announced his verbal commitment to attend Notre Dame as well as his plan to enroll for the spring semester of 2007.

In a little over 13 months, Weis had done more than simply establish a foundation. He had poured the concrete and inserted the steel rods. He had reaffirmed Notre Dame football as a national power on the field and in recruiting circles. Thirteen-and-a-half months after inheriting a program that seemed to be on the verge of collapse, Notre Dame was back. The Fighting Irish were a certain 2006 preseason Top 5.

Notre Dame was back because of a new, hard-working football coach who had re-established the way Notre Dame football functioned.

A coach who had raised the bar to an old, familiar place.

A coach who, in just one season, had established the *new* gold standard.

······

ACKNOWLEDGMENTS

FOR THE PAST 20-PLUS years, long-time *Blue & Gold Illustrated* associate editor Lou Somogyi has been a source of encouragement and a wealth of knowledge. I drew heavily on both for this project. His influence has helped make me a better journalist and person, and his unconditional friendship speaks volumes about the soul of the man.

Thanks to former *BGI* assistant editor and current Rivals.com editor Pete Sampson, who provided much of the legwork and background information on the hiring of Charlie Weis, as well as the relationship Weis developed with the admissions department at Notre Dame. He is a bright talent in this business, and I look forward to working with him in the future.

Thanks also to Pat Leonard, who helped provide comments from the Notre Dame student body regarding the hiring of Weis and their experiences listening to Weis speak to the students in the Notre Dame dorms.

Photographer Matt Cashore and webmaster Jack Freeman are people of quality and compassion in a world that too often lacks humanity. Thanks, guys.

By casting sharp eyes on my X's and O's, crack researcher-reporter Doug Mittler and amazing line editor Beth Adelman saved me from some costly turnovers.

To my wife Terri and son Eric, whose love, respect, and way of life are inspiring. They are blessings from God. They are my heroes.

And to the rest of my family, especially my brother, Michael, who has supported and believed in me. My modest achievements—as a writer, athlete, and coach—are my way of thanking him for always supporting me.

Finally, I'm thankful for the ideal that is Notre Dame. It has always been and will always be the guiding force in my life.